# ARLINGTON:

## MONUMENT
## TO HEROES

New and Enlarged Edition

## JOHN VINCENT HINKEL

PRENTICE-HALL, INC., Englewood Cliffs, N. J.

To the Members of the Armed Forces
of the
United States of America

American-by-birth or American-by-choice
Black, Red, White or Yellow
Christian, Jew or other faith
Draftee, Recruit or Volunteer

To All Who Served in Our Nation's Wars in
Air Force, Army, Coast Guard, Marines, Navy or Nurse Corps

This Book Is Reverently Dedicated.

ARLINGTON: Monument to Heroes by John Vincent Hinkel

© 1970, 1965 by Prentice-Hall, Inc.

Library of Congress Catalog Card Number: 79-89542

Printed in the United States of America · T
13-046565-8 (casebound)
13-046557-7 (paperbound)
PRENTICE-HALL INTERNATIONAL, INC., London
PRENTICE-HALL OF AUSTRALIA, PTY. LTD., Sydney
PRENTICE-HALL OF CANADA, LTD., Toronto
PRENTICE-HALL OF INDIA PRIVATE LTD., New Delhi
PRENTICE-HALL OF JAPAN, INC., Tokyo

# FOREWORD

THE ARLINGTON NATIONAL CEMETERY IS THE RESTING PLACE OF heroes. Its headstones tell the inspiring story of the men and women of the Armed Forces of the United States who did so much to build and defend this country, often at the cost of their lives.

What is a hero? What constitutes heroism? We know that many of our heroes lie in Arlington, but when we examine their stories we find it difficult to correlate their exploits into a simple explanation on which all would agree.

What is clear, however, is that heroes do not fit any particular pattern, irrespective of their time of service or the war in which they fought. They have no specific creed or color. They come from all ranks and from all stations in life. They have no special bracket of age and no similar origin.

The heroes of Arlington do have one common bond. They wore the American uniform and they wore it in defense of the United States against the forces of evil as those forces armed and formed up in their times.

Arlington is a fitting final resting place for these heroes. It is fitting because it memorializes no special individual or group but all who served their country in its wars. It translates the memory of the selfless service of these heroes into inspiration for all of us. It is our Nation's greatest shrine.

*Earle G. Wheeler*
General, USA
Chairman, Joint Chiefs of Staff

# ACKNOWLEDGMENTS

IN A HISTORY SUCH AS THIS INFINITE CARE HAS TO BE TAKEN IN THE research. That this book is as complete as it is, is due in large measure to the magnificent cooperation received from Government agencies. It is almost impossible to mention all those who have helped. However, I wish to give particular thanks to:

Mr. John C. Metzler, Superintendent of Arlington National Cemetery since 1951, and his fine administrative staff, who rendered every possible courtesy and help. They included Mr. Robert H. Schmidt, Assistant Superintendent, and his successor, Mr. Frank A. Lockwood; also Mr. Joseph M. Frye, Mr. Richard L. Magaha, Mr. Thurman Higginbotham, Mrs. Thomas E. McClain, Mrs. Mary Lee Smith, Mr. William K. Davis, Mr. Anthony Cicoria, Miss Mary E. Rebar and Mrs. Barbara Lewallen.

Colonel Glenn E. Fant, at the time Information Officer of the Military District of Washington, which administers Arlington National Cemetery; his successor, Colonel L. H. Sims, Jr.; Lieutenant Colonel Isabelle J. Swartz, Chief, Community Relations Branch; Mr. Paul C. Miller, Director, Ceremonies and Special Events, and their staffs also provided invaluable assistance.

Considerable assistance and many helpful suggestions were given by Mr. Charles F. Romanus, Chief of the General Reference Branch, Office of the Chief of Military History, himself a recognized military historian and author. Valued help also was given by his principal assistant, Miss Ruth Markwood, Army historian, and other branch staff members.

The excellent staff of the National Capital Region, National Parks Service, Department of the Interior, headed by Mr. T. Sutton Jett, Regional Director, and Mr. Cornelius W. Heine, Assistant Regional Director, was most cooperative. These two officials, both historians and experts on Arlington, and their associates—Mrs. Carol Smith, Mrs. Billie Copeland and Miss Naomi Hunt—aided especially on the Custis-Lee Mansion, which is under jurisdiction of the National

Capital Region. Another who provided much information was Mrs. Agnes Downey Mullins, former historian at the mansion. Photos by Mr. Abbie Rowe, National Parks Region photographer, add considerably to the book.

Miss Helen T. McDonald, Special Assistant to the Chief, Memorial Division, Office of the Chief of Army Support Services, administrator of all national cemeteries under military control, and her associate, Mr. Theodore M. Collier, division historian, furnished much valuable information.

The National Archives produced a veritable treasure trove of facts on Arlington and many noteworthy persons buried there. Mr. Victor Gondos, Archivist in Charge of the Army-Air Force Branch, and Archivists Milton K. Chamberlain, Sara D. Jackson and James Walker, were particularly helpful. So, too, was Navy Archivist Richard A. Von Doenhoff, as well as Miss Josephine Motylewski and Mr. Paul White, Archivists in the Still Picture Section.

The Information Offices of the Army, Navy, Air Force, Marines and Coast Guard were extremely cooperative and helpful in providing research data for use in this volume. Particular mention should be made of Major B. J. Smith, Major Lillian Baker and Mrs. Edna C. Curcio of the Army; Mrs. Betty Shirley, Navy; Lieut. Col. Milton K. Kegley, Air Force; Gunnery Sergeant Wesley Ward, Mrs. V. P. White and Miss Manell P. Brice, Marines; and Captain Henry A. Friedenberg, Coast Guard.

In addition, Miss M. C. Griffin and Miss Rosemarie Purcell, Bureau of Naval Personnel; Chaplain (Brig. Gen.) William J. Moran, Deputy Chief of Army Chaplains; Miss Donna A. Traxler and Mr. Albert A. Buquor, Army Photographic Agency; Mrs. Virginia Fincik, Air Force Aeronautical Charts and Information Center; Dr. William J. Morgan, Naval historian; Mr. Daniel O'Quinlivan of the Marine Corps Historical Branch; Mr. David Schoem, Air Force Historical Division; and Miss Florence E. Oblensky, Technical Information Office, Office of the Army Surgeon General.

The splendid assistance and many suggestions extended by the fine staff of librarians at the Washington Public Library, and especially the help given by Miss Edith Saul, chief of the Washingtoniana Room, and Miss Georgia Cowan, chief of the Biographical Section there, is gratefully acknowledged.

Others who extended unusual courtesies and help were Mr. Carl Stange, Prints and Photographs Division, Library of Congress; Mr. Paul H. Oehser, chief of the Editorial and Publication Division, the Smithsonian Institution; Miss Esther A. Manion, librarian, and Mrs. Virginia C. Hill, Assistant Librarian, the National Geographic Society; Mrs. Elden Billings, librarian, and Mr. Robert Lyle, executive secretary, the Columbia Historical Society; Mr. John Jennings, Director, Virginia Historical Society; the Association of the United States Army, the Navy League and the Air Force Association. The Washington Post and the Washington Star also were most cooperative.

Mrs. Virginia Edwards Hughes did an excellent job of typing, and Mrs. Elizabeth K. Hinkel and Mr. Christopher Hinkel helped with collating the manuscript, and in other ways.

Finally, I wish to thank, in particular, those close collaborators in the preparation of this book, Mrs. Ruth Taylor Hunter and Mr. Patrick E. Hughes. Mrs. Hunter assisted with the research and editing. Mr. Hughes supervised the collecting of photographs, adding to them more than twenty excellent photographs which he himself took at Arlington. Without their dedicated, loyal and unstinted cooperation, the preparation of this volume would have been seriously delayed or made impossible. For that reason, I am deeply grateful to these two faithful friends.

# CONTENTS

# THE HEROES OF ARLINGTON

IN THE SEVERAL YEARS SINCE THE FIRST EDITION OF THIS BOOK much water has flowed down the Potomac past Arlington to the sea, much has happened of purport to our country, many have died in defense of our commitments and ideals.

Yet, there are those who continue to say that patriotism is old-fashioned, that there must be a "free new world" in which there will be no room for love of country, love of family, or love of God.

Arlington National Cemetery is a living denial of these sentiments. Beneath the rows of white headstones rest men who went out boldly and died bravely for their country—heroes all. They are buried with their comrades.

Burial at Arlington is a mark of distinction. There is no gloom at Arlington, sadness yes, but no gloom. Rather is there a sustaining pride. For at Arlington the warriors rest at last in a quiet place of green trees, winding paths, shady lawns, and gently sloping hillsides. Arlington is a peaceful place to visit. It is solemn but not somber. Its graves tell the story of our nation.

In serried ranks on its quiet green slopes lie these honored dead who served their country, and who served it well, in war and peace. They have a common bond to unite them—the oath each swore when he or she entered the Armed Forces of the United States:

> I do solemnly swear (or affirm) that I will support and defend the Constitution of the United States against all enemies, foreign and domestic; and that I will obey the orders of the President of the United States and the orders of the officers appointed over me, according to law . . .

There is also another bond they have in common—a unity of service, the comradeship of those who have, even if only for a short while, put aside personal interests for the common good.

Patriotism to them was not just a word in a book. It was not simply a phrase for orators to declaim on holidays. They regarded patriotism as an act of unselfish devotion to country, of self-sacrifice for an ideal.

Those who rest in Arlington proved their patriotism. Where they served is unimportant. What *is* important is that they served their country where and in what capacity they were ordered to serve—and to the best of their ability—regardless of rank or position.

Arlington stands unique as a memorial to American war dead from the Revolution to Korea and the now continuing and continuous Cold War.

Of those who rest in Arlington, some were loudly acclaimed by their countrymen. Others were bedecked with medals and lived to wear them proudly. For some, the medals were presented posthumously to their next of kin in honor of their bravery. But many more received no medals for merit, even though their spirit and dedication were as great. Any combat veteran will admit that courage and dedication are not always shown by daring deeds, but rather by the faithful doing of the assigned duty—and that all heroes do not receive recognition.

So it is at Arlington. But, judged by the jury of their peers—their comrades in arms—they are heroes all. They fulfilled their destiny. Their deeds are a source of pride, an inspiration for generations yet to come.

A journey to Arlington National Cemetery today is a pilgrimage to a great shrine of our country. Those who lie in that hallowed spot overlooking the city of Washington—planned by a soldier and laid out by a soldier—are but symbols of *all* of America's war dead—those legions who have served honorably in the United States Armed Forces in peace and war.

This book is the story of Arlington and of a few of the noteworthy men and women who are buried there—chosen at random because each is representative of the many.

Once the real significance of Arlington National Cemetery is realized, what American can leave that hallowed spot without a feeling of pride, of intense humility, a determination to be worthy of these heroes of all our wars?

J.V.H.

# THE

# ETERNAL FLAME

Since that bleak November day when all that was mortal of John Fitzgerald Kennedy, thirty-fifth President of the United States of America, was borne to its last resting place on the hillside at Arlington, the line of mourners has never ceased—except for those few hours at night when the cemetery is closed. Even then, on the roads below, the cars move more slowly, that their occupants may see the flicker of the Eternal Flame of Remembrance.

Like a river the line of people flows past the grave. The great of the world come to lay wreaths in the name of the men and women of their countries. The humble come to drop a single flower, or a prayer from their hearts. The old climb slowly. The children stop—in sudden awe of what they feel but cannot comprehend. The great majority are young.

For the most part they are reverent pilgrims, come to do honor to the one whom they felt understood them and their problems and whom they thought they understood.

Treading close upon the heels of the ones before them, they stand patiently in line, sometimes waiting hours for that moment to arrive when they might pass the grave.

What draws them there? Why do they come? What motivates them? Arlington is not a place to which one goes casually or carelessly. It takes time to get there, no matter how one goes. It isn't on the way to any place—it is an end in itself. In many ways it is just as aloof from the city of Washington as it was when George Washington Parke Custis first built Arlington Mansion as a place to house the relics of George Washington. Yet still the people come.

They come by bus. The monster vehicles disgorge them by the dozens. Travel-worn, rumpled, with the inevitable cameras around their necks, they charge toward the grave. Almost as if on signal, their voices lower, their expressions become serious. As they near the grave, there seems to be a sense of unity—they lose their emphasis on self.

They come by automobile. From the North or from the South on the Virginia side of the Potomac, they look across to the whiteness of the buildings of Washington, whose marble facades mark the working areas of the Government, as the marble gravestones at Arlington mark the resting place of the dead who fought in the nation's wars.

Out of the city and around the nation's memorial to the man who was President when Arlington became a Cemetery in 1864, the shrine wherein Lincoln sits brooding over the people whom he loved—around that calm figure the cars go whirling onto the Memorial Bridge. Across the predecessor of the nearby span—the former Long Bridge—thousands of Union soldiers had gone gaily off to war. Across that span they had streamed in panic-stricken rout after the First Battle of Bull Run. And, across the Memorial Bridge, a century and two years later, had slowly passed the funeral cortège of the thirty-fifth President. Across the Memorial Bridge the people now come to his grave.

They come on foot. As individuals they appear small against the great gates of Arlington. As an unending line they have all power, for they are the people—separate, nothing; but together, invincible.

As Commander-in-Chief of the Armed Forces of the United States, John F. Kennedy was entitled to his gravesite—just as was that J. F. Kennedy buried not a quarter of a mile away. That other Kennedy was a Private and the date of his death was May 16, 1864. He was one of the first to be buried at Arlington.

Long before he became Commander-in-Chief, John Fitzgerald Kennedy had earned his burial place there. The story of his service might well be used to represent hundreds of the other young officers of World War II, who now lie in Arlington.

John Kennedy tried to enlist in the Navy in the spring of 1941, well before Pearl Harbor inflamed the nation. An old football injury to his back barred him, so he underwent a course of treatment and finally was accepted in September, 1941. He applied for active duty, but it was not until a year after Pearl Harbor that he was assigned to a Motor Torpedo Boat Squadron.

In August of 1943 PT-109, commanded by Lieutenant John F. Kennedy, was patrolling off the Solomon Islands when it was torpedoed by the Japanese. Kennedy risked his own life to save the lives of several of his crewmen, one of whom he towed through the water for three miles by a life belt which he held between his teeth.

The citation for the Navy and Marine Corps Medal awarded him for this exploit tells the story, in part:

> . . . . Unmindful of personal danger, Lieutenant (then Lieutenant
> Junior Grade) Kennedy unhesitatingly braved the difficulties

In mute sorrow, thousands lined the roadway to the gravesite at Arlington. As far away as television could reach, millions watched the solemn black-draped cortège wend its way to Arlington and a hero's grave.

He was our friend. And we have come to tell him we will not forget him.
Patrick Hughes

The thirty-sixth President of the United States pays honor to the thirty-fifth President.

The John F. Kennedy grave at Arlington.

and hazards of darkness to direct rescue operations, swimming many hours to secure aid and food after he had succeeded in getting his crew ashore.

His outstanding courage, endurance and leadership contributed to the saving of several lives and were in keeping with the highest traditions of the United States Naval Service.

The young Lieutenant belittled his injuries and insisted on staying on duty in the Pacific until he was ordered home and into a Naval Hospital. His back was in bad shape again.

While he was in the hospital his older brother, Lieutenant Joseph Kennedy, Jr., a Naval Aviator, was lost in a flight over the English Channel. The story from then on is a story of the making of a President and familiar to all Americans.

But it is important to remember that, whatever President Kennedy may have been, or whatever he may have done, Lieutenant John F. Kennedy earned—by active service for his country—his resting place in Arlington. Too few of those who pass by his grave to honor the President, remember that he, too, was a service hero—just like the other men who lie near him.

The people still trudge the hillside to his grave. It was not remarkable at first, for the nation was stunned by the manner of his death, and, regardless of political persuasion, filled with sincere sympathy for his family.

The hearts of the world were touched. The sympathies of the world went out to the widow and her children.

But still the people come—as they have ever since John Kennedy, in the prime of his life, with everything to live for, and with a great work he wanted to complete, was slain by an assassin from ambush.

The shock and first grief have passed, and yet still the people travel the weary way to his grave from all over the country—no, from all over the world.

Why do they make this pilgrimage? The best answer comes from one of the young people.

"He gave us a challenge. He did not just bewail the state of the world. He told us if we didn't like it, we had better do something about it. He showed us that the greatest of adventures is in being a good citizen. He took us up to the top of the mountain and showed us the work to be done. Then he gave us a chance to do it. We are alive now—alive to conditions, alive to people. We won't forget that it was John Kennedy who gave us that challenge!"

Perhaps John Fitzgerald Kennedy's "moment of greatest glory" was on that Inaugural Day when he laid a charge upon the American people—when he challenged them to action.

The greatest tribute to his memory—his Eternal Flame—is in the enduring quality of his own words:

> And so, my fellow Americans, ask not what your country can do for you. Ask what you can do for your country.
>
> My fellow citizens of the World. Ask not what America will do for you, but what together we can do for the freedom of man.
>
> Finally, whether you are citizens of America or citizens of the world, ask of us the same high standard of strength and sacrifice which we ask of you.
>
> With a good conscience our only sure reward, with history the final judge of our deeds, let us go forth to lead the land we love, asking His blessing and His help, but knowing that here on Earth God's work must truly be our own.

So spoke the thirty-fifth President of the United States, who, today, rests on an Arlington hillside, but whose spirit is alive in the hearts of freedom-loving people everywhere.

The Eternal
Flame
U.S. Army Photograph

# ALWAYS

# A MEMORIAL

ACROSS THE POTOMAC RIVER FROM THE CITY OF WASHINGTON RISES a high but gently sloping hill. The white-pillared house that crowns the summit seems to brood over the city, giving a sense of protection and peace. Surrounding it are acres upon acres of small white stones which mark the last resting place of those who served their country in its Armed Forces.

They came from every part of the nation, from all ranks of society, from farm and factory, from village and city, from the work bench and the schoolroom. Here there is no question of class, no bar of national origin or race, no differentiation by religion. They lie in peace together—comrades-in-arms—in Arlington National Cemetery which is a grateful nation's memorial to them.

Arlington has always been a memorial. It has been a national cemetery since 1864. But even before that, the sound of marching feet—the quick step of men gaily off to war, and the solemn tread of men bearing their burdens home again—has been in Arlington's background.

More than two hundred years ago, in 1755 to be exact, there landed at the flourishing port of nearby Alexandria, just below present-day Arlington, an expedition that was to be a dress parade for the Revolution.

"His Excellency Edward Braddock, Colonel of the 14th Regiment of Foot, Major General and Commander-in-Chief of all His Majesty's Forces raised or to be raised in North America" disembarked with the firm intention of showing the Colonists and the French and Indian enemies just what a British regiment could do. He found himself in immediate difficulties. The Colonists were not impressed; they didn't take orders, and they had the most peculiar ideas of fighting.

However, General Braddock did admit the excellence of his colonial Aide—a tall, broad shouldered planter with strong pock-marked features— who had come to him at the urging of the Governor of Virginia. The Aide had a way of getting things done—though it was disconcerting to hear him called "George" by vagrant scouts just out of the woods.

With the help of this George Washington, the Expedition finally marced out of Alexandria, past the church and the race-courses, past fields of wild ginger, purple-brown in the sunlight, out on the way to Fort Cumberland and beyond that to death in the forest.

Back and forth, from the Army on the march to Williamsburg, sped George Washington, arranging for food, urging assistance to get this unwieldy force on its way and to keep it moving. How his surveyor's eye must have scanned the land as he rode, marking the crop possibilities, the growth of timber, the lay of the land for drainage!

Perhaps in those rides he assessed the land that later was to be known as Arlington, the Custis Mansion, the Lee Mansion, and, little more then a century after he rode by, as "Arlington National Cemetery." Did he note the hilltop and the long view down the river? And did he mark its strategic possibilities?

Even in the formality of a posed portrait, a small boy's devotion shows itself. George Washington —first in war, first in peace and first in the hearts of his countrymen—was not only the light of Parke Custis' world—he was that world.

**National Gallery of Art**

And, some twenty-five years later, in 1780, did he suggest this area to his stepson—John Custis—when, pausing in the conduct of the Revolutionary War, he advised John to spend his patrimony on land, the only real wealth?

It was from the camp near Dobbs Ferry, New York, that Washington wrote young Custis. He had tried to be a wise father to Martha Dandridge Custis Washington's only son. But Martha Washington was the richest woman in the Colonies, and John was her idolized heir. She was so rich that rumor has it that this wealth may have influenced the selection of Washington as Commander-in-Chief, for, as one talkative politician put it, "George won't need any pay." John Custis had known luxury that his stepfather, as a younger son, had never known. But Washington tried to counter Martha's indulgence with sound and practical advice.

Young Custis bought the land that is now Arlington—but he did not live to build a home on it. While serving as an Aide to his stepfather at the Siege of Yorktown in 1781, John Custis became ill and died of the deadly "camp fever."

The heart-broken Washingtons adopted John Custis' two younger children and their hopes and dreams centered on the boy—George Washington Parke Custis. It was a glamorous existence for a small boy as the adopted son of the most important man in the new nation—the United States. Not only were there the great public ceremonies—the inauguration of the First President, for example—but there was also a constant stream of important guests coming to pay homage. Even a small boy relegated to the background would have been affected—and there is no record that George Washington Parke Custis ever stayed in the background!

Marriage was a serious business transaction in the days when George Washington Parke Custis espoused sixteen-year-old Mary Lee Fitzhugh.

**KNOW all men by these Presents,**

That we *George Washington Parke Custis and William Fitzhugh*

are held and firmly bound, unto the United States of America, in the full and just sum of one hundred and fifty dollars, to the payment whereof, well and truly to be made, we bind ourselves, our heirs, executors and administrators, jointly and severally, firmly by these presents: Sealed with our seals and dated this *fifth* day of *July* ———————— 1804

THE CONDITION of the above obligation is such, that whereas, there has this day issued a License from the Clerks office of the Circuit Court of the District of Columbia for the County of Alexandria, for a Marriage intended between *George W. P. Custis and Mary Lee Fitzhugh*

Now, if there is no lawful cause to obstruct the said Marriage, then the above obligation to be void, or else to remain in full force and virtue.

Sealed and delivered  }
in presence of            }

He tagged at the great man's heels, and Washington tried to teach him the principles by which he regulated his own life—the fundamental truths of what was right and what was wrong, the value of the pledged word, and that the true wealth was in land, and that land gave out in proportion to what was put into it. These lessons Custis never forgot. He was to put them to good use at Arlington.

When Martha Washington's death in 1802 followed upon that of his adored foster father in 1799, George Washington Parke Custis determined to carry out the ideas and ideals of his mentor on his own acres— bought by his father and, as yet, having only one building of the former owner.

Custis' plans for Arlington were vast. He had originally planned to call it Mount Washington, but was dissuaded, and named it Arlington after the Custis family estate on the eastern shore of Virginia. But he definitely decided to make it a memorial to George Washington, and a fitting place in which to house the many Washington relics he had both bought and brought from Mt. Vernon. He took twenty years to build the house, while at the same time he laid out his lands in accordance with Washington's teachings.

The mansion he built showed the Greek influence of the times in its pillared front. The two wings balanced the imposing center so perfectly that even today when the thousands cross the bridge to pay their homage to the soldier dead, they see it not as a house that was completed in 1818, but as the properly coordinated structure needed to crown the hillside above the white-marked graves.

Custis married Mary Lee Fitzhugh in 1804 shortly after he began his memorial-home. Descended from the Lees, Fitzhughs and Randolphs who had been noted for generations for their integrity and ideals of service, she was the perfect chatelaine for the beautiful new mansion, for which she planned and planted the famous rose garden. Though only sixteen when she married Custis, Mary assumed the full responsibilities of her position and fulfilled her manifold duties admirably.

Perhaps it was a full knowledge of the demands made upon the mistress of such an estate that prompted Mary Randolph, her cousin, to write The Virginia Housewife. It was a best seller for generations and contained everything from "How to Dress a Turtle," "Pickled Nasturtiums," "Ginger Beer" to "What to do for Rheumatism"! It also included valuable information on how to make candles, and the importance of getting up early.

Mary Randolph, who died in 1828, was the first person to be buried on the grounds at Arlington. Her red-brick tomb is only a stone's throw from the mansion. She and her husband had been frequent visitors and her husband was the inventor of the special stucco used on Arlington Mansion—a stucco which has defied the passage of time.

Just as Custis spent twenty years building the home to house the relics of Washington, so did he prepare the rest of his estate to be a memorial to Washington's beliefs.

He farmed as he had been taught. He kept careful records—open to other farmers. He varied crops. He tried out new methods and reported on them faithfully to any who cared to learn from his experience. Many were the guests who came to Arlington in his day. They ranged from Lafayette, who made two visits, to the farmers who came to observe the new methods and the guests at the annual sheepshearing.

Custis' attitude at Arlington was not that of an owner, but of a trustee of a public place, the curator of a shrine. He welcomed those who came to Arlington—even when it was just for a picnic at Arlington Springs, which had long been a favorite recreation spot for their friends in the neighborhood and those from Washington. He took delight in setting up for them the tents that had sheltered Washington at Yorktown. He was always ready to make a speech on Washington—not so much for the pleasure of orating, as in a sincere belief that everyone was interested in his favorite subject.

In this belief he brought up his daughter, Mary Anne Randolph Custis, the only one who survived of his four children. She was taught to think of herself as Washington's granddaughter with the responsibility of living up to his precepts. She was carefully trained with the understanding that in time she would be entrusted with the care and preservation of the memorial to the first President.

Had Custis and his daughter known what the end of their beloved Arlington would be, perhaps they would have understood and rejoiced in the knowledge that George Washington—who bound his men to him in bad times as well as in good because they knew he thought of their welfare before his own—would have asked no greater memorial than this beautiful resting place for those who had fought for their country.

# THE

# LEE MANSION*

T HE HEIRESS TO ARLINGTON, MARY ANNE CUSTIS, MIGHT WELL
have used Washington's yardstick of integrity when, from out
of her many suitors she chose Robert E. Lee.

What was there about this man that made such an impress upon people
that no one has been able to besmirch or debunk him? Why was it that the
storied white house rising above the Potomac has been enshrined in the
hearts of millions of Americans as the Custis-Lee Mansion?

It was not Lee's—and never was. George Washington Parke Custis built
it to house the relics of another Virginian-soldier, George Washington. He
left a life interest in it to his daughter, wife to Robert E. Lee. But he entailed
it in perpetuity to his grandson, George Washington Custis Lee, asking that
he take his "arms and name."

Perhaps the reasons can be found back in the days when Arlington was
virgin forest and the Lees first came to Virginia. They were always outstanding
people.

Lee's father, Light Horse Harry Lee, was a hero of the Revolution. At
twenty-two he first distinguished himself in battle and went from success to
success. After the war he married Ann Carter, from an equally distinguished
family, and became a three-time Governor of Virginia. Robert, born in 1807,
was the youngest son of this marriage.

In 1812—when Robert was five—his father again gave proof of his daring by coming to the aid of freedom of speech and of the press in the defense of a newspaper editor in Baltimore. Attacked by a mob, Light Horse
Harry Lee was brutally beaten, crippled for life, disfigured, and—what was
worse for him—rendered incapable of rallying to the colors when the

---

* Custis named his estate Arlington and, formally, the mansion was known as Arlington
House. During the War Between the States it was referred to as the Lee Mansion by Union
soldiers stationed in the area and by others who knew it only as the former home of Robert E.
Lee. Although the mansion became part of Arlington National Cemetery in 1864, this term—Lee
Mansion—was still used to describe it until 1955 when its name was officially changed by Congress to the Custis-Lee Mansion. Congress has been petitioned by fourteen patriotic groups to change
the name back to Arlington House.

When the Lees were young, and their love was new, and the future was rose-colored, these portraits were painted for her mother and father and adorned the walls of Arlington Mansion.

British swept down from Canada. He never recovered his health and died in 1818 on his way home from the West Indies.

Familiar with his father's book on *Memoirs of the War in the Southern Department* and brought up in Alexandria, a town rich in memories of Washington, it is not surprising that Robert's thoughts turned to the Army as a career. His education would cost his widowed mother nothing—and he really did like mathematics. In 1825 Calhoun signed the appointment of Robert E. Lee to West Point and so began that long march which led, at the end, to Appomatox.

Even though his class at the Military Academy was noted for its brilliance, he was among the first rank and kept to his resolve to have no demerits. His scholarship was such that he won entry into the Engineering Corps as he had hoped. And in his final year he reached the most coveted honor— Adjutant of the Cadet Corps.

It was the summer he graduated from West Point that he started courting Mary Anne Custis whom he had known all his life. Custis objected at first. Mary Anne was the heiress of Arlington and due to be trustee of the Washington Memorial—Arlington. A junior officer in the Engineering Corps, who flatly stated that his wife must live on his salary and as his co-workers lived, was not what Custis had planned for his daughter.

But Mrs. Custis was a Fitzhugh and a Randolph and a Lee. To her a man to whom fidelity, honor and integrity were a way of life, was just what she wanted as a husband for her only daughter. Mary Anne had already made up her mind, so Custis had to give in. He wanted to help the young couple financially, but his assistance was politely, but firmly, refused by both.

On June 30, 1831 Mary Anne Randolph Custis was married to Robert Edward Lee at Arlington Mansion in the midst of a torrential rain storm.

They say that a house is not hallowed until there has been a wedding, a birth, and a death. Arlington had all three.

The wedding was that of the Lees, the births those of six of their seven children, and the deaths, many years later, those of George Washington Parke Custis and his wife.

In spite of the bad omen of the rain, the marriage was a singularly happy one. They liked so many of the same things—gardens, the beauties of nature, books—and they were both deeply religious. Their personalities complemented each other. He was quiet in his statements, she apt to be fiery in her opinions. They both liked people, but never needed companions other than each other. He was neat and painstaking, she was neither—but they both had a keen sense of humor.

Sidney Lee—the naval officer—signed for his brother, together with the father of the bride. Thirty years later the Lees had left Arlington forever, Custis was dead, and Sidney was an officer of the Confederate Navy.

Lee soon found out that not only had he married Mary Custis, but he had also married Arlington. Fortunately, Washington had always been his hero, too. He could take traditions in his stride, and he was proud that Arlington would be part of his children's heritage.

As the years passed by, Lee was at Arlington only when on leave. His duties as an engineering officer took him all over the country and often into places where he could not take Mrs. Lee—particularly as, after the birth of her second child, the illness which was to cripple her, evidenced itself. However, his children grew up at Arlington, played on the lawns and under the great oaks as their mother had done.

When in 1846 the Mexican War broke out, Lee was called up and posted first to General Wool and second to General Scott. He won promotion after promotion, rising to brevet Lieutenant Colonel, and serving with many of the men with whom and against whom he was to fight in the dark days ahead.

The years passed, and Mrs. Curtis died in 1852. Custis grew more and more feeble—and not always wise in his choice of overseers for his farmland. Lee was stationed in Texas in 1857 when the word came of Custis' death.

Lee was the executor of the Custis estate. Arlington was left to Mrs. Lee with entail to their eldest son, Custis. The plantations on the Pamunkey went to the two other boys, Rooney and Robert. Ten thousand dollars cash was to go to each of the girls—Mary, Anne, Agnes, and Mildred. The slaves were to be freed—but this could not be done until the estate was settled, for by law they were part of the estate.

There was only one thing to do—and Lee did it. He settled down at Arlington to learn the facts about successful farming. His mathematical brain saw through the twisted figures of the men Custis had hired to run the properties. He hunted through records to disprove claims against the estate. He planned for the legal freeing of the slaves and also arranged that they be trained for freedom, rather than turned loose to fend for themselves.

Custis Lee, seeing his father's predicament, wanted to turn Arlington over to him, so that Lee would have complete freedom to act, but Lee refused. His children had inherited the estates and he was trustee. It was as simple as that.

Perhaps this influenced his ultimate decision in 1861. And yet, there were other considerations. Few of the citizens of other states have been as conscious of state entity as those in Virginia. It was to them the *Dominion* of Virginia, and it had been a dominion before national lines were drawn. The men of Virginia who framed the Constitution of the United States felt that in advocating its adoption, they were not giving up their rights to other states, but were joining with these states to protect their rights.

In 1861 Virginia was neutral until threatened with a call to invade her sister states. Then she withdrew from the Union, but did not yet join the Confederacy.

The travail of spirit through which Lee went before his decision to cast his lot with his home state was made, is shown in a letter to his older sister, Ann, who was married to a man with pronounced Union sympathies. He wrote:

> With all my devotion to the Union and the feeling of loyalty and duty of an American citizen, I have not been able to make up my mind to raise my hand against my relatives, my children, my home. I have therefore resigned my commission in the Army, and, save in defense of my native state, with the sincere hope that my poor services may never be needed, I hope I may never be called upon to draw my sword.

That night of April 19, 1861 he had walked around Arlington for hours, then spent a long time on his knees in prayer before he came to his momentous decision.

In that night-vigil he must have realized he was saying good-bye to the place he loved so much, and of which he had written:

> Arlington . . . where my affection and attachments are more strongly placed than at any other place in the world.

But he could not decide otherwise and live with himself. On that day of decision, Lee had been offered the command of the Union Army of the Potomac. He had refused it, as definitely if not as vehemently as he had refused the command of the Texas Confederate troops when Texas had seceded some months before.

He did not want secession. He had disapproved of the stand taken by the Virginia Assembly. But he was loyal to Virginia, and left Arlington to offer his services, hoping only for a defense post in his native state. He did not go—as so many hurried historians have inferred—to take command of the Confederate forces. Virginia had seceded, but was not then a part of the Confederacy. When she did become a part, Lee was sent to South Carolina, not to be recalled until a year had elapsed and his tactical skill was needed.

He only saw Arlington once more—and that was after the war and from the window of a passing train. But there is one memorial at Arlington which would have meant much to him.

It is not the Confederate War Memorial, fine as that is. It is the rows of graves of the Confederate dead, which from 1871 on, have been decorated each Memorial Day equally with the Union graves.

The flag of the United States—the flag he served so well for so long—
flies over them. The scars of battle are healed at long last. And the nation is
one nation indivisible. That is the memorial Lee would have wanted.

For Lee felt, to use his own words to a former Captain in the Confederate
Navy written shortly before his death in 1870:

The war being at an end; the Southern States having laid down their arms, and
the questions at issue between them and the Northern States having been decided, I believe it to be the duty of every one to unite in the restoration of the
country, and the reestablishment of peace and harmony.

The surveyors move in to turn Arlington Estate into Arlington
Cemetery—1864.

Mathew Brady

The dome of the Capitol rises on the Washington skyline as seen from
the porch at Arlington in 1872.

Library of Congress

# ARLINGTON BECOMES

# A CEMETERY

WHEN LEE LEFT ARLINGTON IN 1861 TO GO TO RICHMOND, MRS. LEE had remained there with her daughters. He had advised her to move to the White House on the Pamunkey, for Lee knew war and its effect on property. Even if he had decided for the North instead of the South, strategically-located Arlington was sure to be taken over. And Mrs. Lee was becoming increasingly crippled.

However, Arlington was the property of a non-combatant and there would be no resistance to its being occupied. Under the existing laws it would remain Mrs. Lee's property. As a matter of fact, in 1882 the Supreme Court confirmed Lee's evaluation of the situation and declared the property to belong to Custis Lee as heir in entail. But by that time the house was uninhabitable, being with its immediately surrounding acres used as a cemetery; and much of the rest of the estate had been taken for Fort Myer, so Custis Lee relinquished his title to the United States Government for the sum of $150,000, and Arlington ceased to be private property.

Shortly after her husband left, Mrs. Lee was informed privately that Arlington would be occupied, and she departed for the Pamunkey. Left behind in attic and cellar were all that she could not carry with her, including many of the priceless Washington relics. It never occurred to her that there would be any interference with her property. She would have been just as indignant at a trespass from the South as from the North. She had been brought up to believe that Arlington was ground hallowed to Washington. Away from it, she was Mrs. Robert E. Lee. But at Arlington she was Mary Anne Custis Lee, granddaughter of George Washington.

Fortunately for her, Arlington became the headquarters for General Irvin McDowell, who tried in every way to protect her property. But there were always militia around and too many of them were irresponsible and undisciplined. McDowell, and later on General Heinzelman, when he succeeded to the command, were shocked to find that things were disappearing.

Finally McDowell had what remained packed and sent to the Patent Office for safekeeping.

Lee tried again and again in his letters during the war years to explain to his wife that the exigencies of war would be such that they could not expect to return to Arlington as it was, that the mere fact of the camps logically placed on the heights overlooking the city of Washington would entail the use of wood, the cutting down of trees, the baring of lands, and so forth—and that she must not expect too much.

Mrs. Lee was not to be assuaged. She felt that somehow she was failing as a trustee of the Washington Memorial. Had everyone forgotten who was the "Father of His Country"?

Then a further blow fell. In 1862 Congress passed a law under which it levied direct taxes on real estate located in the "insurrectionary" districts within the United States. Commissioners were appointed to assess and collect the taxes.

Since the real aim was the confiscation of property belonging to Southerners—both men and women—the Commissioners refused to accept taxes from anyone except the direct owner.

Mrs. Lee was, as was well known behind lines of both South and North, an almost helpless invalid confined to a wheel chair. A cousin appeared for her and offered the amount of taxes imposed, which was $92.07 plus 50 percent. The Commissioners refused to accept the payment and went ahead with a "sale for default," buying Arlington for the "Government" for $26,800.

In 1861 Arlington was occupied by Union troops under Major General Irvin McDowell. Here he stands on the steps of the East Portico, surrounded by his dashing officers, in what they trusted were military poses.

Looking as though he were about to cross-examine a recalcitrant witness, is Edwin M. Stanton, Lincoln's Secretary of War, who sincerely believed he was ordained to conduct the war single-handedly.

There were those in the Government who did not hold this type of chicanery constitutional—as the Supreme Court later ruled—but the radical elements were in control. In fact, as many of the officers stationed at Arlington thought, there was more bitter fighting in the city at their feet than on the battlefields—which these political fighters took care never to approach.

Lincoln had tried to create peace in the ranks of his own party by giving cabinet posts to his rivals for the Presidency. His Secretary of State and closest rival, was Seward, who kindly offered to relieve him of the duties of the Presidency. Lincoln reckoned that since he was elected, he'd better do the President's job. However, as his first selection for Secretary of War had proven highly incompetent for that important post, he accepted Seward's recommendation of Edwin M. Stanton.

Lincoln had tangled with Stanton in a law case some years previously and knew him for a shrewd, hardworking lawyer. Unfortunately he had forgotten that before the case was over Stanton was on the outs with everyone concerned. Stanton was a "smart" man—never corrupt in the matter of money, but with an overwhelming ego and a chronic dislike of Lincoln, the Cabinet, all Southerners, the Regular Army officers who thought they knew more about waging war than he did, and anyone who ever ventured an opinion contrary to his own. He seemed to delight in indulging in small nastinesses—such as making the President come to him for information, and then keeping him waiting.

Stanton had the perfect foil in his Quartermaster General—Montgomery Meigs. Meigs was a competent man with an infinite capacity for detail, but imbued with an idea of his own importance. When a former Secretary of War had wanted to courtmartial him for an act of insubordination which might well have proved fatal in any European Army, Seward saved him—and even had him promoted from Captain to Colonel. Meigs was indignant. He felt he should have been made a General.

Hon. Edwin M. Stanton,

Secretary of War:

Sir:

I have visited and inspected the grounds now used as a cemetery upon the Arlington Estate.

I recommend that interments in this ground be discontinued, and that the land surrounding the Arlington Mansion, now understood to be the property of the United States, be appropriated as a National Military cemetery, to be properly enclosed, laid out, and carefully preserved for that purpose; and that the bodies recently interred be removed to the National Cemetery thus to be established.

The grounds about the Mansion are admirably adapted to such a use.

I am, very respectfully, your obt sevt

M C Meigs

D. M. Genl.

1125 —

The famous letters of June 15, 1864 whereby the land around Arlington Mansion—and the Rose Garden—became a national cemetery. For the record let it be said that burials had been made in other parts of the estate for more than a month previous to the June date.

National Archives

---

The Arlington Mansion and the grounds immediately surrounding it are appropriated for a Military Cemetery.

The bodies of all soldiers dying in the Hospitals of the vicinity of Washington and Alexandria (after the grounds now used at Alexandria are filled) will be interred in this Cemetery.

The Quartermaster General is charged with the execution of this order. He will cause the grounds, not exceeding two hundred acres, to be immediately surveyed, laid out, and enclosed for this purpose; not interfering with the grounds occupied by the Freedmens Camps.

June 15. 1864

Edwin M Stanton

Secretary of War

In fact Meigs wanted to command the Army of the Potomac on its march into Virginia. However, he finally settled for Quartermaster General. After all, the Quartermaster General could make or break any combat commander by issuing or holding back on supplies.

Shortly after beginning to work with Stanton, Meigs became very antisouthern. He had been brought up in Georgia and owed all of his previous promotions to the sponsorship of Jefferson Davis and the southern congressmen. Now he hated them all, including his brother who had remained in the South. But he kept his most violent diatribes for his own previous commander—Robert E. Lee.

This was the man who was Quartermaster General and upon whom devolved all authority for hospitals, cemeteries, supplies—in short, the responsibility of housekeeping for the Army and the District of Columbia.

The city of Washington had become a hospital center. Most of the buildings confiscated for hospitals were inadequate, poorly equipped, incompetently staffed and badly regulated. Indeed, there was so much carelessness and inefficiency in the handling of the wounded, dying and dead in the Washington area that gradually public sentiment throughout the North was aroused. Once aroused, it made itself felt on Congress, and then on Stanton who, having drawn unto himself all authority, was forced to accept all responsibility. So Stanton ordered Meigs to do something about the matter of cemeteries. He did.

Arlington still stood above the Potomac. To Stanton it was a defiance, besides which the officers posted there liked it as headquarters. To Meigs, it had sheltered a man recognized at West Point and in the Army as his superior.

Meigs made no survey of sites. He recommended to Stanton, *in writing*, on June 15, 1864, that Arlington Mansion be made a cemetery and on the same day, *in writing*, Stanton gave orders. Unheard of efficiency—in the days before typewriters.

The estate was large—1,100 acres. Freedmen's Village, housing seven hundred freed Negroes, occupied but a small part of it. Contrabands were buried on the grounds in large numbers. These were men, women and children, who had come to Washington for help—as though to the Promised Land—when freed by the advancing Union armies. No proper provision had been made for their care, and they were put into hurriedly planned camps. Disease was rampant among them and they died and were buried within sight of the marble buildings of their Promised Land across the river.

There was still, however, plenty of room for a large cemetery well away from the mansion which was used by the Army as a headquarters.

Mathew Brady took this picture in June, 1864 just after Arlington had become a cemetery. Already the house shows the effects of war. It has become a lonesome-looking place.

Meigs ordered the first burials to take place by Mrs. Lee's rose garden and close to the house itself. The officers in residence naturally objected and countermanded his orders. Perhaps they realized that back of the choice was spite. Perhaps they thought the spite directed entirely against them. At any rate they knew burials there were unnecessary and forbade them.

But Meigs was stubborn and, it is said, determined that the house where Lee had lived be made uninhabitable for his former chief. So he went to Stanton, asking to have those interred elsewhere, reburied around the house. Needless to say, Stanton agreed. To strike at both the Regular Army and Lee at one time was an accomplishment!

So it began. The death knell of Arlington as a home was sounded. But out of this welter of spite and hate, out of the notions of lesser men, grew something big. Something as big as the man for whose relics it was designed. Something as big as the man who had lived there—and who was revered and liked by the men of the Regular Army as much as they deplored and regretted his choice of allegiance.

The first two soldier-dead were interred in Arlington National Cemetery on May 13, 1864. On June 15, Stanton formally designated the mansion and two hundred acres around it as a cemetery for the burial of soldiers from the hospitals in the area.

So it was. Arlington, named for the Custis estate on the Eastern Shore, built to house the relics of Washington, home for a while of Robert E. Lee, was a victim of the War Between the States.

But out of its grave grew a thing of beauty—a symbol of unity, a memorial to which the yearning hearts of those who lost loved ones in any of our wars could turn again for the sign of remembrance, the torch of immortality for heroes all.

# HEROES FROM
# THE PAST

F ROM ITS VERY BEGINNING THE SHADOW OF WAR FELL UPON WHAT
was eventually to become Arlington National Cemetery. The
Revolutionary War was being fought when John Custis bought its acres.
When George Washington Parke Custis first moved there, the Barbary
War was being waged to establish for all time that Americans would not
pay tribute.

Even as the walls of Arlington Mansion were being raised, the War of
1812 was begun on a dozen battlefronts. From Arlington, Custis went to
join the defending troops at nearby Bladensburg against the invading British.

There were always Indian wars on some frontier as the land-hungry
settlers surged forward. To the frontier in the West went Robert E. Lee,
leaving his family at Arlington. During the Mexican War 1846-1848, they
remained in its peace, while he went on to battle.

When Arlington became a National Cemetery in 1864, the remains of
many of those who died in these wars were reinterred with their comrades
at Arlington. Here are the stories of a few of those who represent the heroes
of the early wars.

Among the graves of those who fought in the Revolutionary War are
three of the original founders of the Society of the Cincinnati—the first
great patriotic organization of veterans. The title came, of course, from
Cincinnatus, the Roman patriot who left his plow to go to the defense of
Rome—and returned to his furrows when Rome had defeated her enemies
under his leadership.

The experiences of these three were very different. Perhaps the best
known is Pierre l'Enfant, whose marble tomb overlooks the city he planned.
He needs no great monument. Indeed, the old Latin line suffices—*Si monu-
mentum requiris circumspice* or "If a monument is needed, look around and
see."

Not his public honors, not his death as a martyr to freedom of the press—but his war-time record—is cut deep on the tomb of James McCubbin Lingan. To him, the fact that he had served his country was the most significant act of his life.

**Patrick Hughes**

How many of those who look out over the city realize that he was one of the Frenchmen who came to join in the fight for liberty, drawn by a vision of a bright New World; that he fought from 1776 to the end of the war and became a friend of George Washington, for whom he drew up the plans for the capital city.

Like most visionaries he was derided by many for his "overly ambitious" plans, for he envisioned a city for "fifty states, not thirteen." In death he has found the recognition denied him in life.

Quite different in experience was that of another founder of the Cincinnati—Colonel John Green, who was born and died in Liberty Hall, Culpepper County, Virginia. He was among the first to follow Washington, and he, too, fought all through the war in battle after battle, serving with distinction. He was Colonel of the Sixth and Tenth Virginia Regiments of Volunteers—backbone of any corps to which they were attached. He was a soldier's soldier, with a record to which his descendants can point with pride.

The third member of the Cincinnati was James McCubbin Lingan, who, at the time of his death in 1812, was Collector of the Port of Georgetown. He had been among the first to go to war and was captured after service in the Maryland and Virginia Continental troops. For three long years he was a prisoner on the infamous British prison ship, the *Jersey.* He could have been released—in fact he was offered release and high rank if he would change sides. But even though related to British Admiral Hood, he stood firm and endured the imprisonment.

In 1812 he—together with Lighthorse Harry Lee—came to the defense of a free press in the person of a newspaper editor in Baltimore, who, a Federalist as were they, did not believe the war with Britain necessary, and felt that Napoleon and the French Revolution constituted the greater menace. Lingan was present when the mob attacked this editor and was instantly killed, a martyr to freedom of speech and of the press.

In the same year in which Lingan was killed, there was a small group of Marines stationed on the Florida frontier, then under Spanish domination, to keep the supply lines open between the Regulars, who were slowly moving in to take possession. The Indians were fighting with and for the Spaniards. They ambushed a wagon train and mortally wounded a young U. S. Marine Captain, John Williams. What is significant—and representative—about his grave is that the stone was originally erected in Georgia by his own men as their tribute to a gallant officer who, according to the Marine Commandant, embodied the highest ideals of the Corps.

In the War of 1812 the Navy played a most important part—on inland waters as well as at sea. At Arlington there are graves of two distinguished naval officers who fought with distinction in this war, and who are equally important because they stand for all service families.

Captain Thomas Holdup Stevens led the assault on Black Rock and, although wounded, brought his men safely back across the Niagara. He served with Perry at the Battle of Lake Erie, in command of the *Trippe*. Later he fought West Indian pirates under David Porter, and at the time of his death he was Commandant of the Washington Navy Yard. For 110 years the Stevens family gave to the United States gallant officers in both Army and Navy.

Captain Stephen Cassin was himself part of a service dynasty. His father was John Cassin, Commander in the Navy of the infant republic. Cassin fought on the *Ticonderoga* at the Battle of Lake Champlain—and fought so well that he was chosen by McDonough, the commander of the American forces, to carry the captured battle flags to Washington. His descendants have kept up the service traditions of the family.

Not all the valiant deeds were done in war. Consider Charles Wilkes who rose to the rank of Rear Admiral in 1866. His moment of greatest glory was back in 1838 when, but a Lieutenant, he was placed in command of an expedition to explore and survey the Southern Seas—the first scientific expedition ever fitted out by the United States Government. For five long years Wilkes supervised the making of surveys of 280 islands, of eight hundred miles of the Pacific Northwest Coastline, and of 1,500 miles of largely unexplored Antarctic coast. It was Wilkes who discovered that Antarctica was a continent—which was confirmed by Shackleton's discoveries nearly a century later.

The outcome of his explorations appeared in nineteen volumes which proved of incalculable value to mariners who rounded the Horn, and to the whalers who hunted in the Antarctic seas.

By the time the War Between the States began, Wilkes was a Captain, and in command of the USS *San Jacinto*. Then it was that he acquired his

Philip Kearny and his horse—an excellent example of arrested motion, for the gallant General seems straining to ride forth again to defend the nation he loved so well, and for which he fought so valiantly.

Patrick Hughes

best known claim to fame—he stopped the British Mail Steamer, *Trent*, and removed the Confederate Commissioners to England—Mason and Slidell. His action was hailed by the North—although it nearly started a war with Britain.

Like Cassin and Stevens, the service strain repeated itself in another generation. His great grandson, Vice-Admiral John Wilkes, was a submariner in two world wars—an explorer beneath the sea as his grandfather had been among the polar ice.

The Mexican War has often been called the training field for the War Between the States. Certainly most of the commanders who fought in the later war had a good grounding in their craft in Mexico. Much of the strategy and tactics utilized in the War Between the States were worked out by trial and error in the Mexican War. And much of the knowledge of what an officer would do, given a certain situation, was acquired there. After all, the rolls of the Aztec Club of 1847—the equivalent of the Society of the Cincinnati in the Revolutionary War—included Jefferson Davis and Ulysses S. Grant, Robert E. Lee and George B. McClellan, Stonewall Jackson and George Meade, and many others whose moments of glory came in the later wars.

But there was one man whose greatest moment of glory, perhaps, was in this war, even though his life afterwards was also distinguished. That was Philip Kearny, who had always wanted to be a soldier.

His grandfather, James Watts, who was also his guardian, refused to let him go to West Point and tried to turn his thoughts toward the ministry or law, but to no avail. And when his grandfather died, leaving him almost a million dollars, he was off immediately to join his uncle, Stephen Kearny, as a Second Lieutenant.

In the course of time he was sent to the French cavalry school at Saumur and later saw service with the celebrated Chasseurs d'Afrique. Then he came back to the Army on the western frontier.

In the Mexican War he was commanding a troop of dragoons. Like another cavalry-minded general nearly a hundred years later, George Patton, he had the interests of his men at heart. He had mounted them on uniform dappled gray horses—which he had procured at his own expense. They became one of the most daring cavalry groups in a day when calvary was at its height.

At Churubusco, Kearny's dragoons charged—too far ahead to hear Retreat being sounded—and, according to many observers, saved the day. But on the return to the American lines, grapeshot shattered his arm and it had to be amputated.

This did not stop Philip Kearny. Later he went back to France and was in the Franco-Italian war at Solferino. When the War Between the States broke out, he returned to offer his services to the Union. He had difficulty getting in at first, but finally wangled it and became commander of the Third Division of the Army of the Potomac, which included many of the foreign born who were strong believers in the Union cause.

His men adored him—for he understood them and expected from them the same devotion and daring he gave. He was always ahead of them—never behind. His little figure mounted on his big horse was a familiar sight and when the charge was sounded, Kearny rode ahead, his kepi at a jaunty angle, the reins held between his teeth and his right arm free to wave them on.

He ranged too far ahead at the Battle of Second Bull Run and was killed at Chantilly. Under flag of truce General Lee immediately returned his body, and later his horse and sword.

Over his grave is a statue of Kearny on horseback—as though he were ready to ride again at a call from the nation he loved. As tumultuous as his life, was that of the fort named for him. Near Fort Phil Kearny on the Bozeman Trail, Montana, occurred the Fetterman Massacre, and later, in 1867, the Wagon Box Fight where thirty-two troopers stood off 1,500 Indians— and won the day.

But it is not for his daring alone that Kearny is selected as a representative. Kearny distinguished the men of his division by furnishing them with a red patch for their kepis—the forerunner of the shoulder patch of today.

"The shadow of war fell on Arlington."
Patrick Hughes

This distinguishing mark was a great help in rousing the *esprit de corps* so vital in the building of an army.

When Kearny was killed, his men wanted something more than a patch. They wanted a medal for each to wear to prove they were Kearny's men. This was done, and a year later, Major General David Birney, Kearny's successor in command, went further and obtained another medal—the "cross of honor," known as "Kearny's cross"—which was given for exceptional valor in battle to noncommissioned officers and privates.

From this came the Medal of Honor—the highest decoration that can be given to an American serviceman.

# THEY FOUGHT
# FOR THE UNION

FROM THE FIRST SHOT FIRED ON THE HITHERTO QUIET WOODED slopes of Bull Run, to the surrender of Lee at Appomattox, each battle of the East sent its men to rest within the boundaries of Arlington.

First Bull Run, Peninsular Campaign with Fair Oaks, the Seven Days Battle, Second Bull Run, Antietam, Fredericksburg, Chancellorsville, Gettysburg, the Wilderness to Petersburg, and Cold Harbor—from these and many another skirmish, less famous but just as deadly, the wounded came to linger for a while in the hospitals and then to lie at rest on the green slopes of Arlington. They were joined after the war by veterans of the battles in the West.

For the legions of the daring, whose deeds have come down through the pages of time, there is Philip Henry Sheridan, cavalryman, leader of men, and finally General. Sheridan, the son of Irish immigrants, was a born fighter. Indeed, he nearly brawled himself out of West Point and was suspended for a year. He fought in the Northwest and on the Rio Grande, then later became Quartermaster for Halleck at Corinth. He was in the bloody fighting at Chickamauga and Missionary Ridge before he was ordered east after Halleck took command.

Sheridan is, perhaps, most famous for his ride to turn back the fleeing troops in the Valley. "Sheridan's Ride" used to be a required recitation piece in school—"And Winchester twenty miles away." He was a dramatic character—he did not have to dress oddly like Custer and McClellan, for he always looked the part. He was no tactician, but he never stopped fighting and he could always be found where the battle was hottest, and the odds greatest.

His naval counterpart was Rear Admiral David Dixon Porter, son of the David Porter who had taken the *Essex* into the Pacific in the War of 1812, and who had befriended David Farragut. Porter served under Farragut on the Mississippi. It was Porter who ran the gauntlet of the Confederate batteries at Vicksburg and who succeeded where so many had failed.

Gideon Welles, Secretary of the Navy, had pretty well sized up young Porter, feeling that, like his father and brother, he was hard to keep under discipline, but was intelligently daring when given sole command. So, when the other Admirals had failed at Fort Fisher through undue caution, Welles raised Porter to Admiral's rank and ordered him to take the fort— which Porter promptly did, and then looked around for new battles to win. His outstanding record was a shining mark to his descendants in later wars.

One who also had the benefit of a service dynasty was Major General Edward Otho Cresap Ord. His father had been an officer in the United States Navy for a short time and during the War of 1812 was a Lieutenant in the Army. Ord was descended from Colonel Daniel Cresap of Revolutionary War fame, and, it is rumored, from George IV of England. But he made his own history.

A West Pointer, he fought against the Seminoles in Florida in 1840. He was in California on duty for the next decade. In the 50s he fought in Oregon against the Rogue River Indians. On a trip back East, he was sent to Harpers Ferry under Lee to arrest John Brown. In the War Between the States, he led volunteer troops in defense of Washington and against Jeb Stuart. Later, transferred to the West, he fought at Corinth where he was wounded, then at Vicksburg where he was on Grant's staff. He was transferred to Sigel's and to Crook's campaigns in the Shenandoah, and then commanded a Corps before Richmond. In short, wherever there was fighting, there Ord was—a competent leader even of untrained troops. He died of yellow fever in Havana in 1883.

Another good soldier was Abner Doubleday. His grandfather had fought in the Revolution and had been imprisoned on the Jersey. His father was an editor, and both of his brothers were Colonels during the War Between the States. Doubleday graduated from West Point in 1842. Later he joined Zachary Taylor to fight in the Mexican War at Monterrey. He was present at the outbreak of the War Between the States. In fact, he fired the first shot from Fort Sumter in reply to the Confederates. His aim was good—but the shot glanced off its target. Active in the defense of Washington, he fought at Second Bull Run, at Stone Mountain, at Antietam, and at Fredericksburg, becoming a Major General in 1862.

After the war Doubleday was stationed in California, and while in San Francisco started the first cable car company. But what he is best known for to most young Americans is that he is credited with inventing the game of baseball. That far outweighs with them his outstanding record as a soldier.

A General who nearly became President lies at Arlington. William Starke Rosencrans was a sixth-generation American, whose ancestor had arrived in 1637. Rosencrans graduated from West Point in 1842. He resigned from the Army in 1854 but when war broke out became a volunteer Aide to McClellan. It was due to his successful campaign that the Confederates were driven out of West Virginia. Assigned next to the West he was at Corinth and Holly Springs, before being ordered to relieve Buell in Kentucky. Rosencrans succeeded against Bragg at Murfreesboro, but had bad luck at Chickamauga and was removed from command. He had already offended Stanton and Halleck by plain speaking and they did not miss the opportunity to sidetrack him.

It was during this period that he nearly became President. Rosencrans had been asked to run against Lincoln for the Republican nomination in 1864. He refused and was offered the Vice-Presidency. He accepted by wire; but Stanton, having seized the telegraph lines as Secretary of War, received the wire of acceptance and did not pass it on. The result was that Andrew Johnson was nominated.

Symbolic of the many foreign-born at Arlington is Major General H. Julius Stahel-Szamwald, a Hungarian patriot who came to the United States as a refugee in 1859. At the outbreak of hostilities, he, with General Blenker, formed the 8th New York Volunteer Infantry Regiment, composed of the foreign-born who believed so strongly in the Union cause that they volunteered to fight for it.

General Stahel's regiment, when the retreat was ordered at Bull Run, stayed behind to fight a delaying action. Some experts thought this action saved Washington. He was again outstanding at Cross Keys and this won him a promotion. For heroism at Piedmont, under General Sullivan, he received the Medal of Honor.

Perhaps even greater in his eyes was another honor he received. President Lincoln specifically requested that Stahel attend him on the trip to Gettysburg when he made his immortal address—of which a New York newspaper, printing Edward Everett's oration in full, said "The President also spoke."

Brigadier General William A. Hammond represents the merciful. He was a physician—one of the Army doctors who typified the highest ideals of service. His work in the field attracted the interest of the Sanitary Commission, which dissatisfied with the conduct of the hospitals, used pressure to have Hammond made Surgeon General. Stanton did not like the Sanitary Commission which had criticized *him*. He was not prepared to like Hammond and didn't.

Hammond for his part believed hospital corpsmen should accompany the ambulances—not bandsmen furnished by the Quartermaster General.

From the vantage point of Horatio Wright's grave are seen the Washington Monument, which he completed as a memorial to George Washington; the Lincoln Memorial in which the magnificent statue of the war-time President is enshrined; and, just below Wright's tomb, is the throng of sorrowing visitors around the grave of John F. Kennedy.

Patrick Hughes

He believed in sending emergency aid equipment and supplies to the battlefield, and he pointed out that there were ample supplies neatly stored in Washington by the Quartermaster General.

Hammond went right ahead reforming the hospital service. He was courtmartialled in 1863, but it was so obviously a frame-up, that he was acquitted. However, the following year he was dismissed by a military court, and a henchman of Stanton's was put in his place. The courtmartial was reversed in 1878 and his record completely cleared.

Typical of the Marines buried in Arlington is one of their Commandants, Charles Heywood. As a young Lieutenant he was ordered to duty on the Cumberland at Norfolk and with that vessel took part in the destruction of the Navy Yard. In May, 1861—as a First Lieutenant—he landed with the Marines at Hatteras Inlet and was at the capture of Forts Clark and Hatteras. As Captain he was in the duel between the *Cumberland* and the *Merrimac* in March of 1862, when the destructiveness of the iron-clad changed the course of sea warfare. He fired the last gun in this fighting and saved himself only by jumping overboard as the *Cumberland* went down with her flag flying. His gallant conduct resulted in his promotion to Major, and later at Mobile Bay, to Lieutenant Colonel.

In January, 1891 Colonel Heywood became Commandant of the Marine Corps, where he set up officers' schools which still continue. In fact, much of the Marine's current training program is based on his plan.

John McAllister Schofield reached the rank of Lieutenant General and, for a short time, was the Secretary of War. He had thought of studying law before he won his appointment to West Point, and he brought to all he did a judicial outlook.

When the War Between the States broke out, he became chief-of-staff to General Lyon and then, after Lyons' death, was eventually given command of the Army of the Frontier. Politics kept his confirmation from going through, so, instead of complaining, he asked for transfer in order not to disrupt the troops who were fiercely loyal to him.

He next went to the Army of Tennessee where he took a prominent part in one of the most dramatic campaigns. Confederate General Hood was sweeping west with plans to retake Nashville. Union General Thomas, in command at Nashville, was in the process of being axed by Stanton's cohorts because of his Virginian birth and his peaceful, though firm, occupation of Nashville.

Schofield was ordered to delay Hood, while Thomas prepared for defense. Schofield lured Hood—who was always overdaring—to chase him. Apparently retreating to Nashville, Schofield turned suddenly at Franklin and fought just such a battle that would weaken Hood without sacrificing his own troops. Thomas in the meantime gathered his forces and presented a strong front. Hood fled and the threat to the Union forces in Tennessee was over.

Next Schofield went to join Sherman's forces, and later he helped in the negotiations with Johnston for surrender. The peace terms given were as Lincoln had ordered, but immediately upon the assassination of the President, Stanton abrogated the terms.

At the close of the war, Schofield was sent to France to arrange for the removal of French troops from Mexico—a most delicate diplomatic task. Then he served as Secretary of War for a short period of time, resigning when Grant was elected.

Later, while serving as Commandant of the Military Academy at West Point, he conducted the second courtmartial of former Major General Fitz-John Porter, who had incurred Stanton's enmity by his loyalty to McClellan. Upon sifting all the evidence, he and his fellow officers on the Court, saw plainly that the first Court had been rigged for conviction, and therefore they completely exonerated Fitz-John Porter from all charges.

In front of the Custis-Lee Mansion is the grave of Major General Horatio Gouveneur Wright, who, when he retired in 1884 was Chief of Engineers. His grave looks down over the city of Washington, which the troops of the VI Corps under his command saved from Jubal Early's raiders in July of 1864.

Wright had been in the war from the beginning. On April 20, 1861 he was captured in a daring raid to destroy the dry dock at the Norfolk Navy Yard, but soon gained his release. He participated in every battle of the Wilderness and bore the brunt of the fighting at Bloody Angle—before he was rushed off to repel Early's raid on Washington. It is interesting to note how many took the credit for his accomplishments. At Cedar Creek he held the line until Sheridan arrived—and Sheridan was given the credit. His troops were the first to pierce the lines at the bloody battle of Petersburg. And from there he was sent to command the Department of Texas.

After the war he concentrated on important engineering tasks, building the East River Bridge in New York, the Sutro Tunnel in Nevada, the Delaware Breakwater Harbor of Refuge, the South Pass jetties on the Mississippi, and the achievement toward which his grave faces—the Washington Monument, which he completed. A good soldier, a fine engineer—and a brave man!

With the burial there of such heroes—representatives of the more than 19,000 Union dead—Arlington became truly God's Acre, where there were no more wars, and where vanquished and victor were laid to rest together.

John Marthon fought with Farragut at Mobile Bay— and was proud of it.

Patrick Hughes

# THEY FOUGHT

# FOR THE SOUTH

NEVER WAS THERE A WAR IN WHICH FEELING RAN AS HIGH ON BOTH sides as in the War Between the States. Yet, when it was over, the scars faded with the passage of time. This does not overlook the terrible losses on both sides, nor the devastation with which the South was faced, nor the dark days of the Reconstruction period.

Lincoln was assassinated—a tragedy for the whole nation—especially for the South, but there still remained some levelheaded statesmen who remembered his words:

> With malice toward none, with charity for all . . . to do all which may achieve and cherish a just and lasting peace among ourselves . . .

Lee was defeated—but in defeat showed his true greatness. He did not repine—that was not his nature. But, by his calmness, by his acceptance of what must be endured, he led his followers to peace, as he had led them in war.

Julia Ward Howe, who wrote the stirring words of "The Battle Hymn of the Republic," paid tribute to Lee in two memorable lines:

> A gallant foeman in the fight, A brother when the fight was o'er . . .

Lincoln and Lee—the two whose names have stood the test of time— the two who, though neither is buried in Arlington, have had greater impress on it than those who claimed to have created it.

There were Confederate dead buried there even before its formal inception as a cemetery. For the most part they were prisoners of war or civilian prisoners from the Old Capitol Prison. Like so many of the young soldiers who fought for the Union cause, they died of disease. Were the civilian prisoners spies or sympathizers? Or were they merely in somebody's way? No one knows, for there are no existing records. This much is known. One of the first names appearing in the records is that of "John Leacock, Citizen." He is listed as "State Prisoner" in contrast to others who simply have "prisoner" after the word "citizen"—though some omit the "citizen." Who were they, one wonders. Then there are some that have the fateful PW after their names—probably prisoners of war who were so ill they had to be sent to a hospital.

One of the first Confederate soldiers buried at Arlington was Irish-born Michael Quinn, Corporal of Company F, 13th Mississippi Infantry. After three years of fighting, he was wounded on May 8, 1864, at Spotsylvania— just the day before Major General Wright took over the Union troops on the death of General Sedgwick. Quinn died in a Washington hospital on May 16, and was buried at Arlington two days later. One of the ironies of war is that he enlisted in Corinth, Mississippi, then deep in the heart of the Confederacy, but, by the time of Quinn's death, fought over as hotly as the contested Virginia territory where he fell.

The record of the first Confederate officer buried in Arlington could be duplicated many times in the Federal ranks. He was Adjutant David E. Brown of the 14th South Carolina Infantry and he hailed from Townville, South Carolina. He was wounded in a skirmish in Virginia on May 12, 1864 and he died on May 25 at Judiciary Square Hospital in Washington. He was just twenty-three years old. If the Philippine Insurrection at the turn of the century was known as the "Lieutenants' War," what could the War Between the States be called? The "Boys' War"? They were all so terribly young.

At first, under General Meigs, the bitter man who controlled the Arlington National Cemetery—even more bitter now because his beloved son had been killed while on patrol—there was short shrift for those who wanted to cherish the Confederate graves.

When, on the occasion of the first Decoration Day in 1868, some Southern women asked permission to place flowers upon the Confederate graves at Arlington, they were curtly refused and even denied entrance to the Cemetery.

The Union graves there were heaped high with flowers on this first Decoration Day—but the Confederate graves were left bare and forlorn. Then nature, or the spirits of the Union dead, took a hand. That night there was a blustery wind—and in the morning, as report has it, the sentries found the Confederate graves buried under flowers blown from the Union graves.

But, as the years passed by and ex-Union soldiers began to fill the halls of Congress, replacing the radical rabble-rousers and carpetbaggers who flourished after Lincoln's death, the attitude changed. These men had fought. They knew what war meant. They did not hate their foes.

Then, in the year 1900, as a gesture of goodwill—due in part to the way in which so many Confederate veterans had rallied to the flag in the Spanish-American War—Congress authorized a Confederate Section in Arlington, and the many Confederate dead were gathered from all over the Cemetery to rest together. Before another year had passed the bodies of all Confederates buried in Alexandria and at Soldiers' Home Cemetery were reinterred at Arlington. Since then, by another Act of Congress, ex-Confederate soldiers or sailors, who died in and around Washington after the war, have been buried there.

The next step was permission to erect a memorial at Arlington to the hundreds of Confederate dead. The plan was first approved by President Taft, who himself is buried at Arlington, and later by Congress.

The money was raised dollar by dollar by the United Daughters of the Confederacy. When they selected the sculptor, they chose unusually well— for Moses Ezekiel was not only one of the great sculptors of his day, but a Confederate veteran, one of the Virginia Military Institute cadets who fought at New Market and around Richmond. Ezekiel contributed his fee and accepted only the costs.

Peace is the central theme of the 32½ foot high monument. It is surmounted by the heroic-sized figure of a woman, crowned with olive leaves, her face turned toward the South. In her outstretched left hand is a laurel wreath, and in the right hand is a plough stock and a pruning hook. Carved around the memorial is the verse from Isaiah:

They shall beat their swords into plowshares, and their spears into pruning hooks.

A circular frieze of thirty-two life-sized figures shows Southern soldiers going off to war. Their sad homecoming dominates the middle part of the monument. Over it are carved the seals of the Southern states.

The south side of the monument bears this simple dedication:

To our dead heroes, by the United Daughters of the Confederacy. "Victrix causa diis placuit sed victa Catoni." (The victorious cause was pleasing to the gods, but the lost cause to Cato.)

On the north side of the monument is the beautiful inscription written by Dr. Randolph Harrison McKim, who went from the ranks of the Confederate Army into the Ministry, and who was rector of Epiphany Church in Washington for thirty-two years. The inscription reads:

Not for fame or reward, not for place or for rank, not lured by ambition or goaded by necessity, but in simple obedience to duty as they understood it, these men suffered all, sacrificed all, dared all, and died.

A memorial to all the Confederate dead—a memorial in defeat. This is the working of a true democracy, of a republic which has endured.

Patrick Hughes

When the cornerstone of the Monument was laid in 1912 one of the speakers was Corporal James A. Tanner, Commander-in-Chief of the Grand Army of the Republic, the New York schoolteacher who had lost both legs at the first battle of Bull Run. He, too, is buried at Arlington.

The Monument itself was dedicated on June 4, 1914 with President Wilson, himself a Southerner, making the principal address before an audience that included several thousand Confederate and Union veterans.

Three years later Moses Ezekiel died, but his body was not brought from Rome to rest in Arlington until four years later when the First World War was ended. His was the first funeral in the then newly-completed Arlington Memorial Ampitheatre.

Of Sephardic ancestry, Moses Ezekiel was born and brought up in Richmond. He early showed an interest in art; and, although his family were Orthodox Jews, forbidden by their religion "to make any graven image," they were liberal enough not to discourage him. However, he felt that it had to be an avocation, for the generosity of his father toward the poor had put the family fortunes in a bad way. Then the war came. He was too young to enlist and went instead to Virginia Military Institute.

There was his moment of greatest glory. He took part in the gallant charge of the VMI cadets in the Battle of New Market, Virginia, when they went to help the forces of General Breckinridge—former U. S. Senator, Vice-President of the United States, and unsuccessful candidate for the Presidency against Lincoln. With the aid of the cadets, Breckinridge defeated General Sigel's troops—and the cadets returned to Lexington to find that VMI had been raided and their books were torn and trampled in the mud of the parade ground.

After the war Ezekiel returned to VMI to graduate. In 1869, he went to Europe to study, first in Berlin and afterwards in Rome.

The King of Italy knighted him—so technically he was "Sir Moses Ezkiel," creator of two hundred great sculptures—but he knew what honor pleasured him most. He was buried at Arlington, at the foot of the Statue he had created, and the bronze plate on his footstone reads :

Moses J. Ezekiel

Sergeant of Company C, Battalion of Cadets
of the
Virginia Military Institute

Three Confederate officers, deceased since the monument was erected, keep Ezekiel company at its base. They are Lieutenant Harry C. Marmaduke of the Confederate Navy, Captain John M. Hickey of the Second Missouri Infantry, and Brigadier General Marcus J. Wright of Cheatham's Brigade.

General Wright had commanded his brigade with the Army of Tennessee and was wounded in the battles of Shiloh and Chickamauga. In 1864 he was commander of the district and post of Atlanta. He lived to be ninety-one—and wrote such books as a *Life of General Winfield Scott*.

Within the confines of the plot of a Union officer at Arlington, lies the grave of a woman to whom Robert E. Lee wrote: "You have done more for the South than all the women." Juliet Opie Hopkins was the Florence Nightingale of the South. The wife of Judge Arthur Francis Hopkins of Mobile, she began serving in the hospitals shortly after the outbreak of hostilities. Her husband, who was twenty-four years older than she, was also interested in the work; but she was the active one, and proved that she had not only a sense of mercy, but an ability to organize and administer. She not only nursed, she found buildings for a hospital, equipment to supply it, and nurses to staff it. Both her private fortune and much of Judge Hopkins' were used to further this work. She was so well known that her picture appeared on one hundred-dollar bills issued by the Confederate State of Alabama.

After the war, her adopted daughter, who was also her niece, married Union General Romeyn B. Ayres. He died in 1888 and was buried in Arlington. Some two years later his mother-in-law, on a visit to Washington, died and was buried in the same plot. The United States Army accorded her full military honors, presumably because of her works of mercy during the war.

Also ranking among the Southern contingent is Fighting Joe Wheeler. During the War Between the States he had been a Major General in the Confederate Army, one of Bragg's cavalry corps commanders in the battles around Chattanooga, and had cut the Federal supply lines before the battle of Lookout Mountain. He had also been with General Joseph Johnston and had harassed Sherman's Army in the advance to Atlanta.

In the Spanish-American War, he and Fitzhugh Lee, also a former Confederate Major General, returned to their first allegiance to fight under the flag of the United States and again distinguished themselves for bravery. There is one good story which went the rounds about Wheeler. In the excitement of the attack at San Juan Hill, he urged his men forward against the Spaniards with the Rebel Yell and the shout "Get those damn Yankees, boys!"

Whether or not the story is true, one thing *is* certain. When the War Between the States was over, it was over. And as President McKinley said in Atlanta, Georgia, in 1898:

> Every soldier's grave made during the unfortunate Civil War
> is a tribute to American valor.

# THEY WIDENED
# THE HORIZON

When the War Between the States ended, the Regulars went back to their prewar task, which was primarly that of keeping the peace on the frontier, but in so doing they fought over nine hundred pitched battles with the Indians. Settlers were moving into the West—those who wanted farm land; those who wanted extensive acreage for cattle; hide hunters, who killed off the buffalo for their hides and left rotting on the ground the meat on which the Indians lived; meat hunters, who were contracted to feed the men working on the railroads; prospectors; promotors; adventurers looking for a place beyond the reach of law. It was the Army's job to protect them all. And, though cut to the bone, the Army did just that—with old equipment, while the Indians were supplied, by those who would make a profit out of anything, with the newest of rifles, which had been destined for the Army.

Here are some of the men of those days, who returned, at long last, to Arlington.

There was George Crook, called "The Grey Fox" by the Indians. At the close of the Mexican War he left West Point to go to the Northwest where he alternated in exploring and in fighting the Indians. In 1861 he went to war as Colonel of the 36th Ohio Volunteers. From then until the end of the war, he had several brevet promotions, each earned by hard fighting and intelligent use of the men in his command. He was at South Mountain and Antietam. In the Army of the Cumberland he commanded a cavalry division and beat Wheeler at Framington, Tennessee. Then Grant snapped him up and sent him to break railway communications. He commanded a Corps of Sheridan's Army of the Shenandoah and was at Winchester, Cedar Creek and Fisher's Hill. It was for his conduct at Fisher's Hill that he received brevet Major General rank.

In the postwar reorganization he reverted to the rank of Lieutenant Colonel and, without complaint, went off to Idaho to finish an Indian war that had been raging for several years. This done, he was sent to do the same with the Apache War which was also of several years' duration. Next, when gold was discovered in the Black Hills of the Dakotas, which had been set aside for a Sioux Reservation as being worthless for settlement, trouble was expected and he went to meet it, in command of the Department of the Platte. The war with the Sioux was a series of running, vicious battles, but it did prepare both Crook and his troops for another Apache war to follow.

The Indians called him "The Grey Fox" because he could move as quickly and as silently. His men were trained to travel on a minimum of equipment and rations and to cover prodigious distances. There was no fuss and feathers about Crook. He even blacked his own boots and wouldn't have an orderly.

He was ahead of his day in his thinking about Indians—and they trusted him because he never broke his word to them.

John Gibbon, Major General of Volunteers, was another great Indian fighter. He had had a little experience fighting the Seminoles before the War Between the States began. His three brothers went with the Confederacy, but he remained loyal to the Union. He was at South Mountain and Antietam and was severely wounded at Fredericksburg. He was at Gettysburg and in all the heavy fighting of the Army of the Potomac during the Wilderness campaign.

He was particularly noted for his ability to take raw troops and make fine fighters out of them. Once he deprived three regiments of carrying colors until they should regain the privilege by their behaviour in later battles.

After the war, like Crook, he went to the Frontier in command of a new regiment. There he rescued the survivors of the forces under Custer, and buried the dead of the Battle of Little Big Horn. One of these, Lieutenant Donald McIntosh, was later brought back to rest at Arlington. Gibbon remained in active service, primarily in the Northwest, until 1891.

Successor to Crook's mantle was Nelson Appleton Miles, who rose to the rank of Lieutenant General. Not a professional soldier at first, he proved in the War Between the States that, as his ancestors had in the Revolution, he could acquire military knowledge rapidly. His record, from his first appearance as a captain of volunteers in Colonel Henry Wilson's 22nd Massachusetts Infantry, was excellent. He received his first commendation, and his first wound at Fair Oaks, and for his conduct at Chancellorsville he received the Medal of Honor. At the age of twenty-six he became a Major General of Volunteers. At the close of the war he was made custodian of Jefferson Davis at Fortress Monroe.

Following this he went into the Regulars as a Colonel and was ordered to the Frontier. For fifteen years he fought Indians—Cheyennes, Kiowas,

Comanches, Sioux. He chased Sitting Bull across the border into Canada, and dispersed the bands of Crazy Horse. He succeeded General Crook in both his post and his fight with Geronimo whom he finally captured. His last great Indian battle was in 1891 at Wounded Knee in the Dakota Territory.

Governor's Island in New York harbor was his next command—quite a change from Indian fighting. But there was more to come. The Spanish-American War broke out and, while he was not allowed to take an expeditionary force to Cuba as he wished, he did get to Puerto Rico with reinforcements. After his retirement in 1903 as a Lieutenant General, he was a familiar figure around Washington, where he lived to the ripe old age of eighty-six. He rests in one of the two mausoleums at Arlington—and was very particular to specify that no one be buried in front of it.

Lovell Harrison Rousseau also went into the Army from civil life. He was a lawyer when the Mexican War began in 1846. He enlisted in the 2nd Indiana Infantry, became a Captain and was mentioned for gallantry at the battle of Buena Vista. He went back to the practice of law in Louisville, until the War Between the States broke out, when he began recruiting—but across the Ohio so as not to disturb Kentucky's neutrality. He is given

Robert Todd Lincoln, only son of President Lincoln to live to maturity, rests under this massive stone. He had served as Secretary of War to another assassinated President, Garfield.

**Patrick Hughes**

credit by many for keeping Kentucky in the Union. He fought at Shiloh, Perryville, Chickamauga and in many other battles. Again he went back to the bar after the war, but soon became a Congressman, fighting the extremists both figuratively and literally. Once when attacked verbally by Grinnell of Iowa, he replied with a cane—the House, egged on by Thaddeus Stevens, censured him. Whereupon he went home and was reelected to the House. In 1867 he rejoined the Army as a Brigadier General, and, with the brevet rank of Major General, was sent to Alaska to receive the surrender of that immense territory from the Russians, which extended the American horizon to the North.

There is something about service in the Army or Navy that makes good explorers. Major General Adolphus Washington Greely was no exception. He enlisted as a private in the Nineteenth Massachusetts Infantry in 1861 and rose steadily in rank. Wounded at Antietam, he was mustered in as a Second Lieutenant with the 81st United States Colored Troops in 1863. He went up to Major in the Volunteers and then started all over again in the Regulars after the war, rising to Major General before retirement.

Greely spent the greater part of his service in the Signal Corps—laying telegraph lines. In the three years from 1876 to 1879 he constructed 2,000 miles of telegraph line in Texas, Montana and the Dakota Territory. The importance of this is seen in the fact that it was the only means of communication between Army posts—and when the line was dead, the troops knew the Indians were out.

In 1879 upon the recommendation of the Hamburg International Geographic Congress, General Greely was placed in command of a United States expedition to establish a chain of thirteen circum-polar stations.

The expedition of twenty-five sailed from Newfoundland on July 4, 1881 and reached farther north than any previous expedition, discovering new land north of Greenland and crossing Grinnell Land in the Polar Sea. Then the party was marooned on Arctic ice. Two relief expeditions failed. Supplies became exhausted and all except seven died of starvation. The survivors were finally rescued in June of 1884 by Captain Winfield Scott Schley of the Navy, later of Spanish-American War fame, who is also buried at Arlington.

Greely retired in 1908 and, nearly thirty years later, was awarded the Medal of Honor "for his life of splendid public service."

Closely related to Greely's expedition was William Babcock Hazen, who, from the day he entered West Point until his death some thirty-six years later, was a professional soldier. Hazen was not a tactful man—whatever he thought, he said. But his men could always rely on him for justice.

Hazen started the War Between the States as a Captain, but soon, in company with his boyhood friend, James Garfield, later to be President of

Medal of Honor: the nation's highest award for heroism.

the United States, he had won his regiment. He was at Shiloh, at Chickamauga, Missionary Ridge, the march from Atlanta to the sea, and the return march through Columbia, South Carolina. When the Grand Review was held in Washington on May 24, 1865 he marched at the head of the XV Corps in the Army of Tennessee.

After the war Hazen saw long years of service on the Frontier as a Colonel in the Regulars. It was while in service on the Plains that he restrained Custer from wiping out the friendly Kiowa camp near Fort Cobb. An Indian was an Indian to Custer and better dead—but not to Hazen, as not to Crook. Later he commanded at Fort Buford—that forlorn outpost for the defense of the Bozeman Trail and the protection of the telegraph line—in the Dakota Territory. The Indians had discovered that if they lassoed the wires and raced away with their horses, they could drag the wires for a long distance and leave them in a hopeless snarl.

It was while Hazen was at Fort Buford, that he wrote most pointedly about the exaggerated claims of the land speculators along the railroad's right of way. He also hit hard at the corruption apparent in the post-trader system then used, and later substantiated his claims before a committee of the House. This, needless to say, did not endear him to his superiors, particularly when he was called as a witness in the investigation of General William W. Belknap who was Secretary of War. The House Committee recommended impeachment, but Belknap tendered his resignation to President Grant and the case was dropped. General Belknap is buried near Hazen in Arlington. His moment of glory had been in the War Between the States when he had served General Grant well.

In 1880 President Hayes made Hazen Chief of the Signal Corps—which also included charge of the Weather Bureau, probably because all the western weather news came by telegraph. He, therefore, had the duty of command over the Greely Expedition, and took the matter of relief ships most seriously. The first relief expedition failed. The second was caught in the ice. They were about to set out again when the then Secretary of War, Robert Todd Lincoln, eldest son of the martyred President, decided it was too late in the year to send out a relief ship and Greely spent a third winter in the Arctic until rescued by the Navy in the spring. It was during this last winter that so many died of starvation.

Hazen was indignant and wrote another tactless letter. This time he was courtmartialed and reprimanded for "captious criticism"—but the feeling was general among the experts, including Greely, that Hazen had been right. The courtmartial did not seem to affect his position and he was still Chief of the Signal Corps when he died in 1887.

As a postscript, Hazen, Lincoln and Greely are buried near each other at Arlington.

Crook's exploits as an Indian fighter overshadowed his excellent leadership in the Civil War and made him the idol of all small boys.

**Patrick Hughes**

# THEY FOUGHT
# ON FOREIGN SOIL

THE TURN OF THE CENTURY WAS MARKED BY A SERIES OF TUMUL-
tuous incidents. The first of these was the War with Spain. The
revolution in Cuba in 1898 was nothing new. There was sympathy for Cubans
in the United States, as there usually is for the underdog, but, outside of
individual help and a few diplomatic protests over the actions of some
officials, nothing was done.

Then came the catalyst. The USS *Maine* was blown up in Havana Harbor
on February 15, 1898. By whom, or by what party, no one knows. But
Spain was blamed by the newspapers—and the war was on. "Remember the
*Maine*" joined "Remember the Alamo" as a slogan—just as "Remember
Pearl Harbor" rallied the people some forty years later.

Rear Admiral—then Captain—Charles Dwight Sigsbee was in command
of the ill-fated ship. He died in 1923, and has joined the 257 of his crew
who were the first members of the United States Armed Forces to be killed
abroad and brought back to rest in Arlington.

Schoolboys also thrilled to the account of the dash around the Horn
of the USS *Oregon*, captained by Charles E. Clark, later Rear Admiral, who
today lies in Arlington. It was known that the Spanish Fleet in the Atlantic
was large, but, if the *Oregon* could arrive in time the advantage would be on
the side of the United States. It was March 19 when the *Oregon* left San
Francisco and headed south, away from spring into fall and to winter gales
around the Horn. The next that was heard of the *Oregon* was when, sixty-
five days later, Captain Clark reported at the telegraph station at Jupiter
Inlet, Florida, that the *Oregon* had arrived and was ready for action.

The Navy distinguished itself in the Atlantic. Rear Admiral William T.
Sampson was in command of the forces. He had graduated from Annapolis
in the class of 1861, and was immediately tapped as an instructor, when the
Naval Academy was removed to Newport for safety. It was 1864 before
he finally managed to get away to sea as a Lieutenant on the USS *Patapsco*,

"Remember the *Maine*" was the rallying cry of the nation. The anchor is part of the memorial to those whose bodies were raised from Havana Harbor and brought back to Arlington National Cemetery.

Patrick Hughes

an ironclad which was blockading Charleston Harbor. As Executive Officer he was charged with removing mines from the harbor. He was in the turret when suddenly the ship was blown up. He had the unpleasant experience of soaring a hundred feet in the air and landing in the waters of the harbor. Only twenty-five men were saved, the other seventy having gone down with the ship.

War with Spain broke out while Sampson was in command of the North Atlantic Fleet and with twenty-six ships he set forth to blockade the north coast of Cuba. Here he was joined by Commodore Winfield Scott Schley in command of the Flying Squadron.

The Spanish Fleet which had been coaling in Santiago Bay, sailed out to do battle on July 3, under command of Admiral Cervera. On July 4, 1898 Admiral Sampson sent his famous message to Washington:

> The fleet under my command offers the nation as a Fourth of
> July present the whole of Cervera's fleet.

Also in the fight against Cervera's Fleet was Robley Dunglison Evans, later Rear Admiral—but most affectionately known to the Navy, men and officers alike, as "Fighting Bob." Evans went to Annapolis in 1860 and came out just in time to be at the bombardment of Fort Fisher, where he was severely wounded. The naval surgeons wanted to amputate both legs—but Evans drew his pistol and "dissuaded" them. Even at nineteen he was a fighter. He wanted to stay in the Navy, which he did, though his peculiar walk, as a result of his wounds, earned him his first nickname of "Old Gimpy." The "Fighting Bob" nickname was won at Valparaiso during the Chilean Revolution, when he went in, breathing fire, to uphold the honor of the United States.

In command of the USS *Iowa* he was part of Admiral Schley's Flying Squadron until attached to Admiral Sampson's Fleet during the Battle of Santiago. In 1905 he became Commander-in-Chief of the Atlantic Fleet, second only to Admiral Dewey in rank. President Theodore Roosevelt picked him to lead the "Great White Fleet" around the world. He circled South America but was ill by the time he reached San Francisco where he died. On the stone to his memory in Arlington is the line "The path of duty was the way to glory." Sigsbee, Clark, Sampson and Schley rest near Evans in Arlington.

Meanwhile, what was the Army doing? Just as in the Revolution and the War Between the States, it was hurriedly rebuilding what had been dispensed with by an economy-minded Congress. Kipling's bitter poem on "Tommy Atkins" might well have been paraphrased for the American Army many times before the Cold War made a permanent defense force necessary and desirable.

> For it's Tommy this, an' Tommy that, an'
> "Chuck him out, the brute!"
> But it's "Saviour of 'is country" when
> the guns begin to shoot.

There was no need for a draft in the War with Spain. The trouble was just the opposite—there were too many volunteers, all eager and untrained. Nelson Miles was the Commanding General of the Armies. Russell Alger was Secretary of War. To put it mildly, they did not like each other. Alger refused to let Miles lead the expeditionary force, relegating him to the background, and putting in command Major General William Shafter, who, thirty years before, had won the Medal of Honor at Fair Oaks. General Shafter was elderly, enormously fat, and easily affected by heat. He had a good plan for the campaign—but it was summer in Cuba, the supplies did not arrive, the transportation was lacking, the landing place was ill-chosen, and the food was bad. And, the volunteers were volunteers. There was one exception—the hard-boiled group of mixed gentlemen and cowboys, the Rough Riders, recruited by the former Assistant Secretary of the Navy, Theodore Roosevelt. Instead of taking the top command for himself, an

Captured Spanish cannon at Arlington
Patrick Hughes

amateur soldier, he wisely turned command over to one of the most level headed of Regulars—Leonard Wood.

Leonard Wood had gone into the Army as a Contract Surgeon, but his administrative qualities and his ability to lead had caused his use in a wider field. He had won the Medal of Honor in the West in the days of the Apache wars. He had volunteered to take dispatches through Indian territory, covering seventy miles in one night and thirty the next day. Finding an officerless troop, he took command and fought valiantly.

Wood led the Rough Riders in their first battles and at San Juan Hill where they distinguished themselves in the famous charge. He accomplished so much with this untried regiment that he was put in charge of a province, then later made Military Governor of Cuba. It was well that he was a physician, for the greatest enemy the Army had to fight was disease.

Leonard Wood went from Cuba to the Philippines and its toughest assignment, that of Military Governor of one of the Moro provinces. When the pacification was accomplished, he returned to the States to become Chief of Staff of the Army. He was a Major General by this time, Senior Officer of the Army, and was apparently slated to head the Expeditionary Force in World War I. However, he was passed over for General Pershing. Wood, as a good soldier, did not complain and buckled down to train a division, from whose command he was removed on the eve of embarkation. After the war and a change of Presidents, he returned to the Philippines as Governor General. In 1927 he died and was buried in Arlington, where rest so many of the Rough Riders he led.

The founder of the Army Nurse Corps, Dr. Anita Newcomb McGee, is also buried at Arlington. She held the proud title of an Assistant Surgeon in the United States Army, the only woman so honored.

At the request of the Surgeon General, George M. Sternberg, Dr. McGee was given the task of passing upon the qualifications of those who sought appointment as contract nurses in the Spanish-American War. Dr. McGee helped to write the bill creating the Army Nurse Corps and also established the Nurses' Reserve, which proved so valuable in World War I. An officer of the Daughters of the American Revolution, Dr. McGee was always most interested and active in their work. Full military honors were paid Dr. McGee at her funeral.

When the war with Spain was over, Cuba was granted her independence, but the United States paid $20,000,000 for the Philippines. Aguinaldo, the Philippine patriot leader, who had fought side by side with the Americans, entering Manila with the troops, was more than indignant. He had thought that the Philippines like Cuba, would be made independent. Guerrilla warfare began almost immediately and before the Insurrection was put down, there were more casualties than had occurred from enemy action in Cuba.

There were few pitched battles—but many skirmishes, much like the Indian wars on the Frontier. Finally, by a ruse, General Funston captured Aguinaldo, delivering him to Major General MacArthur, who persuaded Aguinaldo to make peace.

The heroes of the Philippine Insurrection who came back to rest in Arlington were many—but perhaps these two are typical of the others.

First, there was General MacArthur. As a boy of sixteen Arthur Mac-Arthur had enlisted in the Union Army in the War Between the States. He had served with Sheridan at the battle of Chickamauga and led a charge up Missionary Ridge, planting the flag on the crest amid a hail of bullets. He was seriously wounded, but for this gallant act he was awarded the Medal of Honor.

He had come to the Philippines at the head of an army—but stayed as Governor General, to endear himself to the Filipinos by his justice, tempered with mercy, as his son was to do many years later. Incidently, the two MacArthurs, Arthur and Douglas, were the only father and son to win the Medal of Honor. Arthur MacArthur died in 1912 while delivering a speech in Milwaukee to his old regiment from the War Between the States. He is buried at Arlington as is his elder son, Arthur MacArthur, a Captain in the Navy.

Fortunately for the country, there always seems to be a Porter present whenever there is a war. David Dixon Porter of the Marine Corps, was the sixth generation of a distinguished naval family. His great-grandfather, David Dixon Porter, was the hero of the *Essex* hegira into the Pacific during the War of 1812. His grandfather, also David Dixon Porter, was the Lieutenant who ran the gauntlet at Vicksburg, and the Admiral who took Fort Fisher in the War Between the States. This David Dixon Porter, a Marine as was his father, while yet a Captain, earned the Medal of Honor by also doing the impossible. In Samar, he led his men up a two-hundred-foot cliff by means of bamboo ladders and drove the enemy from an almost impregnable position. Having done this on one side of the river, he crossed and repeated the same heroic deed on the other side, destroying positions which, according to prisoners, had taken three years to perfect and which no foreigner had hitherto penetrated.

Later Porter served in Panama, Haiti, Santo Domingo and in World War I. Upon retirement he was made a Major General. Like his grandfather, the Admiral, he is buried in Arlington.

In the midst of the troubles in the Philippines came the Boxer Uprising in China, also known as the China Relief Expedition. A fanatical Chinese group called the Boxers, rose against foreigners. A number of missionaries and some members of legations were killed. The foreign legation area of Peking was besieged for fifty-five days. In that time, American forces were dispatched to China to join with the British, French, German, Italian, Russian and Japanese troops to lift the siege. When the Relief Expedition won through, the United States, alone of the participating nations did not press for huge reparations and for extraterritorial concessions.

At Peking there was a Marine—John T. Myers, later Lieutenant General. As a Second Lieutenant he had led a landing party on Guam during the Spanish-American War. As a Captain he had commanded a landing expedition during the Philippines Insurrection. In 1900 Myers was ordered to Peking with a force of forty-eight marines and three sailors, along with detachments of British, Russian, French, Italian and Japanese Marines. They reached Peking at eleven o'clock on the night of May 1—just before the city was encircled by Chinese troops. During the siege the Boxers built a tower, reaching well above the wall around the Legation area so as to permit firing at will into the grounds already crowded with refugees. The Americans suggested an immediate attack on the tower to which the British Ambassador, who had overall command, agreed. Myers was picked to lead the attacking force. The assault on the tower was successful but Myers was wounded. Full credit was given to him, for later, when a monument was erected in London to the Royal Marines, a bas-relief was included showing Myers leading the British Marines to the attack.

During World War I Myers was Fleet Marine Officer, as well as Counter-Intelligence Officer on the staff of the Commander of the Atlantic Fleet. A Major General when he retired, he was promoted to Lieutenant General in the retired list in 1942, when Congress passed a law authorizing such promotions for officers who had been specially commended in combat.

Also buried at Arlington is another soldier killed at the Relief of Peking—Captain Henry J. Reilly, of the 5th U. S. Artillery. It was "Reilly's Battery" which blasted open the gates of Peking. And Reilly gave his life that August 15 in 1900. On his tomb is carved the verse from Second Timothy:

> I have fought the good fight.
> I have finished my course.
> I have kept the faith.

These words could almost be carved over the great entrance to Arlington.

Leonard Wood fought the Spanish on San Juan Hill, but he fought the greater enemies of yellow fever and leprosy in both Cuba and the Philippines.

Patrick Hughes

# IN A DECADE OF PEACE

THE TUMULT AND THE SHOUTING DIED. THE NEW CENTURY WAS TO be a century of peace and prosperity—or so the perennial optimists assured the public. But the Armed Forces of the United States are never off guard. To them a decade of peace was a misnomer. There were still battles to be fought and another war with its defeats and victories. This was the war against disease, against the same "camp fevers" that had laid low John Custis at Yorktown in the Revolutionary War, that had filled the Washington hospitals and the graves at Arlington in the War Between the States, that had slain more men than had bullets in the War with Spain.

Disease was hampering the building of the new Canal across the Isthmus of Panama, from whose farther shore Balboa had first gazed upon the Pacific. Disease was devastating the occupation troops in the Philippines. Disease was striking at the Marines at Peking.

So it had been. But no more was it taken as a necessity nor as an adjunct of war. Now there were soldiers fighting disease in the laboratories. They were men who sought causes that they might be eradicated. They were men who were not content with merely alleviating suffering.

Here are the stories of a few of the heroes of the decade of peace, who now rest in Arlington.

It has already been told how Leonard Wood, while cleaning up Santiago, had also spurred the search for the causes of the epidemic diseases which had proved so devastating.

Fortunately the Surgeon General at that time was a scientist, conversant with the problems of research and oblivious of the criticism of those who, to cover up their own shortcoming, wanted to blame the Medical Corps for lack of sanitation, bad food, disease—and probably floods, fire and thunderstorms as well.

George Miller Sternberg—bacteriologist, epidemiologist and Surgeon General of the United States—was the son of a Lutheran minister in New

York's historic Schoharie Valley. Sternberg taught school, and studied medicine in his spare time, finally getting his degree from Columbia in 1860. When the War Between the States began, he immediately enlisted as an assistant surgeon and was at Bull Run, Gaines Mill and Malvern Hill. His devotion to his work had earned him the brevet rank of Major before the war ended.

In 1893 Sternberg became Surgeon General of the Army. During his nine-year tenure he established the Army Medical School, the Army Nurse Corps, the Army Dental Corps and many hospitals. He also set up the Typhoid Fever Board and the Yellow Fever Commission headed by Walter Reed. The inscription on his monument in Arlington is headed by the words "Pioneer American Bacteriologist."

Walter Reed's father was also a minister, but in the South. He earned his medical degree at the University of Virginia before he was eighteen, then went to Bellevue Hospital Medical College for a second degree. In 1874 he joined the Army Medical Corps as assistant surgeon with the rank of First Lieutenant. In the eleven years he spent on the Frontier, he laid the foundation for his work as a scientist, as Sternberg had done.

At the newly organized Army Medical School, he taught bacteriology and clinical microscopy, serving also as curator of the Army Medical Museum. Just prior to the Spanish-American War, having worked on the bacteriology of erysipelas and diptheria, he came out in favor of antitoxins and Government control of biologic remedies.

When an epidemic of yellow fever broke out in Havana in 1900, he headed the commission to study it. With him were his assistants, Dr. James Carroll, Dr. Jesse W. Lazear and Dr. Aristedes Agramonte. Reed, with this staff, commenced the controlled experiments which were to evenually wipe out the plague. Dr. Finlay had already suggested the mosquito as the killer. Now the theory was tried on volunteers. Dr. Carroll was bitten but recovered with a damaged heart. He died some years later and is buried at Arlington. Dr. Lazear was bitten accidently and died. Twenty-two volunteers went willingly through the experiment and lived, and others volunteered to try other means of infection, which proved negative. The war on mosquitos began. As a result, whereas in 1900 there were 1,400 cases of yellow fever in Havana, in 1901 there were thirty-seven. But, in his preoccupation with bacteriology, Reed neglected warning symptoms for himself and, shortly after his return to Washington, died suddenly of appendicitis.

Younger than these physicians, but destined to carry on the ideals of their work, was William Crawford Gorgas, who also was to become Surgeon General of the United States Army. His father was a Brigadier General and Chief of Ordnance in the Confederate Army. Young Gorgas spent the four years of war in Richmond. He wanted to go to West Point, but could not get an appointment. A medical degree seemed to be a way into the Army, so he attended Bellevue Hospital Medical College and then joined the Medical Corps.

Like Sternberg and Reed he was sent from one border post to another, finally getting yellow fever at Fort Brown, Texas. On his recovery, being then immune, he was constantly being drafted for service where yellow fever existed. Following the occupation of Havana in 1898, he became chief sanitary engineer of Havana. The Reed Commission reported on the finding of its controlled tests, and Gorgas went after the mosquitoes with the results already stated.

It was only natural that he was selected as santiary engineer when the plans were developed for the Panama Canal. By that time he was a Colonel. He studied the previous attempt to build the canal, planning his fight against the diseases which had routed the French. However, the first Canal Commission was so determined to avoid extravagance and corruption that it cut down on sanitary disbursements, as a luxury, perhaps. Not until there was an epidemic of yellow fever could Gorgas get any support for his program. President Theodore Roosevelt stood by him, however, for he had seen first-hand the effect of epidemic diseases on his Rough Riders in Cuba. After a visit to Panama, Roosevelt made Gorgas a member of the Canal Commission with broad powers. But when General Goethals was made Chairman and Chief Engineer, he centered his attacks upon the expense of Gorgas' sanitary work. Notwithstanding this opposition, Gorgas was recognized as the leading sanitary engineer of the world, and his services were eagerly sought by other countries. But he remained as Surgeon General of the Army until after World War I, when he retired and devoted himself to work for the International Health Board. While on a mission to Europe he was taken ill in London, where he died. His funeral was held at St. Paul's Cathedral, after which he was brought home for burial in Arlington.

One of the nurses who had served with General Gorgas died in 1954 at the age of ninety and was buried at Arlington. As a Spanish-American War nurse, Anna E. Turner of Carbondale, Pennsylvania, preceded the days of the Army Nurse Corps. She was first assigned to Fort Monroe, Virginia, where the medical equipment consisted of twenty cots, one hand basin, a water pail and dipper, and one bed pan. Anchored off Old Point Comfort were ships loaded with sick troops returning from Puerto Rico. The hospital consisted of four tents placed together, and it housed one hundred men ill with typhoid.

In 1899 Miss Turner went to Cuba on a cattle boat with 1,400 men, 720 horses and mules and nine other nurses. There she spent two years in the Yellow Fever Hospital in Havana under General Gorgas. While there, she caught malaria and was sent back to the United States—but when General Gorgas went to the Panama Canal Zone, she did too. Miss Turner was aboard the first ship to pass through the Canal after it was completed— a small, but satisfying reward for her work.

Ever since the days of Admiral Wilkes and his mapping of Antarctica, the Navy has furnished great explorers to the nation. Rear Admiral Robert E. Peary was one of the best known of these.

Peary entered the Navy as a Civil Engineer with the rank of Lieutenant, after two years with the Coast and Geodetic Survey. His first assignment was in the tropics, surveying a route for the proposed Nicaraguan Canal. Perhaps it was the tropics that turned his mind to the North, for he made his first expedition to Greenland on a six-month leave of absence in 1886.

During the next twenty-three years he led various expeditions into the Arctic. It was on his eighth expedition—April 6, 1909—that, at long last, Peary reached his goal. On that historic occasion, he dropped into a small crevice in the ice, a small glass bottle in which was sealed the note:

> I have this day hoisted the national ensign of the United States of America at this place, which my observations indicate to be the North Polar axis of the earth, and have formally taken possession of the entire region, and adjacent, for and in the name of the President of the United States of America.

His wire announcing the event said: "Stars and Stripes nailed to the North Pole. Peary." His monument at Arlington was dedicated by the President of the United States, the Chief Justice, the Secretary of War, the Secretary of the Navy, the Dean of the Diplomatic Corps and the Board of Trustees of the National Geographic Society. The latter had investigated and approved the claims for the discovery.

Since the sea and the earth and the diseases thereon had been charted, there remained but the air—or so it seemed. Much controversy had risen about whether or not flying would ever become practicable, and while aviation did not come into its own until World War I, still the first steps were being made and carefully watched.

George Owen Squier was a soldier, scientist and electrical engineer. He graduated from West Point as a Second Lieutenant of Artillery in 1887— and kept right on studying for several years. That he was given this opportunity, proves that those in authority recognized his talents. During the Spanish-American War he was a signal officer. He must have been a good one, for after the war, he was assigned to the Signal Corps to lay the cable and superintend the telephone lines in the Philippine archipelago. He was a born researcher and had a series of discoveries to his credit.

Over the parade ground at Fort Myer and above a gate to the cemetery flew Orville Wright in one of the first flights. Then he took up a passenger —the resultant crash was just outside the gate now named for that passenger, Lt. Thomas Selfridge, the first Army Aviation casualty.

As early as 1908 he became interested in aviation, like another Signal Corps officer, General Adolphus Greely. While serving as Military Attaché in London at the outbreak of World War I, he made a study of military aviation in Great Britain and France, which was invaluable to the United States when it entered the war. By 1917 Squier was Chief Signal Officer of the Army and a Major General, supervising the cable and radio communications between military headquarters in the United States and the AEF abroad. Such was the man who did so much for the aeronautics work of the Armed Forces.

One of the tragic events of Army flying happened in 1908. Few of those who go into Arlington through the Selfridge Gate know why it is so named, or read the bronze plaque at the side. It was in September of that year that Orville Wright began tests of his plane at Fort Myer. Flying was so new, that the tests drew great crowds of sightseers. After several trial flights, Orville Wright suggested that he might take up an observer if the Army authorities so desired. Lieutenant Thomas Selfridge begged for permission to go with Wright. Permission was granted and the young officer was buckled into the open cockpit. The plane started to rise. Then something happened to the propellor. The horrified onlookers saw the plane crash, fatally injuring the observer. Lieutenant Selfridge thus became the first air casualty in the United States Army. His grave lies within sight of the Fort Myer Parade Ground on which he crashed.

Already there were rumbles of the approaching storm on the horizon. There was unrest in Latin America. There was unrest in the Far East. As usual, the Marines were sent to keep the peace.

John H. Russell was Commandant of the Marine Corps and a Major General when he retired. His performance of duty on the USS *Massachusetts* during the Spanish-American War had brought commendation from his superiors—and more difficult tasks to perform.

In 1908 he was sent from Hawaii to the Canal Zone to command the Marines stationed at that critical spot. In 1910 he left the Naval War College for Peking to command the Marine Detachments at the American Legation. During his three years in that post, the Chinese Government changed from an empire to a republic, with all of the attendant disorders in and around Peking.

In 1914 he was at Vera Cruz on the Mexican dispute. In 1917 he was ordered to the Dominican Republic and later to Haiti. In both places his task was to keep the lid on the boiling pot while the United States was at war. Repeatedly he asked for transfer to the fighting front in Europe. He was too valuable where he was. In fact, in 1922, he was appointed American High Commissioner to Haiti with the rank of Ambassador Extraordinary, serving there until 1930. In 1934 he became Commandant of the Marine Corps, serving in that capacity until his retirement.

Was it a decade of peace? In the light of the two World Wars to come, what happened in those years may seem trivial. But in their own way, the deeds of those years were as important as the more dramatic episodes of wartime. It is sometimes easier to be a hero in the excitement of battle than it is in peace. But the good soldier, sailor or marine is the one who does his assigned task thoroughly, intelligently and consistently. Such a man is a true hero.

Robert E. Peary, the discoverer of the North Pole, rests under a massive globe of the world.

Patrick Hughes

# THEY FOUGHT
# IN LITTLE WARS

THE ASSASSIN'S SHOT AT SARAJEVO IN 1914 ECHOED AROUND THE world. It sounded the beginning of the "Great War," "The World War" or "World War I." What it is called depends upon the age of the speaker.

It drowned out the clamor of the little wars—or the period before the United States joined the Allied powers in 1917.

The little wars may have been forgotten by the general public, but little wars have their heroes just as often as do the great wars. A bullet is just as lethal as a bombardment to the one it hits. Many who fought in the little wars, lived through them to fight again on the battlefields of Europe in the Great War. In those earlier struggles they learned what war meant and in them, and in the days of preparation for Armageddon, they had their moments of glory.

Here are the stories of some of these heroes, who, now that their wars are forever ended, lie on the peaceful slopes of Arlington.

There was tension and unrest in the Caribbean and in Central America. The Monroe Doctrine warned off European nations from entering into the area even to protect their nationals. Therefore, it was up to the United States to provide this protection. Between 1906 and 1917, for example, the United States had been forced to send troops into Cuba eight times. Panama, Nicaragua, Haiti, the Dominican Republic—in all of these United States troops, usually Marines, had had to keep the peace.

President Wilson had decided that the United States would no longer recognize any government which had come into power by unconstitutional means. Out of this decision arose the Vera Cruz incident in the spring of 1914. Before Madero—the elected President—had a real opportunity to institute reforms, he was murdered by the followers of a General named Huerta, who promptly proclaimed himself "El Presidente." He was not recognized by the United States and resented it both vociferously and vehemently.

At Tampico, early in 1914, a boat crew from a U. S. naval vessel on maneuvers went ashore to buy supplies. The Mexican Governor immediately arrested the men and threw them into jail. Though they were shortly released, it was without an apology. Then word came that a German freighter was bringing arms and ammunition to Huerta at Vera Cruz. The Marines were ordered ashore. Matters worsened. The Marines and the Navy had to take over Vera Cruz—a short, bitter fight—and hold it until the Army under General Funston arrived.

One of the heroes of the Vera Cruz campaign was Wendell C. Neville, who later became Major General Commandant of the Marine Corps. He was one of the most decorated Marines in the history of the Corps. During the thirty-eight years of his service he saw action in Cuba, Mexico, China, the Philippines, Nicaragua and France. For his valor and leadership he won the Medal of Honor, the Brevet Medal—once the Marines' highest honor —the Army Distinguished Service Medal, the Navy Distinguished Service Medal, the Cross of the French Legion of Honor, five Croix de Guerre with three stars and two palms, five citations and eight campaign and expeditionary awards.

Neville graduated from the Naval Academy in 1890. At the outbreak of the Spanish-American War his battalion was hurried to Cuba where it staged a daring attack under fire at Guantanamo Bay. Neville received the Brevet Medal for this deed and was promoted to Captain. Next came China and four battles during the Boxer Uprising. Reassigned to the Philippines, he became Military Governor of Basilan Province. In quick succession followed Cuba, Nicaragua, Panama and Hawaii.

In 1914, as a Lieutenant Colonel, he was in command of the Marines' landing at Vera Cruz. His citation for the Medal of Honor says:

> . . . he exhibited conspicuous courage, coolness and skill in his conduct of the fighting. Upon his courage and skill depended in great measure, success or failure.

Perhaps that was his greatest moment of glory, though he repeated his actions again in World War I. He had gone to France in 1917, upon his return from China where he had commanded the combined Allied Guard at Peking. On January 1, 1918 he took command of the Fifth Marine Regiment and in May moved into action at Belleau Wood where Germany's big drive was decisively halted. The action of the Marines at Belleau Wood caused the French to change its name to *Bois de la Brigade de Marines*.

Also at Vera Cruz was Admiral Jonas H. Ingram—though it was still a number of years before he would receive Admiral's rank. He was already famous, however—and had been ever since his Annapolis days. A varsity football star during his last year, he had scored the only touchdown in Navy's first victory over Army in seven years! That was in 1906. In 1914 he was at Vera Cruz on the battleship *Arkansas*. As turret officer he had established a world's record in the firing of the twelve-inch turret guns. And at Vera Cruz, he earned the Medal of Honor "for skillful and efficient handling of artillery and machine guns."

For the two years before the United States entered World War I, he was back at the Academy as Head Football Coach, but when war was declared he became Aide and Flag Lieutenant on the staff of Admiral Hugh Rodman. He was present at the German surrender and won the Navy Cross for his actions during the war.

By 1941 Ingram had reached the rank of Rear Admiral and was put in command of the South Atlantic Fleet the following year. He didn't like this assignment—he wanted to go to the Pacific where the war was hotter. In fact, he is reported to have told President Franklin Roosevelt that he (Roosevelt) was making a third-class diplomat out of a first-class fighting man. Just the same, Ingram did a fine piece of work directing the fight against the German submarine and surface forces prowling off the South American coast. The last year of the war, with rank of Admiral, Ingram was Commander-in-Chief of the Atlantic Fleet, directing the flow of men and material overseas.

The situation in Mexico grew steadily worse. Carranza, who came into power after Huerta, could not keep order. His former ally, Pancho Villa, revolted and raided where he chose. In March, 1916 the place he picked was Columbus, New Mexico. A number of American soldiers and civilians were killed in the raid and much property destroyed before U. S. Cavalry drove the raiders off. President Wilson then ordered Brigadier General John J. Pershing to lead a Punutive Expedition into Mexico to assist the Mexican Government in capturing Villa.

The Mexican Government, while it did not want Villa, also did not want American help, as Pershing soon found out, and there were some clashes between the Federalistas and Pershing's troops.

The rehearsal for the main battle had come. Here the airplane had its first testing, and it was seen that much remained to be done both in training and in getting the proper planes. As for the Army, many of those who handled Divisions, Corps and Armies in World War I and II, learned their profession in the deserts and hills of northern Mexico. In all, and through all, there was John J. Pershing.

Kenyon A. Joyce, later Major General, was with Pershing on the Punitive Expedition into Mexico. He had enlisted as a Private in the Spanish-American War, serving both in Cuba and the Philippines. He was decorated for his service in what was one of the last Indian Wars in Montana, and then went to the Mexican border.

During World War I, he was again with Pershing, this time in France, where he was Chief of Staff of two divisions. In savage fighting during the Meuse-Argonne Campaign he was wounded by a grenade and did not again have full use of one hand.

The Arlington area where he rests is not new to him, for from 1933 to 1937 he commanded the 3rd Cavalry at Fort Myer and supervised the design and construction of the post chapel where his own funeral was held, and which is so integrally a part of Arlington. General Joyce retired in 1949 after serving as President of the Allied Control Commission in Italy in World War II.

Who was the man called Pershing? Why was he chosen to head the Punitive Expedition to Mexico? And later the American Expeditionary Force? Was he austere, domineering, stubborn? Did he earn his position or get it because his father-in-law was a Senator? Was he a really great General?

To dispel the myths, look at his record. John J. Pershing's boyhood was that of Tom Sawyer, or of any small boy in a one-horse Missouri Town. His father had started out as a section hand on the railroad and built up

"Black Jack" Pershing and his men cross into Mexico during the Punitve Expedition. This is the Pershing his men remembered—rather than the "General of the Armies" of his later triumphs.

his fortunes without help until he owned a store—which he later lost in the panic of 1873—and became town postmaster. Pershing taught school before he took the examinations for West Point. He didn't have any pull for an appointment—he earned it the hard way, and he took his work there seriously.

When he graduated in 1886, he joined the Cavalry and was on the Frontier in the sporadic Indian Wars. At the beginning of the War with Spain, Pershing was at West Point as Assistant Instructor of Tactics—he would need this in World War I. He had also served for six months on the staff of General Miles; and that crochety individual mercilessly sized up men, carefully recording his impressions.

In the Santiago campaign, Pershing distinguished himself and then, requested active service in the Philippines. There he had one difficult assignment after another—all requiring exercise of both tact and firmness. He was dealing with the Moros—the Moslem Filipinos, who were fighters to the last ditch.

It was after he came back from the Philippines with his record already established that he met and married Senator Francis Warren's daughter. Another difficult assignment followed—that of military attaché at Tokyo. When he returned to the States, Pershing jumped from Captain to Brigadier General. The disgruntled whispered "pull" and "favoritism." To the initiate, however, the variance of his assignments and their difficulty was explanation enough. President Theodore Roosevelt had his own methods of reforming the Army. Leonard Wood and Tasker Bliss had both been tried out and jumped up in rank.

By 1909 he was back in the Philippines, again at Mindanao, this time as Governor of the Moro province. His tactful handling of a delicate situation resulted in pacification of lawless tribes and establishment of stable civil government.

When Pershing returned to the States in 1914, he hoped for active service, but instead went first to the Presidio in San Francisco and then to El Paso. His wife and children were to join him in Texas, but just before they were to arrive in 1915, tragedy struck. In a fire at the Presidio, his wife and three little daughters perished, leaving only his six-year-old son. Is it any wonder he became austere and self-contained? Or that when ordered on the Punitive Expedition, he threw himself into it completely?

The Mexican situation was potential dynamite. President Wilson needed a commander who could be both firm and cautious—who would not seek after personal glory, but would remember the position in which the United States was placed. Pershing had the training and the ability; so he was the man chosen.

To a soldier it was not a great campaign, but in it the men who were to command the AEF learned how to work together. It is interesting to note that while Pershing was called domineering, the men who worked under him were not subservient. For instance, Patton was his Aide in Mexico, and they became lifelong friends. The men who worked with Pershing grew in stature and when the time of their testing came in World War II, they were ready.

Thus was John J. Pershing hammered on the anvil of fate. Thus was he made ready for the day when he should lay a wreath on the tomb of Lafayette, while his Aide said the famous words—"Lafayette, we are here!"

Fame lay ahead, and the plaudits of the crowd. At the end, in 1948, there was a hilltop at Arlington, and, at his own request, a plain GI headstone. John J. Pershing, General of the Armies, would lie among his men.

Years later, sitting beside President Roosevelt as he spoke at Arlington, did General Pershing think of the days of the Little Wars and the gallant officers who learned their trade under him then?

**National Park Service**

LeJeune was only a young officer in the days of the Little Wars, but it was then he learned the skills that made him tops in World War I.

**Patrick Hughes**

# THEY FOUGHT

# FOR DEMOCRACY

IT WAS 1917. GERMANY ANNOUNCED UNRESTRICTED SUBMARINE warfare, thereby miscalculating the sentiments of the American people. The sinking of the *Lusitania* had partially blasted the public out of its apathy. The Black Tom explosion in New York Harbor and the Zimmerman note, suggesting an alliance between Germany and Mexico against the United States, provided the final awakening.

The Selective Service Act was passed and young America was drafted for war. General Pershing was made Commander-in-Chief of the AEF. Admiral William S. Sims gathered up what Congress had left of the Navy and went off to England to start work. The Marines were ready for orders. The Coast Guard was *semper paratus*—"always prepared."

There were some who remained in Washington, closely connected with developments in the planning days of war, who now rest in Arlington.

General Tasker Howard Bliss, the Chief of Staff, had had quite a variety of experiences. Graduated from West Point in 1875, he had served in the Artillery, and in 1888 served as Aide to General Schofield, the Commanding General of the Army. With General Schofield he traveled extensively, then became Military Attaché at Madrid—a good experience for his later diplomatic work in France.

When Bliss was retired as Chief of Staff at the end of 1917 he was immediately recalled to duty by the President, who made him American representative on the Supreme War Council in France. Because of his diplomatic background, he opposed Pershing's insistence on retaining the American forces as a separate entity. For a time he was inclined to yield to the British and French demands that the American soldiers be turned over to them to be used as replacements under their command. Pershing stood firm—it was as an American Army that the troops had been raised, and it was as an American Army that they would fight!

The white marble figure looks out upon the hundreds of Army and Navy nurses who so valiantly earned their right to lie at Arlington. Among them rests Jane Delano, who contributed so much to the nursing profession.

Patrick Hughes

With Wilson, Lansing, White and House, General Bliss served on the American Peace Commission after the war. He retired from active service in 1920.

Succeeding General Bliss as Chief of Staff was General Peyton C. March —a mere youngster who had graduated from the Point in 1888. A decade later upon leaving the Artillery School he formed the Astor Battery and sailed with it for the Philippines where he was four times cited for gallantry in action. In 1898 he was Aide to General Arthur MacArthur in the Philippines, during which time he received the surrender of Aguinaldo. As did General Pershing, he served as Military Attaché and was with the Japanese troops during the Russo-Japanese War.

After the United States entered World War I, March was ordered to France with his regiment. He commanded the Artillery of the AEF under Pershing, who was training his token force overseas. When the Secretary of War wanted March to replace Bliss, Pershing did not want to give him up, but was finally forced to do so. General March had already proven by his organization of the Artillery that he was a good planner, and he has been credited with much of the organization work entailed in the creation of the new Army out of untrained civilians. General March retired in 1921, but was a familiar figure around Washington until his death in 1955.

While the military was being organized, there was also a woman who made plans—for which she would be blessed by thousands of servicemen and their families. She was Jane Delano, Second Superintendent of the Army Nurse Corps, from 1909 to 1912.

Her father's death in the War Between the States turned Miss Delano to Army nursing. She graduated from Bellevue Hospital in 1886 and returned as superintendent in 1897. In that decade, besides other posts, she had served as superintendent of a yellow fever hospital.

During the Spanish-American War she had joined the Red Cross and became interested in securing nurses for enrollment in the Red Cross Nursing Service. When she was offered the Superintendency of the Army Nurse Corps, she accepted, believing that it would bring a closer relationship between the nursing services of the Army and the Red Cross. Miss Delano devoted herself to reorganizing and improving the Army Nurse Corps, and to increasing the pay so as to attract the best class of nurses. She finished her work by making the Red Cross Nursing Service a Reserve of the Army Nurse Corps, then resigned and devoted her time to the Red Cross. There her work was particularly heavy due to the great demand for nurses during the war. It was on an inspection trip to France that Miss Delano died. She was awarded a posthumous Distinguished Service Medal for her work in obtaining and transferring to the Army Nurse Corps 18,732 nurses to serve during World War I.

When Admiral William S. Sims, Commander of the U. S. Naval Forces Operating in European Waters, first went overseas, he realized how little was known at home of the havoc wrought by German submarines. Upon his shoulders would rest the responsibility for combatting this menace. As was usual with him, once he had the facts in hand, he prepared a plan. But let's go back a bit in this story of the stormy petrel of the Navy . . .

After several years at sea following graduation, Sims was appointed Naval Attaché to Paris, St. Petersburg and Madrid. During the War with Spain he continued duty in Paris and St. Petersburg and in this assignment had charge of American secret service work in Spain, Russia and Italy.

While on the staff of the Commander-in-Chief of the U. S. Asiatic Fleet in 1901 and 1902, he met Captain Percy Scott, the British officer responsible for the British Navy's remarkable progress in gunnery. Sims was not content until he had learned Scott's procedure and proved for himself that it would work.

With the naivety of a very young officer, he elatedly wrote a report to the Navy's Bureau Chiefs. No answer. He wrote to the Secretary of the Navy. No answer. He wrote to the President—Theodore Roosevelt. Things began to happen. Roosevelt ordered a test in target practice, looked at the results, and cabled China, ordering Sims home at once. Upon Sims's arrival, he was made Naval Aide to the President and given charge of naval target practice. During the years he held this post, the rapidity of hits increased 100 percent and the general effectiveness of fire increased five times. In 1913 he was assigned command of the Torpedo Flotilla, Atlantic Fleet, to examine its efficiency.

In March, 1917 Sims was designated the representative of the Navy Department in London and Commander of the U. S. Naval Forces operating in European waters. With his Aide he left for England, incognito, for it was the week before war was declared. By the time he arrived war had begun and Admiral Sims's task was to cooperate with the Állied Powers.

Sims surveyed the situation, cabled the Navy Department regarding the urgency of action, and asked that all destroyers and other light craft in the Navy be sent immediately to where they could do the most good—Queenstown, Ireland. The first destroyers arrived on May 4, 1917. Commander Joseph K. Taussig was asked by the British Port Admiral when the force of six destroyers he commanded would be ready for sea. He replied, "We are ready now, sir." And so they were. With what Sims could get overseas—and it was not all he wanted—he did a remarkable job. Commander Taussig, later a Vice-Admiral, is at Arlington near his old chief.

The convoy system Sims laid out worked, greatly reducing sinkings by submarines. The Navy planes, and there were precious few of them, were eyes for the Fleet. The battleships served as watchdogs. Eventually mines and depth bombs were developed which worked so well they proved to be a contributing cause of the mutiny in the German Navy.

In 1918 only a small part of the U. S. Army had arrived in France and Germany had superiority on the Western Front. The American and British Navies had to meet the emergency. And they did. By July, American soldiers were being transported by the tens of thousands. In all of this, Admiral Sims was the guiding genius—directing and keeping in touch with the American naval forces scattered from Constantinople to the Azores and from Murmansk to Gibraltar. Besides this, he served on the Allied War Council.

This monument was erected as a memorial to the 192 officers and enlisted men of the Coast Guard Cutter *Tampa* who went down with their ship during World War I.

**Patrick Hughes**

When Sims returned to the States, it was to become President of the Naval War College. The Secretary of the Navy in his annual report published the list of decorations given. But Secretary Daniels had so radically changed the list from what the Board of Awards and Admiral Sims had recommended, that the stormy petrel of the Navy refused the Distinguished Service Medal offered him. His men had been ignored, and he didn't propose to stand it!

"Plan I, Acknowledge"—that was the dispatch received by all Coast Guard units on the morning of April 6, 1917. It meant that the fifteen cruising cutters, over two hundred officers, and 5,000 men of the Coast Guard were to go into action with the Navy. Their task for the most part was to convoy cargo ships and screen transports. And, of course, the Coast Guard would not neglect its peacetime job of saving lives. Many Coast Guard men died during World War I—but few came back to Arlington. They went down with their ships. In their memory is a very beautiful memorial dedicated to all in their service.

Typical of the Coast Guard was Rear Admiral Harry C. Hamlet, who was Commandant of the Coast Guard in the 1930s. He was a second-generation Coast Guardsman, for his father had been a Captain in the Revenue Cutter Service, the predecessor of the Coast Guard. Hamlet was commissioned in 1896. The next year, in the historic cutter *Bear*, he was on what is known to the service as one of the most arduous and perilous rescue expeditions to the Arctic. Up to the beginning of World War I, with the exception of time spent in special courses at the Naval War College, he served in the Far North.

October of 1918 found him in command of the USS *Marietta* at Brest, France. Some months later—on April 28, 1919, to be exact—the USS *James* was sinking off the coast, when Hamlet maneuvered the *Marietta* alongside and saved the entire crew of two officers and forty-five men. For this skillful and gallant rescue, he was awarded the Congressional Gold Life Saving Medal of Honor from the Secretary of the Treasury and a Special Commendation from the Secretary of the Navy. When Hamlet was made Commandant in 1932, he had served in the Coast Guard for thirty-eight years, in virtually every area and in every type of Coast Guard work.

While the Navy and Coast Guard were setting up their protective screens, and while the new Army was being trained in the States, General Pershing with a "token" force had gone to France. With the customary single-mindedness for which he had been selected, he was determined to stick to his orders, to "command an American Army in France." To him that did not mean turning Regiments, Divisions, or Corps over to be integrated into French or British Armies. If he were to avoid conflict, much would depend upon his choice of an Aide. Everyone waited to see whom he would select. And there was much surprise when, instead of a West Point intimate, he reached out into the Philippine Constabulary "graduates" for a relatively obscure Major.

He could not have made a better choice. In fact, the Secretary of War, after inspection trips to France on which he carefully scrutinized all available Generals, decided that if anything should happen to Pershing, his successor would be James G. Harbord.

Harbord was not a West Pointer. He was a teacher in Kansas schools until 1889 when he enlisted in the U. S. Infantry. He served as Private, Corporal, Sergeant, and Quartermaster Sergeant before he was commissioned a Second Lieutenant of Cavalry in 1891. He served in the West until the War with Spain, by which time he was a Major.

Three years later he went to the Philippines and by 1906 was the Assistant Chief of the Philippine Constabulary in various isolated places. This force was the American Army's method of teaching the Filipinos how to set up and maintain their own law enforcement agency, the first step to freedom. Harbord was back at the Army War College when General Pershing decided to make him his Aide.

Until May, 1918 Harbord was Chief of Staff at the General Headquarters of the AEF. He then persuaded Pershing to give him command of the Marine Brigade. He liked Marines and they liked him. In this capacity he carried through at Belleau Wood, Chateau Thierry and Soissons, before Pershing insisted on his taking command of the Service of Supply which was breaking down due to the great amounts of material needed, and the war-torn conditions of French roads and railways. After the war, General Harbord followed General March as Chief of Staff, remaining in that post until his retirement in 1921. Upon leaving the Army, General Harbord became Chairman of the Board of the Radio Corporation of America.

Another of Pershing's Generals was Charles P. Summerall, well known for his oft reiterated credo "Artillery exists only to protect and support the Infantry." As successor to March in command of Pershing's Artillery he proved the efficacy of his theories and was a potent factor in breaking the deadlock on the Western Front.

Summerall had graduated from the Military Academy in 1892. When the Philippine Insurrection broke out, Captain Henry J. Reilly requested Summerall's assignment to "Reilly's Artillery." He was cited for gallantry in the Phillippines and accompanied Reilly to Peking where Reilly won immortal fame, and Summerall was again cited.

By the time World War I broke out, Summerall had served in almost every Artillery post, including teaching artillery tactics at West Point. In

France he commanded the First Division during the Aisne-Marne, Soissons, St. Mihiel and the first phase of the Meuse-Argonne offensives. In 1926 he was made Chief of Staff of the Army. He retired in 1931, becoming President of the famous Citadel in Charleston, South Carolina.

One of the most colorful characters in World War I was Lieutenant General John A. Lejeune, later to be the thirteenth Commandant of the Marine Corps, and often referred to as "the Greatest of all leathernecks."

Lejeune was already an alumnus of Louisiana State University when he went to the Naval Academy, from which he graduated in 1888, being commissioned a Second Lieutenant in the Marine Corps two years later. During the War with Spain, he saw action on the USS *Cincinnati*. In the fall of 1903 Lejeune, then a Major, was dispatched, with a battalion of Marines, to Panama where conditions had become critical during the revolution against Colombia. He served in the Philippines, then led two expeditions into Cuba to restore law and order. The Expedition to Vera Cruz followed in 1914.

On arrival in France in June of 1918, immediately following the attack at Soissons, he took command of the Fourth Brigade of Marines of the Second Division. A month later, he was given command of the Second Division—the first Marine officer ever to hold an Army divisional command. Following the Armistice, he led his Division in the march into Germany.

Shortly after his return to the States and the demobilization of the Second Division, he became the Major General Commandant of the Marine Corps. At the end of 1929 he retired to accept the Superintendency of the Virginia Military Institute.

Only a few of the many heroes from World War I are mentioned here. They are no greater heroes than others who lie beside them at Arlington. Like the Unknown Soldier, they are but symbols of the men who served their country and who, perhaps, lie in hallowed ground across the Atlantic, or with their ships beneath the seas.

The Argonne Cross was erected in 1922 by the American Legion Auxiliary to commemorate the more than 5,000 U. S. servicemen who died in World War I and whose bodies were brought back for burial in Arlington.
**Library of Congress**

# BETWEEN

# THE HOLOCAUSTS

WORLD WAR I WAS OVER. THE BATTLE OF THE PEACE TERMS WAS joined. Even as the victorious Allies dismembered the Central Powers and quarrelled over sovereignty, even as President Wilson stressed his Fourteen Points, there was another war still being fought, a war in which American troops were dying in the bitter wastes of Siberia.

It was an unpopular struggle, fraught with terrific consequences. Germany was in a great measure responsible. In 1917 the German General Staff had conceived the idea of taking Russia out of the war by fomenting Revolution—and to that end had sent, from Switzerland through Germany in a sealed train, a man who called himsel Nicolai Lenin. The end result of this strategy was to be, in 1945, a divided Germany and a dismembered Berlin. The Cold War was in the making.

But the Allies, including the United States, were not entirely guiltless. They had seen the Kerensky pro-democratic government go down before the screaming, maddened mobs of Lenin's *Bolsheviki*. They had sent token forces to help—but with conflicting orders. The truth of the matter was that everyone was tired of war. France was bled white. Britain, starting out with a volunteer army, had lost the best of her youth.

The United States Navy, entering the war nearly three years after the Allies—and the Army entering nearly a year later—were relatively fresher. But there was no public sentiment for this Siberian Expedition. Instead, there was agitation for peace and disarmament. There were bright-eyed idealists prating of "The Great Experiment" in Russia, and glossing over the massacres and genocide, which Hitler later was to emulate but not excel, with Tally-rand's famous phrase about the French Revolution: "You can't make an omelette without breaking eggs." And, most of all, the women wanted their sons to come home.

No one seemed to see that here was the beginning of another war, that a fungus was growing that would creep over half the face of the earth.

75

That would mean the Cold War—and American boys dead from the Chosin Reservoir to the Turko-Russian border, from the jungles of Viet Nam to the gray, cold waters of the Bering Sea.

Some of the American dead of the Siberian Expedition stayed there in unknown graves, but there were those who at long last came back to rest at Arlington.

Also there is the Commanding General of the American Expeditionary Forces in Siberia, Major General William S. Graves, a graduate of West Point. When World War I started, he was sent on a special mission to Europe, then later was assigned to the command of the 8th Division at Camp Fremont, California. In August of 1918 he was ordered to Vladivostok to command the Siberian Expeditionary Force. For his work he received the Distinguished Service Medal. General Graves died in 1940.

Near General Graves at Arlington lie the bodies of seven of the men who were brought back from Siberia. There had been three expeditions to salvage the bodies, hampered at first by the lack of diplomatic relations. The second try was made to appear as a personal expedition of the Veterans of Foreign Wars and the State of Michigan, for they had come from the Polar Bear Regiment, the 339th Infantry—Detroit's Pride. Of the 230 Americans dead, most were brought out through Archangel.

The seven who lie near each other at Arlington are a real cross section of American life. They were Private James T. Ida—his brother was a gunmaker in Japan. Private Nikodem Ladovich, Private Elmer E. Speicher, Private Louis A. Szymanski, Private John P. Angove, First Lieutenant Claude B. Hill and Private Boleslaw Gutowski. They were the first American victims of the Cold War with the Communists.

World War I had opened some eyes to the importance of the airplane in war. The Navy had early evinced an interest in aviation. Many of the old-timers felt that it was wasting time better spent on surface craft. But there was a school of thought that felt that if there were going to be planes, the Navy better know more about them than any other arm of the service—and in any event seaplanes might be useful. So the top brass assigned some of the brightest young men to aviation.

One of the earliest of these was Commander John Rodgers, the third of his name in the U. S. Navy, the third of his name at Arlington. His great-grandfather, John Rodgers, had been on board the *Constellation* under Truxton in 1798 and was the ranking naval officer in the War of 1812. His great-uncle also John Rodgers had been a Rear Admiral during the War Between the States and was at Drewry's Bluff and Fort Sumter. His grandmother was the daughter of Matthew Perry whose fleet opened Japan to the West, and the niece of Oliver Hazard Perry.

The Rodgers family tombs are simple—but their deeds were a saga of American Naval History.

Commander Rodgers graduated from Annapolis in 1903 and in 1911 made his first flight—in a man-carrying kite while his ship was underway in Santa Barbara Channel. He remained aloft at a height of four hundred feet for fifteen minutes. His career was determined then and there.

Among the first group of officers to receive aviation instruction—in March, 1911—he was ordered to Dayton for special training under the Wright Brothers. He qualified as a pilot in August, and in September at Annapolis became the Senior Officer of the first Naval Aviation Detachment. In 1916 he was abruptly assigned to Division One, Submarine Force of the Atlantic Fleet, and for two years he commanded temporary submarine bases, then went into the hazardous task of mine-sweeping for which he was awarded the Distinguished Service Medal. Somehow in the early days of the two new branches aviators were made submariners and submariners aviators. Apparently to the dyed-in-the-wool surface men, above or below the sea was one and the same thing.

But in 1921 Rodgers went back to aviation. In August of 1925 he took off from San Pablo Bay near San Francisco for an intended first "non-stop flight to Hawaii." There were two seaplanes in the flight. One was forced down three hundred miles out, but Commander Rodgers went on. Shortage of fuel, however, forced him to land on the sea, four hundred miles from Hawaii. For nine days the seaplane tossed on the waters. The radio was out, so Rodgers devised a sail from the fabric of a wing. There were only emergency rations and Rodgers distilled sea water in a still his mother had given him. They were just fifteen miles off Kauai when Rodgers and his men were picked up by a submarine.

In 1926 he took a land plane from Washington to Philadelphia on an inspection trip. The plane fell into the shallow waters of the Delaware. Rodgers was pinned in the cockpit and so badly injured that he died.

Another one of the early flyers became an Admiral during World War II. John Henry Towers, who graduated from Annapolis in 1906, was one of the first three Naval officers assigned to Aviation. In June, 1911 he entered training under Glenn Curtis, qualifying as a pilot in August. Selected to do experimental flying in seaplanes, he accomplished his mission in safety.

In 1914 Towers commanded the Naval Aviation Detachment at Vera Cruz. Towers and Curtis were planning a Trans-Atlantic flight next, but World War I intervened. It was 1919 before they could go ahead and on May 16, the NC-1, NC-3, NC-4 took off from Newfoundland under Towers' command. The NC-3 which Towers piloted was forced down in heavy seas off Horta, and he sailed two hundred miles to Porto Delgado. Only the NC-4 made it to England.

Towers was commanding officer of the first airplane carrier in the Fleet in 1926. Prior to World War II he was Chief of the Bureau of Aeronautics. In 1942 he became Commander of the Air Force's U. S. Pacific Fleet with rank of Vice-Admiral, his functions being largely logistical and administrative. He received the Distinguished Service Medal for his work.

The Navy did not have the only pioneer flyers. The Coast Guard was also represented, by Admiral Robert Donohue who was head of the Air-Sea Rescue service in World War II. Donohue, who was commissioned in the Coast Guard in 1913, was one of the members of the first class at Pensacola Naval Air Station. In addition to his air-sea rescue work, he also was assigned to the ships sent out against liquor smugglers during the late 20s. In 1935 he served on the Permanent Board of Aviation of the Coast Guard, and set up bases around the country. His Air-Sea Rescue post during the War was continued until he retired in 1946.

It is interesting to note how many of the soldiers whom Pershing honored were veterans of the Philippines. Another was Malin Craig, who graduated from the Military Academy in 1898, and who retired as a full General in 1937.

Until the Boxer Uprising he had served in the Cavalry in the West, then was detailed first to China and next to the Philippines. In 1917 he went overseas, serving with the 41st Division as Chief of Staff. Next he became Chief of Staff for the 1st U. S. Army Corps, where he was Chief of Staff throughout the hostilities, participating in the Aisne and Champagne-Marne Defensives and in the Aisne-Marne, St. Mihiel and Meuse-Argonne Offensives.

General Craig received the Distinguished Service Medal for "his personal influence, aggressiveness, and untiring efforts" at Chateau Thierry, and during the St. Mihiel and Argonne-Meuse Offensives. His first Oak Leaf Cluster was for his work as Chief of Staff where he was responsible for "the greatest peacetime reorientation and modernization of the Army in its history."

Lieutenant General Hugh Aloysius Drum had also served in the Philippines. Commissioned Second Lieutenant in 1898, his regiment was ordered there during the Insurrection. He had active service in the field, and in December of 1900 commanded an expedition which resulted in the capture of the guerrilla chief Guerro. On a second tour of duty there he took part in the capture of Fort Paulus. A third tour of duty found him at Zamboanga and Parang. Back in the States he was sent to the General Staff College, and later was on the Expedition to Vera Cruz under General Funston, whom he later served as Aide. In May, 1917 he sailed for France and was at AEF Headquarters until August, 1918 when he was detailed as Chief of Staff of the American First Army, serving in the Aisne-Marne, St. Mihiel and Meuse-Argonne Offensives.

By 1938 after intervals in Hawaii and Chicago he was assigned to the First Army and Eastern Defense Command in addition to the Second Corps Area, with headquarters at Governors Island. It was during this period that he conducted the famous maneuvers which have been called the finest training exercises for World War II by those officers who participated in them. General Drum retired from active duty in 1943.

An Army needs more than trained men. It must be supplied. The man who was to be Aide to General Marshall on this task was General Brehon Burke Somervell. A graduate of West Point in 1914, he was one of Pershing's young Lieutenants on the Punitive Expedition into Mexico in 1916. After recruiting and organizing the 5th Reserve Engineers, later the 15th Engineers, Railway, he went overseas as Adjutant of that organization in July, 1917. He saw active service during the Meuse-Argonne offensive, but for the most part his engineering talents were used to sort out the supply problems.

In 1925 he was granted leave to accompany Walter D. Hines, Director of Railways during World War I, to Europe to make a survey of navigation conditions on the Rhine and Danube for the League of Nations. Again in the 1930s he was borrowed by the Turkish Government to make an economic survey of Turkey. His work on the Mississippi River and the Florida Ship Canal established him as the outstanding Army Engineer. He was pulled off Army duties again to act as Works Progress Administrator for the city of New York.

In World War II Somervell organized and directed the Army Service forces. He attended all World War II high level conferences and advised the world leaders of the logistical implications of every major strategic move. In addition he was General Marshall's principal staff advisor on transportation problems, planner of major overseas communication lines and troubleshooter on bottlenecks that developed in their construction.

War had already started overseas. The leaders hoped that this time the United States would not be drawn in—but if it could not be averted, they were ready.

Between wars the old soldiers still die and the great Gates of Arlington swing out to meet these heroes who gave their lives for their country as surely as they would have on the field of battle.
                                                            **Patrick Hughes**

# THEY FOUGHT

# ACROSS THE ATLANTIC

HE DISTANT THUNDER OF WAR HAD DIMLY PRESAGED THE STORM
that broke. By the end of 1941, after the attack on Pearl Harbor
by the Japanese, the United States had again joined her European Allies.

The President of the United States is also the Commander-in-Chief of
the Armed Forces. His is the last word, the one upon whom the responsibility rests, upon whom the praise or blame must fall. Therefore, his choice
of advisors is particularly important. Though President Roosevelt does not
lie in Arlington, his top advisors in matters pertaining to World War II
do rest there.

For Naval Affairs, and in other matters as well, Franklin Roosevelt con-
sulted with Fleet Admiral William D. Leahy, one of the elder statesman of
the Navy. Graduating from Annapolis in 1897, Naval Cadet Leahy was in the
Pacific on the USS *Oregon* when War with Spain began. He was in the
heroic dash around the Horn, and also in the operations against the Spanish
Fleet off Santiago. Wherever there was action, there he seemed to be, for
he was in Panama while the Canal was being constructed and in Nicaragua
in 1912. In World War I he was in the Patrol Force of the Atlantic Fleet
guarding against German submarines. Later, when he was in charge of a
vessel transporting troops, he won the coveted Navy Cross.

For more than a decade he went from one important assignment to
another in various parts of the globe. During these years he had seen a great
deal of the President, who, upon his retirement, sent Leahy to Puerto Rico
as its Governor. His stay there was not to be long, however, for after the
Fall of France, Roosevelt sent him as Ambassador to Vichy. Admiral
Leahy's task there was a difficult one. The Vichy regime was naturally
unpopular in this country. The Admiral had to walk a tight-rope in
his dealings with the Petain Government, at the same time being under a
barrage of criticism from street corner diplomats at home. Only the President
and his Ambassador knew the whole situation, or how much Leahy ac-

81

complished for his country during those vital months. When he came back, there was a high post for him, and shortly, the rare title of Fleet Admiral.

General George Catlett Marshall was a master of logistics. In short, he had an uncanny flair for anticipating needs and planning so that what was wanted would be where it was wanted at the time it was wanted. He first came to Pershing's attention when he was a Lieutenant Colonel in France in World War I. Pershing had been particularly pleased with the plans for the Cantigny attack and asked who had devised them. From that time on he kept an eye on this hitherto unknown officer.

Marshall had gone into the Army not from West Point but from Virginia Military Institute. He had served adequate time in the Philippines, Pershing's favorite school for officers, and he had had thorough grounding in many types of work before he came to Pershing's attention.

It was after the Cantigny operations episode that Marshall got his biggest opportunity. To keep interference away from the American Army, and permit it to operate as a unit, Pershing had agreed to a quick turn to the Argonne from the St. Mihiel Offensive which meant the moving out of 220,000 French and the moving of 600,000 Americans—with all equipment, supplies, and so forth neatly laid on. All of this must be done *secretly*. Pershing turned the task over to Marshall, who performed the miracle. A London paper's military advisor said it was "a fine piece of Staff work and no other Staff could have done it better." Many felt it was the greatest achievement of the war. And it *made* Marshall.

The next five years were spent as Aide to General Pershing, under whom he drew up studies of the work of the various divisions and their commanders. In the following decade, he had varied experiences, including nearly three years in China.

Finally, after Pershing had nudged Roosevelt, Marshall became Chief of Staff in 1939 and served through to November, 1945. Upon the Pearl Harbor fiasco, Marshall reorganized the Army headquarters, so that never again would action depend on just one person. He set up a command post —which worked. Marshall would have liked some combat experience—he very much wanted to lead the Armies in the Invasion of the Continent—but he was too valuable where he was, in the eyes of the President, so he did the job set before him to the best of his ability—which was saying a great deal.

In 1945 President Truman sent him to China, where he served with rank of Ambassador for a year and a half. It wasn't his kind of a job, but his Commanding Officer had ordered it—and Marshall was an obedient soldier. When he came back it was to be Secretary of State for two years. In 1950 he was allowed to go back to what he could do best, and he became Secretary of Defense for a year of the Korean War.

To people overseas, General Marshall is best known for the "Marshall Plan"—the economic aid program. He won the Nobel Peace Prize for this plan—the only soldier ever so honored.

Navy, Army—and Air Force. And the head of the Air Force was Hap Arnold. Of course, he was really General of the Army Henry H. Arnold, but it is doubtful that anyone ever thought of him that way. He was Hap Arnold, and he loved flying. The men who flew the Army planes were most important in his eyes.

Maybe it was because he had been one of the early flyers. Arnold had graduated from West Point in 1907, had gone to the Philippines with the Infantry and was back at Governors Island when his chance came. Detailed to the Signal Corps, he was sent to Dayton to receive instruction in piloting the Wright biplane. Once "qualified" he was made an instructor at the new Signal Corps Aviation School at College Park, Maryland, which consisted of three machines and three pilots. In 1912 Arnold established a new altitude record of 6,540 feet. And he went right on establishing records for the rest of his life. There was the flight to Alaska in 1936, for which he received the Distinguished Flying Cross. His Distinguished Service Medal came for the flight from Brisbane, Australia, to Bolling Field, Washington, in 1942.

He had taught, organized and administered from before World War I until World War II broke out, when he was Chief of the Army Air Corps. Tireless in the promotion of an adequate air force, he worked as hard with plane producers as he did in seeing to it that the flyers were properly trained.

(1) The Promise      Hap Arnold      (2) The Fulfillment

When he retired in 1948 he had spent forty-two years in the service of his country—and most of that time in aviation.

A citizen-soldier who served in both wars was William J. Donovan—"Wild Bill" of the 165th Infantry, head of the first "cloak and dagger" agency, the O. S. S., and one of the most decorated war heroes in American history.

A lawyer by profession, he had joined the New York State National Guard, and went with it to France in World War I. Before long he was a Lieutenant Colonel of the 165th Infantry and had won the Medal of Honor for bravery in the field. He also received the Distinguished Service Cross and the Distinguished Service Medal.

Exemplifying by his actions in war, the best type of citizen-soldier, his sense of civic duty enabled the Government to call on him for special service during the years of peace, service such as Chairman of the Rio Grande Compact Commission and of the Colorado River Commission.

When World War II came, he was recalled to active duty and asked to head up the Office of Strategic Services, or O. S. S. as it was familiarly known. He administered this with the same daring he had displayed in battle, and the accounts of the deed done will go down in the history of spy operations.

The successor to O. S. S. was C. I. A. and an Air Force General was to head that new agency. But first, he had had experience in combat and organization.

General Hoyt S. Vandenberg graduated from West Point in 1923 and went into the Air Service. He not only could fly, but he could instruct others to fly—a very different and rare quality. He was shifted from one place to another to teach and then, a few months after the United States entered World War II, he became Operations and Training Officer of the Air Staff.

Next—in 1942—he went to the United Kingdom to assist in the organization of the Air Forces for North Africa, later becoming Chief of Staff of the Northwest African Strategic Air Force, with which he flew on numerous missions during the North African campaign. For this work he was awarded both the Silver Star and the Distinguished Flying Cross. He already had the Distinguished Service Medal. Upon returning from an Air Mission to Soviet Russia, General Vandenberg became commander of the Ninth Air Force.

In January of 1946 he became Director of Intelligence on the War Department General Staff where he served until his appointment as Director of the Central Intelligence Agency. Returning later to the Air Force, he succeeded General Carl Spaatz as Chief of Staff of the Air Force in 1948. He remained in this post until his retirement in 1953.

During World War II the Coast Guard burgeoned suddenly. In personnel it multiplied fifteen times. It participated in every major invasion and its fleet expanded to the point where the Service manned more than 290 Navy vessels, approximately 255 Army vessels, over 750 of the cutter class and 3,500 miscellaneous small craft. The man responsible for the work of the Coast Guard during this time was Admiral Russell R. Waesche.

Waesche was commissioned an Ensign in 1906, having attended the Coast Guard Academy. After serving on the Great Lakes, in Alaskan and Arctic Waters, and on the Pacific Coast, he was—in 1920—appointed U. S. Commissioner for the Third Division, District of Alaska, in connection with his duties during the Bering Sea patrol. During prohibition days, he was out against rum-runners, which was excellent training for his later planning against German submarines and surface craft—both were canny lawbreakers, and shrewd and artful dodgers.

Admiral Waesche served three full terms—twelve years in all—as Commandant of the Coast Guard. During his administration the Lighthouse Service was transferred to and integrated with the Coast Guard and its efficiency increased. When war broke out, besides the increased Coast Guard there was the added responsibility for the 10,000 women added to the service to take the place of Coast Guardsmen needed for security work—for the

General Walter Bedell Smith signing the surrender terms with the Germans as the representative of General Eisenhower. Admiral David F. Burroughs, Commander-in-Chief of the Naval Expeditionary Forces is at his right, and Major General Ivan Suslaparoff of the Soviet forces is at his left.

Coast Guard was made responsible for much of the security of United States Ports. He also organized the Merchant Marine Council as an Advisory Group.

In March, 1946 President Truman announced the formation of an "elder statesman's" organization for national defense. Admiral Waesche was one of the officers selected. Two years previously the Admiral had been elected President of the Society of American Military Engineers.

The bombing of the Ploesti oil fields was one of the great feats of the war, involving as it did unusually long flights over unfamiliar enemy terrain. Bombing Germany was a milk-run in comparison. It was for gallantry in action in the Ploesti raid of June 23, 1944 that Second Lieutenant David R. Kingsley won the Medal of Honor, though he did not live to wear it. He is representative of the many young airmen who rest at Arlington.

Kingsley was a bombardier on a B-17 in the raid into Rumania. On the bomb run the plane was badly damaged by anti-aircraft fire and forced to drop out of formation. The pilot proceeded over target, however, and Lieutenant Kingsley dropped his bombs, severely damaging vital installations.

The aircraft, forced to lose altitude, fell behind the formation on its way back to base, and was attacked by three enemy craft. The plane received more damage and the tail gunner was seriously wounded. Kingsley made his way back to the gunner, and checked the bleeding. He helped remove the gunner's clothes and parachute, wrapped him in blankets and went back to his own post. Another attack, this time by eight planes, damaged the airplane so badly that the pilot gave orders to prepare to bail out. In the meantime, the ball turret gunner was wounded and Kingsley was busy with first-aid.

When the order came to prepare to bail out, Kingsley helped to get the turret gunner's parachute on. But the one for the tail gunner was missing. Without hesitation, Kingsley took off his own parachute and put it on the injured man. It seemed as though the plane would disintegrate any moment and the "bail out" signal was given. Kingsley helped the wounded men out. Their last sight of Kingsley was standing on the bomb bay catwalk. The airplane continued to fly on automatic pilot for a few minutes and then crashed. His body was found later in the wreckage.

> Lieutenant Kingsley by his gallant, heroic action was directly responsible for saving the life of the wounded gunner.

Thus reads his citation.

There was another citation once—exemplified many times by the heroes at Arlington. It is from the Gospel according to St. John and it reads:

> Greater love hath no man than this, that a man lay down his life for his friends.

Like an avenging whirlwind the Army Air Corps flies out on the daring raid on the oil fields at Ploesti—supplier of the Luftwaffe in 1944.

Patrick Hughes

# THEY FOUGHT
# ACROSS THE PACIFIC

WHEN THE GUNS WERE STILLED AND THE RAIDERS OF THE RISING SUN had left Pearl Harbor, there was a stunned and awful silence. Then came the reassessment, pretty much in the same tone Kipling used for England at the time of the Boer War defeats:

> Let us admit it fairly, as a business people should. We have had no end of a lesson. May it do us no end of good.

"Remember Pearl Harbor" became an American watchword after that fatal December 7, 1941. The United States was in the war at last—and determined to win through no matter what the cost. The cost was great, for literally speaking, the United States Armed Forces had to fight their way across the Pacific, step by step, island by island. Many did not come back to Arlington—they now lie where they fell, or in the ocean's depths. To represent them, here are the stories of a few whose journey's end was on the green hillside above the Potomac.

Heroism is not a matter of rank. It is a matter of character. Heroism is a dedication to duty, of acceptance of responsibility to others rather than to one's self. Consider the story of Robert R. Scott who represents the heroes of Pearl Harbor.

Scott, aged 26, was a Machinist's Mate First Class, from Massillon, Ohio. He had been in the Navy for three years when he was killed on that fateful December day. The compartment in the USS *California*, in which the air compressor essential to firing was located, was flooded when a torpedo hit the ship. When the remainder of the personnel evacuated the compartment, Scott stayed at his post. His last words were, "This is my station and I will stay and give them air as long as the guns are going." For conspicuous devotion to duty, extraordinary courage, and complete disregard of his own life, Scott was posthumously awarded the Medal of Honor.

James V. Forrestal, Secretary of Defense, shakes hands with Bull Halsey—the fighting Admiral.

Fortunately for the United States, the aircraft carrier USS *Enterprise* was not at Pearl Harbor on that black Sunday. She had been sent to Wake Island to deliver some planes and was returning when the news came. Planes were immediately launched, but by then the Japanese Fleet had gone. The Commander of Carrier Division Two was flying his flag on the *Enterprise* at the time. Before the war in the Pacific was over, "Bull" Halsey became Fleet Admiral William F. Halsey, Jr., and one of the most popular officers with the enlisted men in the Navy.

His father was a Captain in the Navy, so it was only natural that Halsey should go to Annapolis, from which he graduated in 1904. During World War I Halsey served on destroyers off the Irish Coast and won the Navy Cross.

In 1934—after a decade of various assignments which included several important Naval Attaché posts at Embassies in strategically important areas —he was sent to Pensacola for Flight Training, and won his wings in 1935 at the age of fifty-two. From then on he was in charge of carriers, thus finding himself on the *Enterprise* as Vice-Admiral on December 7, 1941.

In February, 1942 the first raids were made on the Japanese-held Gilbert and Marshall Islands under Halsey's direction. Two months later he became Commander of Task Force Sixteen and in that capacity, still on the *Enterprise*, escorted the aircraft carrier *Hornet* carrying the Doolittle flyers for their raid on Tokyo.

By the end of 1942 he was appointed Commander of the South Pacific Force and the South Pacific area. Army, Navy and Marine Forces were integrated under him for the battle in the Solomons and all the services approved his handling of the operations. It has been said that the battles of Santa Cruz and Guadalcanal turned the tide.

From the Solomons to Tokyo and the surrender of the Japanese Fleet was a long, hard pull. Halsey was in it all the way—from "Chesty" Puller's forward command post on Guadalcanal to the deck of the USS *Missouri*, Halsey's Flagship as Commander of the Third Fleet, when General Douglas MacArthur received the formal surrender of the Japanese Imperial Government. Admiral Halsey retired in 1947.

The second Japanese attack point was the Philippines. Their blitzkrieg tactics had succeeded in demolishing the greater part of the defending aircraft and the debacle at Pearl Harbor had ended all hope of reinforcements. By clever maneuvering all available troops were gathered into the Bataan Peninsula as had long been planned—but the original plans had allowed for air and sea support, now lacking. Under protest, MacArthur obeyed President Roosevelt's direct order to leave for Australia, turning command over to the man whose reputation for enduring courage will last as long as the rocky islet of Corregidor lies off the Bataan Peninsula.

Lieutenant Jonathan M. Wainwright, a West Pointer, was commissioned in the Army in 1906. He first went to the Philippines in 1909, seeing action on the Island of Jolo. For the most part he served in the West, but when World War I broke out he was made Adjutant of the first Officer's Training Camp—a familiar figure to the new civilian soldiers. He went overseas in 1918 and saw action at St. Mihiel and the Meuse-Argonne campaign.

By the time 1941 came around he was promoted to Major General and given the Philippine Division to command. The Army withdrew into Bataan before MacArthur left, but it was General Wainwright who had handled the withdrawal. He was ordered to Corregidor and remained there through the fall of Bataan in April, until he was forced to surrender to the Japanese in May, after a gallant struggle against hopeless odds.

For over three years General Wainwright was a prisoner of the Japanese —through the Bataan Death March and beyond. He was a gaunt shadow of a man when finally he stood with MacArthur to witness the surrender of the Japanese. He received the Medal of Honor for his courageous stand,

The reunion of two old friends—MacArthur and Wainwright. The emaciated Wainwright shows the effect of his years of imprisonment in a Japanese prison camp.

but even more expressive is the General Orders issued from Fort Sam Houston on the day of his death in 1953.

> Excelling in leadership and courage, throughout his forty-five years of distinguished service, he exemplified, in a conspicuously outstanding manner, the ideal combat commander. Through adversity and success his spirit never faltered. To his men, he was a tower of strength . . . He will live in history as the hero of Bataan and Corregidor and as the commander who bought for this country the time needed for eventual victory in the Pacific.

In March, 1942 came the first boost to national morale—the bombing of Tokyo by the "Doolittle flyers" of the Army Air Force. Their story is well known—how from the carrier *Hornet* they brought the war home to

Japan, hitting their targets and then going on into China—some to safety, others to death. Three of the Doolittle flyers—Lieutenant Dean Hallmark, Robert Mader, William J. Farrow—were captured by the Japanese. Two were executed. One died in prison. All three are buried in Arlington.

So is the man who was then Captain of the USS *Hornet*—Admiral Marc Mitscher. Mitscher had graduated from Annapolis in 1910—and from 1911 to 1916 he steadily asked for transfer to aviation. He was one of the first thirteen students at Pensacola and remained an enthusiast until the day of his death in 1947.

In 1919 he was in the NC-1 when Towers made the attempt to cross the Atlantic with the three seaplanes. Like Towers, his plane was forced to land in heavy seas off the Azores.

Before World War II he had had much experience in carriers and was on board the USS *Hornet* when war was declared. This ship was chosen to carry the Doolittle flyers and Mitscher kept secrecy as ordered until the *Hornet*, accompanied by the *Enterprise* with Halsey aboard, was well out to sea. Then he announced the purpose of the raid to the men, who greeted the electrifying news with cheers. After the planes were out of sight he cautioned the men of the importance of secrecy and for many months the "Shangri-la" to which President Roosevelt referred as their base, was not known.

Mitscher won the Distinguished Service Medal for his work as Commander Air, in the Solomon Islands Campaign. Later followed another medal for his assault on the Marshall Islands and later on Truk. By the end of the war he had commanded Carrier task forces against the greater part of the Japanese-held islands.

His fame was great, but perhaps his greatest moment of glory was in the realization that the pilots who flew under his orders had faith in him. When disabled they knew he would not leave them helpless in the ocean— that even if he had to turn lights on in a submarine-ridden sea, he would search for and bring his men home again.

Guadalcanal was a typical Marine invasion in the beginning—"hold on regardless of supplies or equipment, sniping or assault"—just tough Marine fighting only on a larger scale than Haiti or Nicaragua.

Another Medal of Honor winner in the Solomons was the famous "Red Mike" of the Marine Corps, later known more formally as Major General Merritt A. Edson. Edson had enlisted in the Marine Corps Reserves at the outbreak of World War I. He was commissioned a Second Lieutenant in the Regular Marines in 1917 and served in France for over a year.

During his years in the Marines he had been closely associated with the development of small arms markmanship. In the six months prior to the entry of the United States into World War II he concentrated on experimental operations and training in close conjunction with destroyer transports. This led to the formation of the 1st Marine Raider Battalion one month after War was declared.

On August 7, 1943 the 1st Marine Raider Battalion under Edson, then a Colonel, landed on Tulagi in the Solomon Islands and after two days of heavy fighting captured the island. Later transferred across the strait to Guadalcanal he was assigned the occupation and defense of a ridge dominating the jungle. It was for his brilliant action here that he won the Medal of Honor.

After participating in the battle of Tarawa, Edson was made a Brigadier General. Later he retired with the rank of Major General. Both of General Edson's sons are Marine officers and were present when the destroyer USS *Edson* was named in his honor.

The Navy also was represented at Guadalcanal, not only by Admiral Marc Mitcher, but by a descendant of an old and distinguished naval family.

Captain Cassin Young traced his lineage to Stephen Cassin, hero of the War of 1812. Three years after his graduation from Annapolis—in 1919— he went into the Submarine Service, spending most of his time in this branch for the next few years.

In 1939 he took over as executive officer of the Submarine Base at New London. In 1941, however, he went to sea as Commanding Officer of the USS *Vestal*. It was while he was on the *Vestal* at Pearl Harbor that he won the Medal of Honor.

Captain Cassin Young was blown overboard by the explosion on the USS *Arizona* to which the *Vestal* was moored. He swam back to his ship which was listing and on fire in several places. He took command and in spite of enemy bombing moved his ship to a safe distance and beached it, as the only way to save the *Vestal*.

In 1943 he was in command of the USS *San Francisco*, a heavy cruiser when a Japanese fleet approached the environs to Guadalcanal. The USS *San Francisco* silenced and disabled an enemy battleship, sank a destroyer and damaged two other ships. But Captain Cassin Young was killed in action. A destroyer has been named in his honor.

In the meantime there was activity in the China-Burma-India Theater of Operations. In the air there was the fabulous General Claire Chennault. Chennault had taken up flying shortly after he was commissioned a First Lieutenant in the reserves at the beginning of World War I. Transferring to the Regular Army after the war, he flew and taught all over the country.

Shortly after the outbreak of the Sino-Japanese War he went to China to train pursuit units of the Chinese Air Force. In 1941 as a Brigadier General in the Chinese Air Force, he was charged with recruiting the American Volunteer Group of pursuit pilots, more popularly known as "The Flying Tigers," who compiled such a glorious record against the enemy. A year later he went back on active duty in the Army and became Commanding General of the United States Air Forces in China. The citation for the Oak Leaf Cluster to his Distinguished Service Medal says:

> His force contributed beyond expectation, to limiting Japanese air and ground activities and was a major factor in rendering impotent the enemy's air drive in China.

When General MacArthur returned to the Philippines, he had with him as Commanding General of the Eighth Army, Robert L. Eichelberger. There was more than one reason for this selection. General Eichelberger was unusually conversant with Japan and the Japanese, and he knew the Philippines well.

He had graduated from West Point in 1909 and less than a decade later was ordered to Siberia as Chief Intelligence Officer of the American Expeditionary Force. He was in its 1919 campaign and also served as American representative on the Inter-Allied Military Committee. There he learned the tactics of the Japanese, a knowledge further added to by a year in Japan on intelligence duties.

When World War II broke out he was Superintendent of the Military Academy, but in January, 1942 he became Commanding General of the 77th Infantry Division, shortly thereafter reporting to MacArthur in Australia. New Guinea and then the campaign for the Philippines followed, and then the occupation of Japan.

He was much decorated, not only for his organizational work but for personal bravery. He was a General who led his men—and he could and did use a rifle, when it came to protecting them. It was for such actions in Siberia that he received the Distinguished Service Cross.

The air over Luzon was filled with danger in those days before the recapture of Manila by General MacArthur. It was Christmastime in 1944 when Major Thomas B. McGuire, Jr., a leading ace, won the Medal of Honor. On Christmas Day he volunteered to lead a squadron of fifteen P-38's to cover for a bombing raid on Mabalacar Airdrome. His formation was attacked by twenty Japanese fighters. In the ensuing action, like a good leader, he was constantly flying to the aid of his men, driving off enemy assaults and even forcing an enemy plane into a wingman's line of fire. He also shot down three Zeros himself.

The next day he volunteered again. This time the attack was on strongly

A priest-chaplain and his mother kneel at the grave of the brother and son who won the Medal of Honor for heroism at the cost of his life. Army Chaplain (First Lieutenant) Cormac Walsh was decorated six times for heroism in Korea, and was named Chaplain of the Year in 1955 by the Reserve Officers Association of the United States.

**Wide World Photos**

defended Clark Field. Again he exposed himself to attack to save others and finally scored his thirty-eighth victory in aerial combat. On January 7, 1945 he went out for the last time. To save fellow flyer from attack, he tried a risky maneuver which did not succeed. He crashed to his death.

Another Marine who won the Medal of Honor in the South Pacific was Gunnery Sergeant William G. Walsh of the Fifth Marine Division.

Advancing toward Hill 362 on Iwo Jima, his Company was disrupted by machine gun fire. Walsh charged at the head of his platoon, regardless of the fire of Japanese automatic weapons and hand grenades. Thrown back, he again led the platoon forward up the rocky slope to the ridge. There the Japanese made a suicidal attempt to stop the charge by an intense barrage of hand grenades.

One of the grenades fell in the midst of the survivors of Walsh's platoon, huddled in a narrow trench. As his citation reads:

> Gunnery Sergeant Walsh in a final valiant act of complete self-sacrifice, instantly threw himself upon the deadly bomb, absorbing with his own body the full and terrific force of the explosion. Through his extraordinary initiative and inspiring valor in the face of almost certain death, he saved his comrades from injury and possible loss of life and enabled his company to seize and hold this vital enemy position.

Heroism is contagious. His brother, Army Chaplain Cormac Walsh, a Franciscan priest, won four Silver Stars and a Presidential Citation for aiding the wounded under heavy enemy fire in the Korean War. The Walsh brothers came by their heroism naturally. Their father, a Boston fireman, died in an attempt to save people from a burning building.

The final campaign of World War II was the battle for Okinawa. There a Marine General led an Army. General Roy S. Geiger had already commanded both air and ground units during the war. At Okinawa he was in command of the Third Amphibious Corps, but when the Commanding General of the Tenth Army, General Simon Bolivar Buckner—son of Lieutenant General Simon Bolivar Buckner, hero of the Mexican War, and General in the Confederate Army—was killed in action, General Geiger took command and led the Army to the successful conclusion of this last campaign. For his part in this action he was awarded the Army Distinguished Service Medal.

General Geiger had already piled up a noteworthy record before the Okinawa campaign. He had enlisted in the Marine Corps in 1907 and was commissioned in 1909. In Nicaragua in 1912 he assisted in the capture of Coyotepe and Barranca. Then followed service in the Philippines and in China.

In 1916 he was assigned to Pensacola, where he became the fifth flyer in Marine Corps history. Geiger was one of the few who flew in France, where he was the commander of a squadron with the 1st Marine Aviation Force, and a member of the Day Wing, Northern Bombing Group. He was awarded the Navy Cross for this work. After all, the Marines had virtually invented dive-bombing in the rickety planes that were all they had to practice with in the early days.

After World War I came Haiti—twice. There was always trouble in Haiti on the slightest provocation.

When World War II broke out, General Geiger was serving as Commanding General, 1st Marine Aircraft Wing, Fleet Marine Force. He led this group at Guadalcanal in 1942. For extraordinary heroism and as commander of all Guadalcanal based aircraft, he was awarded a Gold Star in lieu of a second Navy Cross.

Recalled to headquarters in 1943 to become Director of Aviation of the Marine Corps, he nevertheless wangled his way back to the front within a few months, this time as Commanding General of the First Marine Amphibious Corps. He led this group in the Bougainville Operation, winning the Navy Distinguished Service Medal.

In 1944 General Geiger again led the group, now redesignated as the Third Amphibious Corps, in the recapture of Guam, and the capture of the southern Palau Islands. For these actions he received two more Distinguished Service Medals. And, as has already been told, he led his men again in the invasion and capture of Okinawa.

In July, 1945 he became Commanding General of the Fleet Marine Force, Pacific, until called home in November, 1946. He died early in January of 1947 and was posthumously promoted to the rank of General by the 80th Congress.

A Japanese bomb explosion cost a Marine General his sight and gave to the blind and handicapped the country over, a spokesman and an inspiration.

Major General Melvin J. Maas, ex-Congressman, retired Marine General, and Chairman of the President's Committee on the Reemployment of the Handicapped when he died in 1964, had a varied career.

On April 6, 1917 Melvin Maas enlisted in the Marine Corps and served with Marine Aviation in the Azores throughout the war. Prior to entering Congress in 1927, he was commissioned in the Marine Reserve. He was twenty-seven when he went to Congress and he served there for sixteen years, from 1927 to 1933, and from 1935 to 1945. His interest in legislation was concentrated for a good part on that affecting aviation, national defense and the Armed Services. He also was the Congressional author of the legislation creating the first military women's reserve.

It was during his early days as a Congressman that he was awarded the Carnegie Silver Medal for Heroism when he disarmed a man in the House Galleries who was threatening the Members with a loaded revolver. There may have been others nearer—but Maas was the one who acted.

General Maas was called back to active duty in 1941 and served on Admiral Halsey's staff. In 1942 he saw service at Guadalcanal on the staff of Admiral Fletcher. He then was assigned to General MacArthur as Marine observer and was awarded the Silver Star for service with the Army Air Corps at the Battle of Milne Bay, New Guinea. He went back to Congress for a while, but returned to active service for the Okinawa campaign where he was in command of the Awase Air Base. It was then that a bomb explosion injured the optic nerve resulting in total blindness a few years later. He was retired in 1951 and advanced to the rank of Major General for having been specially commended in combat.

From that time until his death in 1964 General Maas gave of himself unstintingly to work for the handicapped, particularly those with service connected disabilities. He had been National Commander of the Disabled American Veterans in 1955-56, and of the Blinded Veterans Association in 1960-61.

With V-J Day World War II came to a close. But, somehow, there was not the jubilation there had been at the close of World War I.

# THEY FOUGHT

# IN KOREA

OF COURSE, THE KOREAN WAR WAS NOT REALLY A WAR WAGED BY the United States—it was Police Action by the United Nations. Yet, several thousand victims of that conflict now lie in Arlington.

Why Korea? Korea was one of the oldest independent kingdoms in the world, when, at the close of the Russo-Japanese War, the Western peacemakers handed it over to the Japanese. At the end of World War I Japan was an Ally, so, in the Treaty of Versailles, "the self-determination of nations" was ignored for Korea. At Yalta, the Soviets demanded and received the controlling influence in the northern part of Korea as a price for waging a ten days "war" against Japan. It must not be forgotten that the Soviets remained on friendly trade terms with the Allies' enemy, even while the Communists demanded all-out aid for Soviet Russia—a partner of the Nazis during the first blitzkriegs.

Why Korea? The Nazis asked this question about Poland in 1939 and the answer is the same. There comes a point beyond which free men cannot compromise—when, if they are to live with themselves, they must stand firm. So it was in Korea.

Somehow, good fighters though Americans are, they never expect a war. But, before the ink was dry on the United Nations Charter, the Soviets had started reneging on every promise made; on every pledge given; on every contract, no matter how legal, on every compact, no matter how solemn. With cobra-like gulps, the Soviets devoured nations and people, until President Truman dug his heels in, and said "NO" for Greece and Korea.

The brunt of the combat did fall on the United States. That was natural for it had had two years less of war. It had more manpower and productive resources, and it had made more promises. So the United Nations Police

Force was at first largely composed of American troops already in the area and, by the very nature of things had to remain on the defensive, the most difficult type of war.

There was one supply item in Korea that never seemed to be in short supply, and that was heroism. Here are the sagas of some of the heroes who now lie in eternal honor at Arlington.

It was July of 1950. The Korean War was less than a month old. Taejon had just been lost and the troops were falling back on the Pusan Perimeter. Sergeant George D. Libby of the 3rd Engineers Combat Battalion was in a truck trying to break through an enemy encirclement when fire from a road block disabled the truck and wounded or killed all but Sergeant Libby. He went into action, fighting off the enemy and giving first-aid to the wounded. An artillery tractor came along and he helped the wounded in. The firing continued and, realizing that the driver was the most essential man, he stepped in front to shield him, receiving several wounds. Back the tractor went, Libby helping other wounded aboard as they went through a town. Refusing first-aid, he constantly shielded the driver, while firing at the enemy until he collapsed and died. In the citation for his posthumous Medal of Honor, it says, "Sergeant Libby's sustained, heroic actions enabled his comrades to reach friendly lines."

The brilliant three-pronged campaign so reminiscent of Scott's tactics in the Mexican War of 1847, began with the landing at Inchon. The First Marine Division had joined the Army and had been brought into the Yellow Sea by the Navy, so the three services were fighting together again.

The Chosin Reservoir battle, or battles, was just about as tough as they come. Bitter cold, and no way to really combat it, constant harassment from enemy fire, enemy concentration to keep supplies from moving up the roads —it all added up to one of the worst of the campaigns. A good sergeant was a necessity to keep things going. Such a man was Staff Sergeant William J. Windrich.

Windrich had been a Marine since 1938. He had spent twenty months in the South Pacific as a machine gunner. He had reenlisted in 1945, and the following year participated in the Atomic Bomb tests at Bikini Atoll. After a tour in China he had returned to Camp Pendleton, Oregon, and was on MP duty when war began. He went overseas with the First Marine Brigade and was himself one of the first Marines to see action in Korea.

There Windrich took part in the Inchon Landing and in the capture of Seoul before moving up to the Chosin Reservoir campaign where he won the Medal of Honor—and died. There had been a savage night battle and he had been wounded. He refused to be evacuated—he had his men to look after.

Instead he spearheaded an attack to a knoll and directed effective fire to cover the withdrawal of troops. Seven of his men were struck down and he was wounded in the head by a bursting grenade. However, he made his way to his company's position, organized a small group of volunteers and returned to evacuate the wounded and dying from the frozen hillside.

He redeployed his troops and fought on with his men, though wounded in the leg. Unable to stand, he still refused evacuation, and directed his platoon in setting up defensive positions until, weakened by bitter cold, excessive loss of blood and severe pain, he lapsed into unconsciousness from which he never woke. "His valiant leadership, fortitude and courageous fighting spirit against tremendous odds served to inspire others to heroic endeavor," says his citation. He probably would have said he was just trying to be a good Sergeant.

The third prong of the attack came up through Hamhung and was made by the X Corps. Army Lieutenant Colonel John U. D. Page was a member of X Corps Artillery and attached to the 52nd Transportation Truck Battalion when he distinguished himself "above and beyond the call of duty." Page had gone up to the Chosin Reservoir plateau to establish traffic control of the main supply route. Once finished he was free to go back to Hamhung— but he did not go. He had found an isolated signal station that seemed to need help. Cut off with elements of the Marine Division and after nearly being ambushed, he reached the Marine lines at Koto-ri, already surrounded.

Page next, voluntarily, quickly formed a reserve group of assorted Army and Marine personnel. In order to help evacuate casualties on a hastily devised airstrip, heedless of his personal safety, and twice exposing himself to direct fire, Colonel Page manned a machine gun on a tank and beat back attacks on the rescue plane.

After ten days of continual fighting the Marine and Army units in the Chosin Reservoir area were gathered in and Colonel Page was flown to Hamhung to arrange for transport and support. But he did not stay in safety—he returned to help, and as the column moved south he joined the rear guard. Refugees were pressing close on the troops—and the Red Chinese had infiltrated among these refugees. They had many tricks—and a good man was needed to spot them. When the column was attacked, Colonel Page mounted a machine gun on an abandoned tank and covered the passing vehicles. Later, he put a gun on a hillside and averted an ambush.

On the night of December 10, 1950 the retreating column—it was retreating because the Red Chinese had come into the war and the United Nations was not sure what it wanted to do—had reached the foot of the pass, when it encountered heavy enemy fire at the head. Despite deadly small arms fire, Colonel Page made his way to the front and plunged forward in a surprise attack.

For his extraordinary heroism during these ten days Colonel Page not only received the Medal of Honor but the Navy Cross as well—but both were posthumous.

While one prong of the attack was driving up from Inchon on the West Coast and the X Corps bore up from the East Coast, the Eighth Army was to shoot straight up the center of Korea. For the early part of the war, until his untimely death in an automobile accident near Seoul, the Eighth Army was headed by Lieutenant General Walton Harris Walker. General Walker had had a most distinguished career ever since his graduation from West Point in 1912. He had served under General Funston in the Vera Cruz Expedition in 1914, then on the border patrol during the hectic period before World War I.

In 1917 he organized Company A of the 13th Machine Gun Battalion with which unit he went to France in April, 1918. As a Major in France, he commanded the Battalion at St. Mihiel and in the Meuse-Argonne, where he was twice cited for gallantry in action, and was promoted to Lieutenant Colonel on the battlefield. After the war he was with the Occupation Forces in Germany.

In 1943 as Major General in command of the IV Armored Corps, later to be better known as the XX Corps, he went overseas. There the XX Corps was attached to General Patton's Third Army and was in his famous drive across France. The XX Corps was in the capture of Metz, and later liberated Buchenwald. For gallantry in combat during World Wars I and II General Walker had been awarded the Distinguished Service Cross, the Distinguished Service Medal, the Silver Star with two Oak Leaf Clusters, the Legion of Merit, the Bronze Star as well as many foreign decorations. General Walker was killed in an automobile accident on December 23, 1950 and was succeeded by Lt. General Matthew B. Ridgway.

The beginning of the New Year of 1951 was the beginning of the end for two brothers who had always done things together. Robert M. McGovern aged twenty-three, was killed in action on January 30, 1951; his brother Jerome F., aged twenty-one, February 10. Both had enlisted in the Army immediately upon finishing high school, Robert in 1946, Jerome in 1948. They were not unfamiliar with the Army for they had gone to St. John's College High School (Washington, D. C.) with its 113-year-old tradition of service, and its 1,200 cadets. Robert had been the honor student, Jerome the athlete. Both went to OCS and were commissioned Second Lieutenants.

Both became paratroopers and were in the 187th Airborne when they went to Korea. Both had made the jump into Kimpo Airfield when that important base was captured on the way from Inchon to Seoul. Then their paths diverged for a brief period.

Casualties had been high. Lieutenants, particularly those who could lead, who had been trained, were needed to stiffen up the new troops. Robert was sent to the 5th Cavalry, Jerome to the 9th Infantry.

Robert won the Medal of Honor at the cost of his life. As he led his troops in an attack up a slope, there came a heavy burst of enemy rifle and machine gun fire. Though wounded, Lieutenant McGovern pressed forward. Then came a barrage of grenades. Young McGoven managed to throw back some before they exploded. Disregarding his serious wounds, he charged a machine gun emplacement. When he was within ten yards of the position, a burst of fire ripped his carbine from his hands. Undaunted,he continued the lone-man assault and with his pistol and grenades he managed to kill seven of the enemy before falling mortally wounded.

Before he learned of his brother's death, Jerome had earned the Silver Star for his gallantry. On February 10, in the vicinity of Kumwang-ni his company attacked Hill 442 when it was halted by enemy fire. Lieutenant Jerome McGovern, ignoring a painful wound, reorganized his platoon and resumed the assault. Inspired by his actions, the platoon charged. Then he received his second and fatal wound.

The two brothers were brought back to Arlington together. There they rest under a simple granite marker on which their father had inscribed:

> To their conscience they were true and had the genius to be men.

That truth is more dramatic than fiction is shown by the story of a heliocopter pilot. Lieutenant John K. Koelsch had gone directly into the Navy from Princeton, and by 1944 was designated Naval Aviator.

In October, 1950 he joined the USS *Princeton* as Officer in Charge of the Helicopter Detachment. On July 1, 1951 he was reported "Missing in Action" as the result of an airplane crash while on a rescue mission. Later it was learned that he had been taken prisoner and died of malnutrition on October 16, 1951.

Here is the story of what happened as told by the citation for his posthumous Medal of Honor. It must be remembered that citations deliberately underplay, and since the days of General Terry of Indian War fame, the facts are most carefully checked. This is mentioned because of the sheer drama of the tale.

It was almost dark when word came that a Marine flyer had been shot down and was trapped in mountainous terrain. Lieutenant Koelsch volunteered to go in after him. With an almost solid overcast below the peaks, Koelsch flew his helicopter, unarmed and vulnerable. Fighter cover would not go that low.

The heliocopter was fired upon while he made his search, but he persisted until the pilot was found, suffering from serious burns. Just as the pilot was being hoisted into the heliocopter, it was struck again and crashed into the side of a mountain.

Koelsch quickly got his crew and the Marine aviator out of the wrecked plane and managed to hide. For nine days he evaded the enemy and looked after the burned flyer. Then they were all captured. Koelsch, in captivity, was a continuous inspiration to his fellow prisoners by his courage and fortitude in refusing to yield to Communist mistreatment, which resulted in his death.

The Army and Marines were fighting in Korea, but it was the Navy that took them there and kept them supplied. It was the Navy carriers from which the Navy planes and helicopters flew. And the man who was commander of the United Nations Blockading and Escort Force was Admiral John E. Gingrich.

At the beginning of World War II, Gingrich, a Naval Academy graduate, was kept in Washington as Aide to the Secretary of the Navy. Finally in 1944 he managed to get to the battlefront in the USS *Pittsburgh*. In 1945, in action, he was awarded the Silver Star for towing out of range an aircraft carrier which had been badly damaged and was lying dead in the water, while at the same time, directing fire upon the enemy.

In 1947 he was ordered to duty in the Office of the Secretary of the Navy for service with the Atomic Energy Commission. When the Korean War began, he was assigned to the post of Commander, training Command, Pacific Fleet. From there it was but a step to assuming command of the United Nations Naval forces. Ships from Great Britain, Canada, Australia, New Zealand, the Netherlands, Thailand and Colombia operated successfully under his direction—and he received the Distinguished Service Medal for his work. Admiral Gingrich retired in 1954.

The 35th Marine to be awarded the Medal of Honor in Korea was Second Lieutenant Sherrod E. Skinner, Jr., whose twin brother is a Marine Reserve officer.

The two boys had entered the Marine Corps Reserve Platoon Leaders program, serving on active duty during the summers of 1948 and 1949. Sherrod Skinner was appointed a Second Lieutenant in October, 1951 and was ordered to active duty the next day and to Korea in 1952.

Lieutenant Sherrod Skinner was a forward artillery observer with the 11th Marines, in a vital forward outpost when it was attacked by the enemy, supported by a barrage of artillery and mortar fire which completely severed the communication line of the outpost. Organizing and directing the survivors in defense of the outpost, Skinner continued to call down fire on the enemy by means of radio until this equipment was too damaged for use.

Twice he left the bunker, once to direct accurate fire, once to get more ammunition. Each time he was wounded, but he refused help until all the men received treatment. He led the fight until the ammunition was exhausted and the position overrun by Communists.

When the bunker was overrun, he had his men feign dead for the three hours it was held. Then the enemy, becoming suspicious, threw a grenade where they lay. Skinner smother the explosion with his body, sacrificing his life for his comrades.

When King Frederik of Denmark visited the United States in 1960, he went to Arlington, not only to place a wreath upon the grave of the Unknown Soldier, but to lay a wreath upon the grave of a Marine.

Neils Qvistgaard, son of the Danish Admiral who was Naval Attaché here in 1950, had an unbounded admiration for the U. S. Marine Corps. He had served in the Danish Army and with the British Forces in Germany. Now for the Korean War he wanted to join the Marines. It took a special exemption to waive the citizenship requirements, but it was done. And when he found he was destined for headquarters duty, he begged so hard for a front line post that he was made a forward artillery observer. He was killed by a shell when the Communists attacked in October of 1952. He had said that should he fall, he wanted to be buried with his comrades. This was done at Arlington.

President Truman wrote his father, in part:

> He stands in the unbroken line of patriots who have dared to die that freedom might live and grow and increase its blessings . . . . Freedom lives and thru it, he lives—in a way that humbles the understandings of most men.

Not all combat heroes are fighting men. If heroism is putting others before self, then those who go into battle to succor the wounded and comfort the dying are real heroes—like Francis C. Hammond, Navy Hospitalman, who was not quite twenty-one when he was killed in Korea.

Hammond had enlisted in the Navy as a Seaman Recruit in 1951. He was given training as a Hospitalman and then sent to the Marine Barracks at Camp Pendleton for assignment.

Francis C. Hammond, Jr., is not old enough to know that he has lost his father, but he does seem to like the Medal of Honor being presented to him by Secretary of the Navy Robert Anderson. His mother is holding him while his grandmother, Mrs. Elvira Hammond, looks on adoringly.

*Washington Post* Photo

In February, 1953 he left for Korea as a Hospitalman attached to the Fifth Marines. A little over a month later, near Sanae-dong, he was killed and the manner of his going earned him the Medal of Honor. The platoon to which he was attached was subjected to heavy enemy fire. Resolutely advancing, Hammond administered first-aid, though critically wounded himself, for four long hours. When the unit was ordered to withdraw, he remained to skillfully direct the evacuation of casualties. The area was swept by enemy mortar fire and Hammond again was wounded, this time mortally. "By his exceptional fortitude, inspiring initiative and self-sacrificing efforts, Hammond undoubtedly saved the lives of many Marines." So reads the citation with the Medal of Honor which was presented to his infant son— a worthy inheritance from a brave man.

Like the Philippine Insurrection, the Korean War was a young man's war. Of the Class of 1950 at West Point, forty died in Korea. Among these were three Lieutenants, all of whom were killed in action in less than half a year after graduation. All of them were awarded the Purple Heart, the first two the Silver Star, and the third a Commendation. They were Willard Holbrook Coates of the 7th Infantry, 3rd Division, and William Edward Otis, Jr. and George Everett Foster, of the 32nd Infantry, 7th Division. All three of them were brought back to rest in Arlington.

There is one grave in Arlington on which two names appear—but only one soldier lies there. The additional name is a soldier-father's tribute to a soldier-son.

The father, Brigadier General Don Carlos Faith, Sr., enlisted in 1917 and was commissioned a Second Lieutenant. He did not get overseas in World War I, but instead was sent to the Philippines shortly afterwards, and then to China. Much of his Army duty from then on was in Training Centers—a man with an ability to teach is always in demand. In fact he was awarded the Distinguished Service Medal in 1944 for his administration of the training program for the Women's Army Auxiliary Corps. After his retirement General Faith became Dean of Men at George Washington University.

General Faith's son, Lieutenant Colonel Don Carlos Faith, Jr., a Georgetown University graduate, was killed in Korea. His body was never found, but General Faith arranged to have included on the reverse of his own tombstone the words:

> In memory of
> Don Carlos Faith, Jr.
> Lieutenant Colonel, U.S.A.
> Medal of Honor
> 1918 - 1950

Colonel Faith was awarded the Medal of Honor for his courage in the five days' bloody fight near Hagaru-ri in the Chosin Reservoir campaign of 1950. When an attack was launched against his battalion, Colonel Faith unhesitatingly exposed himself to fire while directing the action. When the enemy penetrated into their position, he led the counterattack.

In an attempt to join up with another unit, Faith personally reconnoitered the route across the frozen reservoir, and directed the evacuation of all the wounded. Taking command of the second unit, he was then ordered to force a way through to still another U. S. unit. Not only had the ranks been decimated till no unit was up to full strength, but there was a dearth of officers, among whom the mortality had also been high.

Although already physically exhausted by the continuous fighting and the bitter cold, Faith rallied his forces and led another attack. When enemy fire halted his men, Colonel Faith led two flank attacks and then a center charge. Mortally wounded during the final charge, he managed to hold on until the enemy roadblock was overrun. Then he fell.

Again it would seem that dedication to service is an inherited quality.

# THEY FOUGHT

# IN THE COLD WAR

THE SHOOTING WAR HAD BARELY CEASED WHEN THE COLD WAR
—the "war" between the Free World and the Slave World—
began in dead earnest. The fact that, without help and arms from the United
States, without Allied fighting forces deterring the Nazis on land and sea,
the Communist Empire would have been shattered when its former ally,
Nazi Germany, surged forward, counted for naught with the Communists.
Treachery and ambuscades had always been their weapons—and they continued to be so.

The victims of the Cold War who now lie in Arlington National Cemetery are many and their numbers increase with time.

The first open attack in the Cold War was in 1946. Vienna was administered by the Allies, including the Soviets. The air route from Vienna to
Udine, Italy, passed over one corner of Yugoslavia, a strip not more than
eighteen miles in length. Tito, having seized power with the Allies' aid, had
established a Communist dictatorship in that Balkan country. On August 12,
Yugoslav fighter planes forced down an unarmed U. S. C-47 with ten persons
aboard, one of whom was badly wounded. The Yugoslav planes gave no
signals, nor warning of attack. Tito, himself, witnessed the incident.

A week later a greater tragedy ensued. Another unarmed C-47 was ambushed and five Americans died. Tito arrogantly claimed that the weather
was clear and the pilot should have known better. But, according to reports,
including those from two American UNNRA employees who witnessed the
incident, the weather was foul. Furthermore, since the strip was not over
eighteen miles wide, there had been no time for the Yugoslav planes to
ascend—unless a deliberate ambush had been planned.

After a long time spent in negotiations, protests, and diplomatic red
tape, Yugoslavia released the bodies of the flyers. The crew members, buried
in one grave in Arlington, were Captain Glen H. Freestone, Captain Harold
F. Schreiber, Captain Richard H. Claeys, Corporal Matthew Comko, and
Corporal Chester L. Lower.

Two years later came the Berlin Airlift—the Free World's answer to the Soviet defiance of all agreements. When the Soviets cut all surface transportation corridors into jointly-controlled Berlin, the United States and the Allies sent in supplies to the beleaguered city by plane. One of the men who participated in this work of mercy was Colonel Howard J. LaBrenz, who was himself to die in a plane crash just outside of Washington in 1964. For his work during the Berlin Airlift, he was awarded the Humane Actions Medal by the U. S. Air Force.

It is interesting to note that the Communist countries to whom so much had been given—and who demanded even more—showed no gratitude whatsoever; but the Federal Republic of Germany, part of the Germany that had fought the United States in two wars, expressed gratitude, not merely in the excitement of the Airlift, but later on. On the tenth anniversary of the Berlin Airlift in 1959, the people of West Berlin established a foundation— *Luftbruckendank*—to aid the families and to help with the education of the children of those who had died flying in relief supplies.

Night and day the supplies were flown into Berlin during the airlift. The Communists had a perfect example of how, when once aroused, the allies would remain allies, and would keep their pledged word.

**U.S. Air Force Photograph**

One of the men largely responsible for intelligence work during part of the Cold War, and who now rests at Arlington, was General Walter Bedell Smith. He went into the Army by way of the National Guard during World War I and was put into Military Intelligence. World War II found him as Chief of Staff to General Eisenhower with whom he served in North Africa and in Europe. In behalf of General Eisenhower he signed the surrender of Italy as well as the unconditional surrender of Germany. After the war, from 1946 through 1949, he was in Moscow as Ambassador to the Soviets.

In 1950 President Truman named Bedell Smith as head of the Central Intelligence Agency. When General Eisenhower became President, he appointed his old comrade-in-arms Assistant Secretary of State. General Smith died in 1961.

In February of 1959 another flight incident occurred. While on a world-wide Air Force project to study radio waves, an unarmed U. S. C-130 Hercules turbojet plane based at Adana, Turkey, was shot down by Soviet aircraft over Kars in Soviet Armenia. Seventeen men were on board. The Soviet, who as usual claimed "spy-flight," returned the bodies of six, of which four were identifiable. The State Department has never been able to find out exactly what happened to the missing eleven. One of the six, Captain Edward J. Jeruss, a Navy flyer in World War II and Korea, is buried at Arlington.

On July 1, 1960 on a routine mapping flight over the Barents Sea, thirty miles outside Russian territory, a U.S. RB-47 was attacked and shot down by Soviet fighter planes. There were six men on board. The Soviets returned only the body of the plane commander, Major Willard G. Palm. His grave is at Arlington.

Still another incident occurred in East Germany. On January 24, 1964 an unarmed R-39 trainer with three officers on board was shot down after inadvertently crossing the border. It was proven that the Soviet planes must have heard the U. S. monitor planes that were instructing the trainer plane to turn back—but the Soviet airmen paid no attention. They did, however, permit the United States authorities to take the bodies out of East Germany. One of the three officers, Lt. Colonel Gerald L. Hannaford, is buried at Arlington.

Vietnam—and the war that is not a war. Those who die there seem to have one thing in common, according to the reports that come back. They believe that Communism must not be allowed to go any further, and they are willing to risk their lives to prevent it. When they have made the last sacrifice, many of them come home to Arlington.

There was Colonel Anthony J. Tencza, aged forty-three, who had spent twenty-one years in the Army. He already held five decorations for bravery in World War II and Korea. He was Senior Advisor to the 22nd Vietnam Division. On July 15, 1962 while on a supply and reconnaissance mission, his helicopter was shot down by the Vietcong. Knocked unconscious by the crash, he was, according to eyewitnesses, shot in cold blood by the guerrillas. Before his requested assignment to Vietnam came through, he had been stationed at Fort Myer, which is, of course, part of the original Arlington Estate. It was only fitting that his funeral should have been from the Chapel on the Post.

PFC Neil Kirk MacIver was only nineteen years old when he was killed in action on May 29, 1963—but he was a veteran of two years' standing even them. The Army was in his blood. He had gone to military school, his father was an Army veteran and his stepmother, who had brought him up from babyhood, was an "Army brat" from Panama, where her father had served with Gorgas.

A week previous to his death young MacIver had been painfully hurt in a bamboo trap set by the Vietcong. He begged so hard to stay with his Vietnamese unit that permission was granted. It was just one week later that there was an ambush in the jungle and he was wounded mortally. Because of his outstanding and hazardous work as a radio operator for a Special Forces detachment, he received a posthumous Bronze Star. He had liked the Vietnamese and had planned after the cessation of hostilities to go back there to try to help the people.

It was on an errand of mercy that Army Captain Howard M. Eakin died in June, 1963. A helicopter pilot, he was wounded while flying in a medical evacuation team, and died of his wounds two days later.

Another mercy errand brought about the death of First Lieutenant Daniel K. Lessig of the Marine Corps. In October, 1963 he had volunteered to take his helicopter out in a search for a downed aircraft with a U. S. Air Force officer aboard. The jungle where the plane went down was alive with Vietcong guerrillas; but he kept at the search until he found the plane. Then he encountered enemy forces and the helicopter was shot down. Posthumously he was awarded the Navy Commendation Medal.

The Vietcong, like all Communist guerrillas, are as willing to kill women and children as soldiers—in fact, they seem to delight in ambuscades. On February 15, 1963 Major Donald E. Koelper of the Marine Corps was told that there was a bomb due to explode in a theater. He could have saved himself, but he didn't. Instead he rushed into the theater, ordered the occupants to take cover under the seats and displayed such presence of mind that he prevented a panic. The bomb exploded. Koelper was killed but many other lives had been saved. For his deed of heroism, Koelper received the Navy Cross.

Major, then Captain, Koelper was also awarded posthumously, a Vietnamese decoration with a citation worthy of repetition:

Captain Koelper was of a courteous character, courageous, energetic, and full of good will, and always stood by this battalion in the communist-repressing operations all over the Vietnamese territory. Captain Koelper had closely co-operated with the Marine Brigade and contributed to the winning of many glorious victories.

Captain Thomas W. McCarthy was another "Army brat." His father was a Colonel in the Army and Thomas was born in the Philippines. Later his father was Military Attaché in Chile, and Thomas went to school there. He graduated from West Point in 1955 and was assigned to Fort Bragg with the 81st Airborne.

Captain McCarthy was killed on March 3, 1964 in action against the Vietcong guerrillas near the Cambodian border. He received the Distinguished Service Cross posthumously, for the gallantry of his actions and the way in which he exemplified the "highest traditions of the United States Army." Perhaps what would have pleased him most, though, was what the Vietnamese General who commanded the Airborne Forces said:

In the confusion that followed the initial outburst of fire, part of the company started to break up. But McCarthy was immediately among them, rallying them together . . . . If we hadn't charged, we would have been annihilated—and McCarthy was right up there with me . . . . He was the bravest soldier I ever knew.

Two Army men who volunteered to fight in Vietnam are buried close to each other. They were among the victims of an ambush on August 13, 1964. Two other Americans were killed with more than two hundred South Vietnamese in what the Army referred to as "sixty minutes of the bloodiest fighting."

The two officers were Captains Byron C. Stone and William David Ragin. Captain Stone had already served one tour of duty in Vietnam and had applied for an extension. Captain Ragin, who received his Captaincy posthumously, had requested a transfer to Vietnam because he felt it was his duty.

Captain Ragin was a graduate of the Citadel, and his wife was the daughter of the Commandant there—an "Army brat" herself who could understand her husband's feeling about duty.

According to the Vietnamese witnesses, Captain Stone, Ragin, Lieutenant James M. Coyle—another "Army brat"—and Sergeant Tom Ward refused to retreat and fought to the end. An American advisor said of them,

"All four of them were professionals. They were made of the stuff that makes men heroes."

One touching note was sounded at their funerals. The Old Guard—the Third Infantry—has long been entrusted with the task of conducting the funerals at Arlington. The officer assigned to Captain Ragin's, was his closest friend, who had been rotated home from Vietnam to Fort Myer just a short time before.

Fighter, protector, rescuer—the planes of the Air Force and Army wing their way across the skies of Vietnam.

**U.S. Air Force Photograph**

# THEY ALSO FOUGHT

AMONG THOSE WHO REST AT ARLINGTON ARE MANY WHOSE FAME in peace was so great that in other times, in other climes, there would have been great memorials, the pride of their communities erected in their honor. But to them, and to their families, the final honor was to be buried in Arlington, with the last volley and the clear bugler call of taps to mark their passing.

Those who made this choice are so numerous that only the stories of a few can be told, briefly, here. They must represent the others as they explain how they earned a resting place under the trees at Arlington.

William Howard Taft was the twenty-seventh President of the United States. As Commander-in-Chief of the Armed Forces of the United States he had the right of burial in Arlington Cemetery. But this was not the only reason. He had held other posts which afforded him that right.

Only eight years old when the War Between the States ended, his formative years were, nonetheless, imbued with the idea of government service, for his father was Attorney General, then Minister to Austria, and later to Russia.

Taft was a judge and a teacher—Dean of the Law Department of the University of Cincinnati—when McKinley appointed him to the presidency of the Philippine Commission, where he had to—as Kipling phrased it for this particular task—fight

> . . . . The savage wars of peace—
> Fill full the mouth of Famine
> And bid the sickness cease . . . .

Four years later he returned to the United States as Secretary of War. His years in that post were hectic, for the Cuban Government fell and the United States had to intervene. Taft himself had to take temporary charge of affairs on that unhappy island. There was protection needed for the Panama Canal. The Philippines still needed troops—but troops indoctrinated with what is now called the science of military government. These were active, productive years.

This is not to say that the four years as President which followed were not hectic and productive—they were. So too, were the nine years from 1921, when he served as tenth Chief Justice of the United States—the first man ever to have been both President and Chief Justice. But perhaps the action and positive accomplishments of his days as Secretary of War intrigued him. Perhaps his choice of burial at Arlington proves what to him was his greatest moment of glory.

John Foster Dulles, Secretary of State from 1953 to his death in 1959, had been an ardent fighter for peace virtually all of his life. His experience had ranged the gamut from the Hague Convention in 1907, through the Versailles Peace Conference, to which he was a delegate in 1919, and the organizational conference for the United Nations in 1945. He knew how much, and how little, peace conferences could do. And he had served the Carnegie Endowment for International Peace as Director.

He knew Government—he had served an interim term as Senator from New York State, and then as a consultant to the Department of State, representing the United States in the General Assembly of the United Nations. With rank of Ambassador he negotiated the Peace Treaty with Japan.

He early took cognizance of the menace of Communism—later so apparent in the Cold War which he fought during his service as Secretary of State.

Yet the inscription on the front of his tombstone reads:


John Foster Dulles
Major United States Army


It is only on the rear that it says "Secretary of State."

Dulles had tried hard to enlist in World War I, but was turned down because of impaired eyesight. Later he was commissioned Captain and directed the economic section of M.I.D. (military intelligence), War Department General Staff. It was as Major that he represented the Army General Staff on the War Trade Board.

Perhaps most expressive of Dulles' beliefs is a statement he made at the time of the Korean Armistice. He said:

In war men make vast sacrifices for peace. And then when peace is won, they fail to make the lesser sacrifices needed to keep the peace. Let us this time, not relax, but mobilize for peace the resources, spiritual and material, which too often we reserve for war.

William Jennings Bryan also served as Secretary of State, but his fame was made as a political leader—at least that is what is said in most history books.

However, Bryan was many-faceted. There was Bryan, the orator, who held Chautauqua audiences fascinated for years by his orotund phrases and dramatic delivery. There was Bryan, the quiet Congressman, who served for four years as a Democrat from a Republican district.

There was Bryan, the pro-Silver advocate, lashing out at his opponents in the famous "Cross of Gold speech." "You shall not press down upon the brow of labor this crown of thorns, you shall not crucify mankind upon a cross of gold." There was Bryan, the politician, winning the nomination for President three times and losing each election.

There was Bryan, the prohibitionist, serving grape juice to the Ambassadors when he was Secretary of State. There was Bryan the Fundamentalist, working to bar the Darwinian theory from the schools.

The great orator, William Jennings Bryan, who held them so spellbound that they forgot to vote for him was, after all, a Colonel of Volunteers. His pacifism was sincere, but he would remember when he was a soldier, even if only for a few short months.
Library of Congress

Whatever Bryan did, he did thoroughly—whether it be eating two plates of tripe for breakfast whenever he managed to get to Philadelphia, or denouncing his political opponents in no uncertain terms.

There was Bryan, the pacifist, resigning his post as Secretary of State because he would not send a strongly worded protest on the sinking of the *Lusitania*, believing that the United States must remain neutral at any cost.

And there was William Jennings Bryan, Colonel of Volunteers in the Spanish-American War. He raised a regiment and was made Colonel of it by the Governor of Nebraska. He did not serve outside the United States— but that was the fate of many others. Their men died in the disease-ridden camps of the South instead of on the battlefield—but all had enlisted for service. All had been ready to fight. A soldier goes where he is sent, not where he wants to go. What Bryan thought of his military service is evidenced by where he lies.

James V. Forrestal, first Secretary of Defense, son of an Irish immigrant, newspaper reporter, bond salesman, was a man of terrific drive.

He had worked his way through school, including a year at Dartmouth and two at Princeton. He was a bond salesman at William A. Read & Company, later Dillon, Read & Company, when World War I broke out. The United States declared war in April of 1917. In May, Forrestal enlisted as a Seaman Second-Class. Before the year was out he was commissioned a Naval Aviator and in 1919 he was discharged a Lieutenant. He promptly went back to making a success as a financier, rising to the presidency of the company.

He was brought to Washington by President Roosevelt early in the 30s to help shape the regulations for the Securities Exchange Commission. Finally he went in as Administrative Aide to the President at $10,000 a year instead of the $180,000 he was said to be earning.

The horse-drawn caisson bearing the body of James V. Forrestal, Secretary of Defense, slowly approaches the amphitheater where his funeral services were held.

U.S. Army Photograph

Next he was shifted to the Navy and the production of ships. That there were enough landing craft for the invasion of Normandy is proof of his drive. As Secretary of the Navy after Knox died, he was indefatigable. He talked to the men in shipyards, and was under fire at Iwo Jima. He studied logistics. He testified before Senate Committees. "Peace without power to enforce it is an empty dream," he said.

As Secretary of Defense he fought hard for the Armed Forces. He condemned warmongers and extreme pacifists alike, holding that "the surest way to avoid war is to make it clear to any possible group of enemies that the risks of engaging us are too great to make it worth while. At the same time we must exercise the patience that should also accompany the possession of strength."

Worn out by overwork, Forrestal resigned in 1949. Now Lieutenant Forrestal, Seaman and Naval Aviator, Secretary of Defense, rests in Arlington.

William Frank Knox was Secretary of the Navy when, in 1944, he died in office. He used to say "This is the first war I didn't enter as a buck private," for he had served in three of America's wars.

A senior at Alma College, when the Spanish-American War started, he enlisted in the Rough Riders commanded by Leonard Wood and Theodore Roosevelt, and, as he didn't mind telling you, was in the charge up San Juan Hill.

He had already served as a Major on the staffs of both the Governor of Michigan and the Governor of New Hampshire before World War I—but when that started he entered the OCS and came out a Captain of Cavalry. He went to France in the spring of 1918 with the 303rd Ammunition Train and with that outfit delivered ammunition to the front line batteries for the St. Mihiel, Meuse-Argonne and Sudan offensives. A Major at the war's end, Knox stayed in the Reserves and was a Colonel on the inactive list until his death.

In 1898 Knox had started newspaper work and kept it up all his life, first in Michigan and then in New Hampshire, where he acquired the *Manchester Union*. For three years he was General Manager for Hearst in New England and then bought the *Chicago Daily News*. He was publisher of the *News* until he succeeded Edison as Secretary of the Navy in 1940—and divested himself of active direction of his newspaper properties.

Knox was a strong believer in preparedness. He had actively fought for it and for Universal Military Training from World War I on, and he never stopped. As he said to an American Legion Convention in 1941, "We now know how futile it is to place our trust in written promises to foresake war . . . In such a world as that of today, sea power for America is more vital, more essential, than ever before in history."

Another publisher who earned his resting place at Arlington in active service for his country was Julius Ochs Adler, nephew of Adolph S. Ochs, late publisher of the *New York Times*. His Ochs ancestors came from Bavaria and furnished soldiers to the United States in both the Mexican War and the War Between the States.

Adler was on the staff of the *New York Times* when he decided to go to the Plattsburg Training Camp in 1915. He went again in 1916 and was commissioned in 1917 the day after war was declared. He was promoted to Captain four months later and in 1918 embarked for France with the Seventy-seventh Division—"New York's Own."

Adler saw action with the 306th Infantry and was awarded the Distinguished Service Cross for heroism in the Meuse-Argonne offensive when in a fire-fight he captured sixteen Germans single-handedly. He emerged from the war a Major—and, in addition to his DSC, received the Purple Heart, the Silver Star with an Oak Leaf Cluster, the Croix de Guerre with Palm and innumerable citations. His first act as a civilian again was to write the history of the Seventy-seventh, in which he became Colonel in 1930. In 1932 he was named Civilian Aide to the Secretary of War in connection with establishing Civilian Training Camps. He had been General Manager of the *Times* since 1919 so his life was a very full one.

In 1940 Adler was ordered to active duty and, as a Brigadier General, went to the Pacific Theater where he remained until 1944 when he was invalided home. He did not lose his interest in the military after he went back to the *Times*, for he pushed preparedness and Universal Military Training. He also took part in the postwar training exercises as Commanding General of the Seventy-seventh Division. In 1948 he was promoted to Major General. Julius Adler died in 1955 and is buried, as he wished, in Arlington with his comrades of two wars.

Another newspaper man who was a citizen-soldier was Joseph Medill Patterson. Like Adler he came from a newspaper family. His father was general manager and later publisher of the *Chicago Tribune*. Joseph Medill Patterson was interested in the reportorial side of newspapers. In fact he took time out from Yale to cover the Boxer uprising in China for the *Tribune*.

After a decade of writing and politics, he went to the *Tribune*, working with his cousin Robert McCormick. His next incursion into war was as a newspaper man covering the Vera Cruz "Incident," Mexican border troubles and the beginnings of World War I in Germany, France and Belgium. But in 1916, he enlisted in the Illinois National Guard, serving on the Texas border as a noncom in field artillery. When the United States entered the War, he went overseas with the Rainbow Division as a Lieutenant.

Later Patterson became a Captain in the 149th Field Artillery. He saw action in the second Battle of the Marne, at St. Mihiel, in the Argonne,

Champagne and Lorraine sectors. His commander Douglas MacArthur, referred to him once as the most brilliant soldier who had served under him —high praise from such an exacting General.

It was after World War I that Patterson, together with Robert Mc-Cormick, founded the *New York Daily News*, the first real tabloid newspaper. Later the cousins divided interests, McCormick retaining the *Tribune* and Patterson the *News*. They had many links, though—except in policy.

In his newspaper career, Patterson was much the same as in the Army— a tough fighter, who demanded much from his men, and would fight for them just as violently.

When World War II broke out, Patterson immediately wrote the War Department, applying for active combat service. After listing his military record, including five years as Major in the organized Reserves, he wound up with "I am sixty-two years old, accustomed to driving a car and in good health."

Like Winfield Scott and Leonard Wood in their days, Patterson was not accepted by the Administration of his time, though he had supported it more than criticized it. But he did use the good offices of the paper to help the Armed Services in every way possible.

The Army meant much to him and it is little wonder that he chose Arlington for his final resting place.

There is a woman who rests at Arlington who has probably given more pleasure to more people than anyone else there. But when at the age of eighty-two she died, there were not many who remembered she had earned her place at Arlington.

When World War I came, Mary Roberts Rinehart and her family went to war. Her sons entered the service, her husband, Dr. Stanley Rinehart, offered his services for overseas duty and she volunteered as a nurse. She was the first to go overseas, but not as she had expected. Dr. Rinehart went into the Medical Corps but his organizational experience was so great he was kept in Washington. While she waited for her orders as a nurse, she was sent for and told that she could be of greater service in a quieter capacity.

In short, she was a trained, accurate observer. Her popularity as a writer opened doors to her that usually stayed shut. If she would go ostensibly to write articles about the war, she might come back with useful information— anyway her picture of things as they were would not be based on preconceived notions but on fact. This she did, carefully and conscientiously as always. The front-line trenches knew her. She talked with poilus and the King of the Belgians. She watched Britain's "thin red line of 'eroes" in the trenches and dined with the great in London. And when the Americans came she shunned the battle of Paris to follow the flag at the front.

It wasn't what she wanted to do. She wanted to nurse the sick as she had been trained to do. But a good soldier obeys orders—and Mary Robert Rinehart was a good soldier.

A veteran of the War Between the States, so famous for what he said and did in the last third of his life that what lay before is almost forgotten, was Oliver Wendell Holmes. To Boston, Wendell Holmes was the son of Dr. Oliver Wendell Holmes, the "Autocrat of the Breakfast Table," co-founder of the *Atlantic Monthly*, author of "Old Ironsides" and "The Chambered Nautilus." To the rest of the world he was Oliver Wendell Holmes, Associate Justice of the United States Supreme Court and "The Great Dissenter."

As a Justice he was probably better known than any member of the Supreme Court with the exception of John Marshall—and Holmes was much more quotable.

But there was another facet to Holmes's life. When he graduated from Harvard with the class of 1861, he straightway enlisted. The previous year he had had training in the militia and, in view of this fact, was commissioned a Lieutenant.

Holmes's first knowledge of war came with the terrible skirmish at Ball's Bluff, with its casualties disproportionate to its importance. There he received his first wound of the flesh, and a deeper wound—knowledge of the horror of war. But, as soon as he recovered, he returned to duty. The grandson of Abiel Holmes and great-grandson of Captain David Holmes—of Revolutionary War fame—could not shirk a task begun, just because it was unpleasant.

Holmes went back—to the Wilderness. The swamps, the tangled under-brush, the mud, the ever-present sickness all took their toll. The flower of his class had been cut down before his eyes. He had earned his Captaincy and took his duties seriously.

There was physical relief as the Army started its march north, but at the end lay Antietam, and his second wound. A bullet went through his neck, miraculously leaving him alive—or just about. With the "walking wounded" he was passed on from one place to another until his father finally found him in Harrisburg. The elder Holmes made an interesting tale of his "Hunt for the Captain" which enhanced his literary prestige—but the story left his son, the Captain, wincing in every nerve.

This time the recovery was slow—the body recovered faster than the mind. He had seen too much and known too much to be able to long endure the attitude of the stay-at-homes who did not realize how very terrible war was. So he went back again to the Army.

It was on the road to Chancellorsville that he received his third wound, this time in his heel. He was to walk with a limp thereafter and weather was to trouble him. The recovery took a long time.

But he went back again—this time to General Horatio Wright's headquarters. That doughty engineer always was given the tough assignments and this was no exception. It was the battle of Cold Harbor—and in three hours Holmes saw 9,000 men fall, with hardly a dent in the Confederate line.

When Wright was called back to defend Washington from Early, Holmes was with him. It was then that the much-quoted Lincoln episode occurred. The basic facts were the following:

Jubal Early's troops were threatening the Capital, and Lincoln went to Fort Stephens for his first view of a real War Between the States skirmish. He was so fascinated that he climbed up on the parapet to see better, and, unwittingly, became the first President of the United States to come under enemy fire while in office.

Mild-mannered General Wright suggested that the President step down to shelter. Lincoln ignored the request. Bullets began to fly as Confederate sharpshooters, five hundred yards away, aimed at the tall figure in the stovepipe hat. An officer standing next to Lincoln was wounded.

Holmes's nerves frayed. "Get down, you fool," he shouted. Lincoln stepped down obediently, looked around and said in a drawl, "Captain, I am glad you know how to talk to a civilian."

Mustered out, Holmes went back to school—Law School this time. His career as lawyer, teacher, judge and justice is too well known to bear repeating here. The wit and sharp insight in his speeches are, like Hamlet, full of quotations.

But once—on Decoration Day in 1884—he made reference to war in a way peculiarly applicable to those who fought in any or all of the nation's wars. He said:

Through our great good fortune, in our youth our hearts were touched with fire. It was given us to learn at the outset that life is a profound and passionate thing. While we are permitted to scorn nothing but indifference . . . we have seen with our own eyes . . . the snowy fields of honor, and it is for us to bear the report to those who come after us.

Holmes had always wanted to be buried at Arlington, but he was, in spite of all his honors, too shy to request it of the Secretary of War. Fortunately, Chief Justice Taft was aware of this desire, and, when Mrs. Holmes died, made the arrangements. For the six years that preceded his own death, Holmes would often go to Arlington and sit there quietly, looking out over the hillside. Perhaps he was remembering his own moment of glory.

# ARLINGTON TODAY

ODAY WHEN THE VISITOR—BE HE PILGRIM OR SIGHTSEER—AP-
proaches Arlington across the Memorial Bridge, the transition
is from the hubbub of a busy city to a place of peace, a city of stone, where
even time itself is stilled.

High above its 620 acres, with their miles of paved roads, miles of walks
and thousands of trees, rises the Custis-Lee Mansion, known also as Arlington
House, its original name. Below it glows the Eternal Flame that marks the
Kennedy grave.

Nearby are Arlington's Main Gates which remind one of Vergil's *Aeneid*:
"There are twin gates of sleep, by men called death!"

Although the Main Gates are again open, the visitor is advised to enter
through the Ord-Weitzel Gate that he may step back into the earliest history
of the Cemetery. (The Ord-Weitzel Gate is the last entrance to the right—
or North—of the Main Gates.) To the left, the twelfth grave in the first row
is that of Private William Christman of the 67th Pennsylvania Infantry.
Twenty-one years old and a farmer near Harrisburg, Pennsylvania, before he
enlisted, Christman was the first soldier to be buried at Arlington—on May
13, 1864, according to the Cemetery's records. Behind his grave, and marked
only by numbered stones, are the graves of two unknowns laid to rest a day or
so later. They were the first of nearly 5,000 "unknowns" at Arlington.

At the top of the slight hill in front of the Ord-Weitzel Gate, and
stretching for several hundred yards along the right side of the road, are the
graves of about 3,800 men, women and children—innocent victims of the Civil
War. They were "contrabands"—Negroes who sought the rewards of their
new freedom in the city of Washington. Herded into camps, some on the
Arlington Estate itself or living elsewhere in dire poverty, they died of disease
and were buried in the outermost limits of the new Arlington National Cemetery in 1864, 1865 and 1866. Most of them weren't even American citizens.
It was the Fourteenth Amendment—adopted in 1868—that conferred the
priceless gift of citizenship on the Negro.

The road winds towards the height on which the stuccoed Custis-Lee
Mansion stands, fronted by classic Grecian columns. Here is one of the most

inspiring sights in America—an unsurpassed vista of the capital city of the nation, the whiteness and beauty of its public buildings standing out majestically against the sky.

The mansion, a landmark for more than a century and a half, is splendidly maintained by the National Park Service. George Washington Parke Custis began it in 1802, and his son-in-law, Robert E. Lee, spent the happiest days of his life there with his family. Fortunately, the historic place has been carefully restored. Extremely capable National Park Service historians give vivid descriptions to visitors of life as it was lived there before 1861. A tour of the place is a "must" for any visitor to Arlington.

One of the first things the visitor notices is the high flagpole in front of the mansion. The flag is lowered to half-staff a half hour before the day's first burial and remains that way until a half hour after the last, to honor the servicemen and women being buried at Arlington that day. Burials are made every Monday through Friday, holidays excepted. Very often the visitor hears in the distance the faint crash of musketry from the firing party and the haunting bugle notes of "Taps" as the nation buries its honored dead. And, daily, bugle calls ring out and a cannon booms at retreat at nearby Fort Myer —they are heard at the mansion and in the cemetery.

Sixty yards away, down the sloping broad expanse of lawn—where Custis and Lee and many famous people of their day walked and where the seven Lee children played—is President Kennedy's grave. Adjoining it on the south is the grave of his brother, Senator Robert F. Kennedy, surmounted temporarily with a simple white cross. The graves may easily be reached by steps leading down from the Custis-Lee Mansion above, or by several roads or paths from the cemetery gates below to the west.

Around the mansion to the north, south, east, and west lie the valiant dead. An L-shaped row of graves marks two sides of Mrs. Lee's famous Rose Garden. The graves were laid out in 1864 to assure that the Lees would never again occupy their much-loved home. The Rose Garden has been beautifully restored by the National Park Service.

The fourth grave in the row stretching from the mansion is that of Captain Albert H. Packard of the 4th Maine Infantry, thirty-three years old, a mechanic in civilian life, and the first officer to rest at Arlington. He died in a military hospital in Washington of wounds received in the Battle of the Wilderness and was buried the same day—May 17, 1864.

The Tomb of the Unknown Dead of the Civil War—containing the remains of 2,111 unidentified Union soldiers who died in the fighting near Washington—"from the fields of Bull Run, and the route to the Rappahannock"—stands in a cluster of oaks a few yards to the southeast of the Mansion. Close by it is the Old Amphitheater, a vine-covered pergola built shortly after the Civil War and used for many years for Memorial Day services.

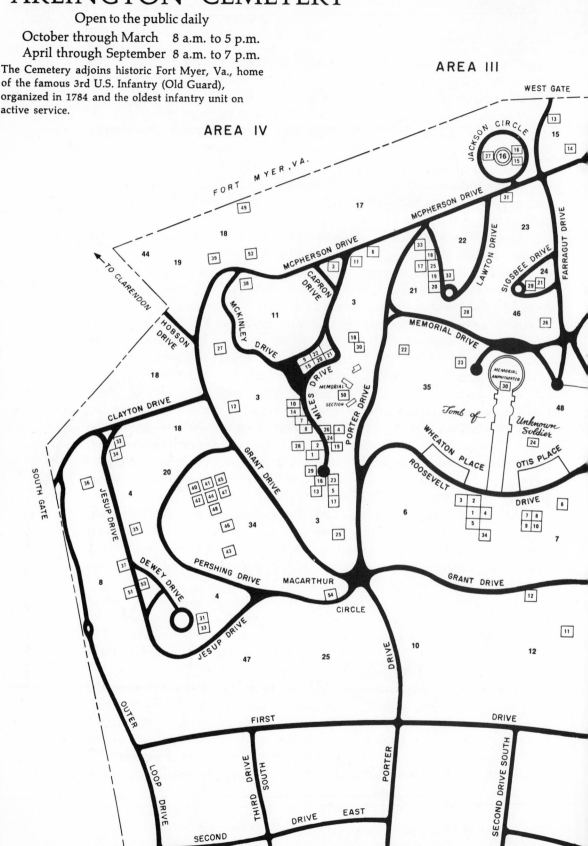

# ARLINGTON CEMETERY

Open to the public daily

October through March   8 a.m. to 5 p.m.

April through September   8 a.m. to 7 p.m.

The Cemetery adjoins historic Fort Myer, Va., home of the famous 3rd U.S. Infantry (Old Guard), organized in 1784 and the oldest infantry unit on active service.

AREA III

WEST GATE

AREA IV

FORT MYER, VA.

TO CLARENDON

JACKSON CIRCLE

MCPHERSON DRIVE

CAPRON DRIVE

LAWTON DRIVE

SIGSBEE DRIVE

FARRAGUT DRIVE

MEMORIAL DRIVE

MCKINLEY DRIVE

HOBSON DRIVE

CLAYTON DRIVE

SOUTH GATE

JESUP DRIVE

GRANT DRIVE

MILES DRIVE

PORTER DRIVE

MEMORIAL SECTION

MEMORIAL AMPHITHEATER

Tomb of Unknown Soldier

WHEATON PLACE

ROOSEVELT DRIVE

OTIS PLACE

DEWEY DRIVE

PERSHING DRIVE

MACARTHUR CIRCLE

GRANT DRIVE

JESUP DRIVE

OUTER LOOP DRIVE

FIRST DRIVE

THIRD DRIVE SOUTH

SECOND

PORTER DRIVE

DRIVE EAST

SECOND DRIVE SOUTH

Established in 1864, Arlington National Cemetery is located opposite the City of Washington, D.C., on the South side of the Potomac River in the State of Virginia. It is administered by the Office of the Chief of Support Services, Department of the Army, under the immediate supervision of the Commanding General, Military District of Washington.

TO WASHINGTON VIA FORT MYER AND KEY BRIDGE

FORT MYER GATE

GARFIELD DRIVE

FORT MYER CHAPEL

TO WASHINGTON VIA MEMORIAL BRIDGE

AREA I

13

70

MCPHERSON DRIVE

DOUBLEDAY WALK

MEIGS DRIVE

HUMPHREYS DRIVE

72

13

SUPERINTENDENT'S LODGE

PARKING AREA

68  69

MEMORIAL SECTION

71

-SON DRIVE

ADMINISTRATIVE AREA

45

FORT MYER, VA.

0  100  200  300  400  500
SCALE IN FEET

N

46  55
27
26
39
43

79

82

SHERMAN DRIVE

29

WARE-HOUSE AREA

PARKING AREA

50

37

-OOK WALK

SHERIDAN DRIVE

26

Custis-Lee Mansion

29
23
73

35  50  60  28  62  44
59  64  54
38  37  65  58  57  44  76  51
33  56  2  78

MEMORIAL SECTION

17

5

13

7

ORD AND WEITZEL DRIVE

28

L'ENFANT DRIVE

MITCHELL DRIVE

ORD AND WEITZEL DRIVE

42

MCCLELLAN DRIVE

9

63
81
80

2

President Kennedy Site

75

45

30

LINCOLN

CUSTIS

68
67

5

11
23  19
24  21

30

38

43

SHERMAN DRIVE

49

LODGE

41

Roosevelt

2

61  41
48  30  31
24  32  52
34  42

36  40

32

74

WEEKS DRIVE

SHERIDAN DRIVE

President Taft Site

WALK

18  9
20  8  15
16  12
14
26  25

22

30

25

36

39

40

27

3  4
2  1

22
21
77

GRANT DRIVE

47  49
25
53

31

MCCLELLAN DRIVE

33

ARLINGTON

RIDGE

ROAD

SHERIDAN GATE

ORD AND WEITZEL GATE

TO WASHINGTON VIA MEMORIAL BRIDGE

SCHLEY DRIVE

27

TO WASHINGTON VIA KEY BRIDGE

EAST

VISITOR'S CENTER

FIRST SOUTH DRIVE

PARKING AREA

MEMORIAL DRIVE

53

51

52

ADMINISTRATION BUILDING

TO WASHINGTON VIA
MEMORIAL BRIDGE

AREA I

FORT

MYER, VA.

N

SUPERINTENDENT'S
LODGE

0   100   200   300   400   500
SCALE IN FEET

29

PARKING
AREA

WARE-
HOUSE
AREA

50

SHERMAN DRIVE

ORD AND WEITZEL DRIVE

MITCHELL DRIVE

ORD AND WEITZEL DRIVE

5

13

7

30

28

L'ENFANT DRIVE

42

CUSTIS

LINCOLN

43

11

23  19

24  21

18  6   9   30

20  8   15

26  16  10  12

14

25

SHERMAN DRIVE

38

DRIVE

49

LODGE

41

President
Taft
Site

22

WALK

SCHLEY DRIVE

36

39

40

27

3   4

2   1

RIDGE                    ROAD

27

TO WASHINGTON
VIA MEMORIAL BRIDGE

SHERIDAN GATE

ORD AND WEITZEL GATE

TO WASHINGTON VIA KEY BRIDGE

53

51

MEMORIAL DRIVE

52

## AREA I

Among Noteworthy Persons Buried in Area I Are:

Note: Number *before* name indicates location on adjoining map; number *following* in parenthesis indicates grave site in section.

### Section 27

1. Pvt. William B. Blatt, Co. B, 49th Pa. Inf.; first battle casualty buried at Arlington, May 14, 1864 (18)
2. Pvt. William C. Christman, Co. G, 67th Pa. Inf.; first serviceman buried at Arlington, May 13, 1864 (19)
3. Pvt. Wiliam Reevees, Co. C, 76th N.Y. Inf.; first draftee buried at Arlington, May 13, 1864 (99)
4. Unknowns, two Union soldiers: first of more than 5,000 "unknowns" now buried at Arlington, May 15, 1864 (96 & 97)

### Section 30

5. Maj. Gen. Anthony Drexel Biddle, WW II leader; ambas. (1172)
6. Gen. Tasker H. Bliss, World War I leader (S-7)
7. Gen. Malin S. Craig, former Army Chief of Staff (S-23)
8. Lieut. James V. Forrestal, USNR; 1st Sec. of Defense (674)
9. Rear Adm. Cary T. Grayson, Chairman, American Red Cross (S-24)
10. Adm. Jonas Ingram, World War II leader (643)
11. Gen. Walter Kreuger, Commander, 6th Army, WW II (794)
12. Gen. Peyton C. March, Army Chief of Staff, WW I (S-17)
13. Gen. Guy Stanley Meloy, Korean War hero (1087)
14. Maj. Gen. Dennis E. Nolan, WW I leader (604)
15. Lieut. Gen. Floyd L. Parks, WW II leader (664)
16. Maj. Robert P. Patterson, USAR; Sec. of War, WW II (612)
17. Mary Randolph, first person buried at Arlington (1828) (near Mansion)
18. Adm. Forrest P. Sherman, USN, Chief of Naval Operations (633)
19. Sgt. Lawrence Steinhardt, USA, WW I; ambas. (728)
20. Gen. Charles P. Summerall, USA, WW I leader (S-16)
21. Lieut. Gen. Richard K. Sutherland, USA, WW II leader (694)
22. President William Howard Taft (S-14)
23. Vice Admiral Joseph Taussig, USN, WW II leader (724)
24. Gen. Hoyt Vandenberg, USAF, AF Chief of Staff (719)
25. Maj. Gen. Keith Ware, Vietnam War leader (2583)

### Section 31

26. Robert Todd Lincoln, former Secretary of War (S-13)

### Section 36

27. Sgt. Medgar W. Evers, USA, WW II—civil rights leader (1431)

*Special Note on Section 27*

Buried in this section—the oldest part of Arlington National Cemetery—are 3800 Civil War "contrabands," the term used for Negro refugees or escaped slaves. Their story is little known because few records are available to tell who they were or how they came to be at Arlington.

The graves of these men, women and children parallel the north side of the cemetery bordering the Fort Myer warehouse area. They are near where Arlington's first recorded military burials, Union soldiers who died of wounds or disease in Washington military hospitals, took place in May, 1864, a few yards from the Ord-Weitzel Gate.

It is surmised that most of these former slaves died of disease in 1864, 1865, and 1866, but a few may have died on the Arlington Estate itself where many Negro refugees lived during and after the Civil War.

In 1863 the Army set up a Contraband Camp at Arlington to care for several thousand "contrabands." The camp sprawled from near the present Amphitheater, through Pershing Hill—Section 34—to its main concentration on the south side of the cemetery.

This became Freedmen's Village in 1865. Its residents were given small plots of ground on the estate to cultivate to support themselves. About 1890 the Government, at the Army's request, financially reimbursed the Negro residents of Arlington—about 800 at the time, and helped them find and move to other locations so Arlington Cemetery could be expanded.

The graves of the former slaves in Section 27 heighten the meaning of Lincoln's sentiment: "With charity for all and malice toward none."

For here at Arlington are buried Union and Confederate veterans, as well as the former slaves. An American flag marks each one of their graves every Memorial Day—touching evidence of our Nation's concern for the dignity of all men.

*Special Note on Section 29*

This section is a reminder of what the areas on three sides of Arlington House—north, south and east—looked like when the Lees lived at Arlington. Many of the towering oaks, black gums, maples and other varieties of trees in Section 29 are over a century old. The original Arlington estate of 1100 acres consisted of 400 acres of woodlands and 700 acres of meadows and fields. The latter were located principally to the east of Arlington Ridge Road, bordering that side of the estate to the Potomac River.

Among Noteworthy Persons Buried in Area II Are:

(Note: Number *before* name indicates location on adjoining map; number *following* in parenthesis indicates grave site in section.)

### Section 1

1. Lieut. Col. Alex. T. Augusta, Negro Army surgeon, Civil War (124)
2. Maj. Gen. Wm. W. Belknap, former Secretary of War (132)
3. Capt. Erastus A. Capron, USA, killed, Mexican War, 1848 (680)
4. Com. Stephen Cassin, hero, Battle Lake Champlain, 1814 (299)
5. Maj. Gen. Abner Doubleday, Civil War leader; invented baseball (61)
6. Maj. Gen. Adolphus Greely, Arctic explorer (129)
7. Maj. Gen. Wm. A. Hammond, noted surgeon, teacher (465)
8. Brig. Gen. Wm. S. Harney, Indian fighter, Mexican War leader (117)
9. Juliet Hopkins, "Florence Nightingale" of South, Civil War (12) (Buried in same grave with Brig. Gen. Romeyn Ayers, her son-in-law)
10. Maj. Gen. Wladimir Krzyzanowski, Polish Legion, Union Army (832)
11. Rear Adm. Samuel P. Lee, hydrographer; cousin, Robert E. Lee (216)
12. Dr. Anita Newcomb Magee, founder Army Nurse Corps; D.A.R. official (526)
13. Brig. Gen. Montgomery C. Meigs, USA; created Arlington Cemetery (1)
14. Maj. John Wesley Powell, US Vols; explorer, scientist, ethnologist (408)
15. Rodgers Family (Navy tradition) (130)
16. Capt. Thomas Holdup Stevens, USN, hero, Battle Lake Erie, 1814 (182)
17. Gen. Lucian Truscott, Commander, 3rd & 5th Armies, WW II (827)
18. Gen. Jonathan M. Wainwright, the "hero of Bataan" (358)
19. Capt. O. S. B. Wall, USA; one of first Negro officers, Civil War (24)
20. Capt. John Williams, USMC; killed by Seminoles, Fla., 1812 (158)

### Section 2

21. Maj. Gen. Wm. R. Arnold, Chief of Army Chaplains, WW II (85)
22. Col. John T. Axton, Sr., first Army Chief of Chaplains (152)
23. Brig. Gen. Hiram Berden, Berden's Sharpshooters, Civil War (979)
24. Adm. William P. Blandy, World War II leader (4964)
25. Adm. Richard E. Byrd, Arctic explorer (4969)
26. Adm. Wm. B. Caperton, led Pacific Fleet, WW I (887)
27. Gen. Claire L. Chennault; led USAAF, China, WW II (873)
28. Maj. Gen. John L. Clem, "drummer boy of Chickamauga" (993)
29. Maj. Gen. George Crook, Civil War leader; Indian fighter (974)
30. Maj. Gen. Wm. J. Donovan, WW I hero; Chief, OSS, WW II (4874)
31. Maj. Gen. Merritt A. Edson, USMC, led "Edson's Raiders," WW II (4960-C)
32. Gen. Robert A. Eichelberger, led 8th Army, WW II (4737-C)
33. Adm. Wm. M. Fechteler, WW II and Korean War leader (1182)
34. Lieut. Gen. Roy S. Geiger, USMC, WW II leader (4964)
35. Maj. Gen. Wm. Gorgas, Army engineer; completed Panama Canal (1039)
36. Gen. Edmond B. Gregory, Army Quartermaster General, WW II (134)
37. Fleet Adm. William F. (Bull) Halsey, led 3rd Fleet, WW II (1184)
38. Maj. Gen. Guy V. Henry, Army Cavalry Chief; Olympic equestrian (1058)
39. Gen. Courtney Hodges, commanded 1st Army, WW II (890)
40. Col. James Jabara, USAF, Korean War hero; 1st jet ace (478-D)
41. Capt. Iven C. Kincheloe, USAF, Korean War jet ace (4872)
42. Frank Knox, "Rough Rider," 1898; Sec. of Navy, WW II (4961)
43. Fleet Adm. William Leahy, Presidential Advisor WW II (932)
44. Maj. Pierre L'Enfant, planned Washington, D.C. (Front of Mansion)
45. Maj. Gen. Philip Kearney, Civil War leader (SW Mansion)
46. Lieut. Gen. Arthur MacArthur, former Gov. Gen. Philippines (879)
47. William Gibbs McAdoo, Secretary of Treasury, WW I (4969)
48. Adm. Marc A. Mitscher, WW II leader (4942)
49. Adm. George D. Murray, World War II leader (4962)
50. Ord Family (Army tradition) (982)
51. Rear Adm. David Dixon Porter, Civil War leader (Front of Mansion)
52. Adm. John D. Price, WW II leader; noted Navy pilot (4968)
53. Capt. Donald Quarles, USAR; Ass't. Sec. Defense (4969)
54. Brig. Gen. John A. Rawlins, Civil War leader (1007)
55. Capt. Henry J. Reilly, killed, Relief Peking, 1900 (844)
56. Rear Adm. Winfield Scott Schley; Spanish-American War leader (1207)
57. Gen. Philip B. Sheridan, Civil War leader (Front of Mansion)
58. Maj. Gen. Hugh L. Scott, noted Indian fighter (Near Mansion)
59. Lieut. Gen. John M. Schofield, Civil War leader (1108)
60. Maj. Gen. H. Julius Stahel-Szamwald, Civil War leader (988)
61. Gen. Brehon B. Somervell, led Army Service Forces, WW II (4946)
62. Army Surgeon Gen. George M. Sternberg, pioneer bacteriologist (994)
63. Asst. Eng. George Westinghouse, USN; invented air brake (3418)
64. Brig. Gen. Joseph Wheeler, USA, Spanish-American War leader (1089)
65. Rear Adm. Charles Wilkes, 19th-century Antarctic explorer (1164)

### Section 5

66. Capt. Oliver Wendell Holmes, USA; US Supreme Court Justice (7004)
67. Lieut. John W. Weeks, USN; Sec. of War (7064)

### Section 13

68. George Washington Parke Custis, creator of Arlington Estate; stepson of George Washington (6513)
69. Mary Randolph Fitzhugh Custis, wife of George Washington Park Custis (6513)
70. Four brothers, Privates Jacob, John, Joseph and Nathaniel McCullough, Co. A, 100th Pa. Inf. (Washington Co., Pa.); two died and two wounded in Civil War (13724)
71. Cpl. Frank S. Scott; USA, 1st enlisted man to die in military plane crash, College Park, Md., 1912, AFB named for him (5331-S)
72. Cpl. Harvey W. Wiley, USA, Civil War; later, famous pure food reformer, chemist, teacher, author and lecturer (5959-B)

### Section 26

73. Capt. Alphonsus H. Packard, Co. G, 31st Maine Inf.; died of wounds, May 5, 1864; first officer buried at Arlington—May 17, 1864 (5203)

### Section 32

74. Field Marshal Sir John Dill, British Army leader WW II. Died on active duty, Washington, D. C., November 4, 1944 (Special Lot)

### Section 45

75. President John F. Kennedy (Special Lot)
76. Maj. Gen. Horatio G. Wright, Civil War leader who saved Washington from capture, July, 1864; later, noted Army engineer (Front of Mansion)

### Memorials

77. *Chaplains (Section 2—crest of hill, near Grant Drive)*
A memorial to 23 Army chaplains who died in service in World War I. This part of Section 2 is known as "Chaplain's Hill" because here rest scores of Army, Navy and Air Force chaplains, both regular and reserve, who served in peace and war.

78. *Memorial Sections*
A & B (Section 2, a few yards SE of Mansion)
G (Section 13, off Wilson Drive, between Farragut and Meigs Drives)
Arlington has seven Memorial Sections. They honor the memories of servicemen who went down with their ships or planes, or whose bodies were never recovered in land or other actions. Each of these servicemen has a Memorial stone similar to a regular G.I. headstone.

78. *Old Amphitheater (Section 26, immediately southwest of Mansion)*
Constructed in 1874, this Amphitheater was the scene of patriotic and religious services commemorating the nation's war dead each Memorial Day from that year to 1921 when the present Memorial Amphitheater was used for the first time. Every President of the United States from President Grant through President Harding, together with hundreds of other notables, participated in these rites.

80. *U.S. Flyers Shot Down Over Yugoslavia in 1946 (Section 2, Grave 3443)*
An unarmed U.S. Army Air Force C-47 transport plane on a routine flight from Vienna to Trieste was shot down without warning by a Yugoslav fighter plane on August 19, 1946, over Yugoslavia. The remains of its five crew members are buried in a single grave in Section 2.

81. *US Submarine F-4 (Section 2, Grave 3387)*
Seventeen dead from the crew of the U.S. Submarine F-4, accidentally sunk at Honolulu, Hawaii, in 1915, are buried at this site.

82. *Unknown Dead of Civil War (Section 26—50 yards SW of Mansion)*
Under this grey granite sarcophagus repose the remains of 2,111 unknown Union soldiers from the two Bull Run battlefields. It was erected in 1866.

83. *Unknown Dead of War of 1812 (Section 1, Grave 299)*
Here, in a single grave, rest the remains of 14 United States soldiers and marines killed in action during the Battle of Washington in the War of 1812 and formerly buried at the Washington Navy Yard.

# AREA III

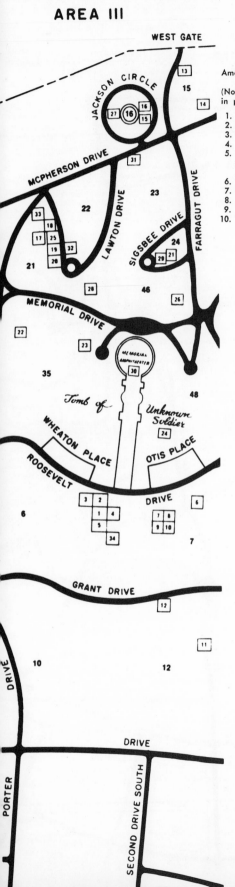

Among Noteworthy Persons Buried in Area III Are:

(Note: Number before name indicates location on adjoining map; number following in parenthesis indicates grave site in section.)

1. Rear Adm. Richard P. Hobson, Spanish-American War hero (5014)
2. Brig. Gen. Hugh Johnson, USA; head, Nat'l. Recovery Admin. (5680)
3. Lieut. Gen. John A. Lejeune, USMC; WW II leader (5682)
4. Maj. Gen. Mason M. Patrick, USAAF; pioneer Army flyer (5692)
5. Maj. Gen. Oscar Westover, USAAF; pioneer Army flyer (5697)

### Section 7
6. Capt. John B. Frazier, first Chief Navy Chaplains (1917–21) (10058)
7. Gen. John L. Hines, Army Chief of Staff (8001)
8. Gen. George C. Marshall, Army Chief of Staff, WW II (8198)
9. Adm. William S. Sims, WW I leader (8002)
10. Gen. Walter Bedell Smith, WW II leader (1897)

### Section 12
11. Pvt. 1st Class Raito Nakashima and Sergeant Wataru Nakashima, brothers; two of 21 soldiers of Japanese-American 442nd Combat infantry Battalion (Honolulu, Hawaii most decorated US unit) killed in Italy WW II—buried at Arlington (5124 and 5125).
12. Maj. Gen. Orde Wingate, British Army Commando, WW II (288)

### Section 15
13. First Lieut. James P. McGranery, USAR; US Attorney-General; US Judge; Congressman (110)
14. James Parks, former Custis family slave; later civilian employee of Army at Arlington; died 1929 in his 80s (2)

### Section 16
15. Moses Ezekiel, sculptor of Confederate Memorial; former Confederate soldier (Special lot—base of Memorial)
16. Brig. Gen. Marcus Wright, Cheatham's Brigade, Confederate Army (Special lot—base of Memorial)

### Section 21
17. Jane Delano, second Superintendent Army Nurse Corps; WW I—nursing leader; high official, American Red Cross (6)
18. Maj. John Foster Dulles, WW I; Secretary of State (31)
19. Rear Adm. William T. Sampson, Spanish-American War (9)
20. Maj. Gen. Leonard Wood, Governor General, Philippines; later, Army Chief of Staff (10)

### Section 24
21. Ignace Jan Paderewski, Polish patriot, statesman and world-famous musician (In base of Maine Mast)

### Section 35
22. Rt. Rev. Bravid Washington Harris, Retired Episcopal Bishop of Liberia (4411)
23. Jeff King, Indian scout for Army; believed to be oldest person buried at Arlington; died 1964—aged 104 (1566)

### Section 48
24. Staff Sgt. William R. Spates, Jr., former Relief Commander, Honor Guard, Tomb of Unknown Soldier; killed in action, Vietnam, 1965 (432)

### Memorials

25. **Army & Navy Nurses Memorial (Section 21)**
Against a background of evergreens, this granite statue of a nurse in uniform was sculptured by Frances Rich. It honors nurses who served in the United States Armed Forces in World War I, many of whom rest among the hundreds of Army, Navy, and Air Force nurses buried in Section 21—also called the "Nurses' Section"

26. **Canadian Cross (Section 46)**
Known as the "Cross of Sacrifice," this 24-foot-high memorial of Canadian granite was erected by the Government of Canada in 1927 to commemorate the several thousand Americans who gave their lives while serving with the Canadian Armed Forces in World War I.

27. **Confederate Memorial (Section 16—Jackson Circle)**
Created by the distinguished sculptor, Moses Ezekiel, who as a Virginia Military Institute cadet fought at the Battle of New Market, this 32½-foot-high bronze statue is a memorial to the 391 Confederate soldiers, sailors and civilian men whose graves surround it in concentric rows—and also to the hundreds of thousands of others who gave their lives for the Confederacy during the Civil War. The memorial was erected by the United Daughters of the Confederacy. It was dedicated in 1914 by President Woodrow Wilson in the presence of several thousand Confederate and Union veterans attending a joint encampment in Washington.

28. **USS Forrestal Memorial (Section 46)**
Inscribed on the front of this gray granite monument are the names of 18 officers and crewmen of the aircraft carrier, the USS *Forrestal*, who rest beneath the memorial. They were among those who died—despite the incredible heroism of their shipmates—when an accident caused explosions and flames to sweep the flight deck of the carrier while it was operating off the coast of Vietnam on July 29, 1967.

29. **USS Maine Memorial (Section 24)**
The mainmast and conning tower of the Battleship USS *Maine* guard the graves of 229 of the *Maine's* officers and crewmen who lost their lives when the *Maine* was blown up at Havana, Cuba, on February 15, 1898. The marble base represents a battleship's turret. Inscribed on its round exterior are the names of all those who died on the *Maine*. This memorial was dedicated on February 15, 1915.

30. **Memorial Amphitheater (Memorial Drive between Wilson and Porter Drives)**
Overlooking the capital of the nation, this classic marble structure is modeled after the Theatre of Dionysius in Athens and a Roman theatre in Orange, France. Seating 4,000 persons, it honors all deceased United States soldiers, sailors, airmen, marines and coastguardsmen at Arlington and wherever else they lie. Honored above all are three, the "Unknowns" of World War I, World War II and the Korean War who rest at the Tomb of the Unknown Soldier, adjoining the Amphitheater. They are guarded proudly day and night every day of the year by the Honor Guard—picked men from the crack 3rd Infantry (Old Guard), which garrisons nearby Fort Myer and is the oldest unit now on active duty in the United States Army.

31. **Rough Riders Memorial (Section 23, off McPherso Drive, opposite Confederate Memorial)**
The famous 1st United States Volunteer Cavalry—raised by Theodore Roosevelt and commanded by Leonard Wood in the Spanish-American War—honored their dead in 1906 by erecting this dark gray granite monument. On its front are listed the names of 62 Rough Riders who died in Cuba in 1898—many of whom are buried among the hundreds of Spanish-American War dead in Section 23.

32. **Spanish-American War Memorial (Section 22, Lawton Drive off McPhearson Drive)**
The memory of all United States soldiers, sailors and marines who died in the Spanish-American War is honored by this tall Corinthian granite shaft surmounted by a bronze eagle—gift of the Colonial Dames of America in 1902. The graves of about 600 soldiers who gave their lives in Cuba, Puerto Rico and the Philippines in that war occupy most of Section 22.

33. **Spanish-American War Nurses' Memorial (Section 21)**
The brave women volunteers who nursed the wounded and sick and who died of tropical plagues in the Spanish-American War are remembered by this memorial—a large granite boulder.

34. **U.S. Submarine S-4 Memorial (Section 6, bordering Section 7, near Roosevelt Drive)**
Eleven officers and crewmen of the US Submarine S-4, sunk in a collision off Cape Cod on December 17, 1927, rest in four graves marked by G.I. headstones.

## AREA IV

Among Noteworthy Persons Buried in Area IV Are:

(Note: Number before name indicates location on adjoining map; number following in parenthesis indicates grave site in section.)

### Section 3

1. Lieut. Gen. Frank M. Andrews, USA; World War II leader (1823)
2. Capt. Frank D. Baldwin, USA; won two Medals of Honor (1894)
3. Lieut. Col. Sosthenes Behn, USAR, founder, Int. Tel. & Tel. (2573)
4. Lieut. Floyd Bennett, USNR; noted aviator & explorer (1852)
5. Adm. Wm. S. Benson, Chief Naval Operations, WW I (1873)
6. Brig. Gen. Fred W. Benteen, commanded relief, Custer Massacre (1351)
7. Maj. Gen. Adna R. Chaffee, Jr., noted tank expert (1944)
8. Lieut. Gen. Adna R. Chaffee, Sr., former Chief of Staff (1945)
9. Lt. Com. Roger B. Chaffee, USN; Astronaut (2502)
10. Davenport Family (Army-Navy tradition) (1990)
11. Lieut. Gen. Hugh A. Drum, WW I leader (1447)
12. Col. Fielding H. Garrison, USA; noted medcial librarian (4621)
13. Lieut. Gen. Amos Fries, founder, Chemical Warfare Service (4021)
14. Graham Family (Army-Navy tradition) (1989)
15. Lieut. Col. Virgil Grissom, USAF; Astronaut (2503)
16. Lieut. Gen. James Harbord, WW I leader; Army Chief Staff (1872)
17. 1st Lieut. Claude B. Hill, USA; Siberian Exped. Force 1918–19 (4165)
18. Col. Robert G. Ingersoll, US Vols; orator, editor, author (1620)
19. Maj. Jonathan Letterman, famous Civil War surgeon (1869)
20. Lieut. Gen. Homer L. Litzenberg, WW II & Korean War leader (2513)
21. Maj. Gen. James W. McAndrew, Chief of Staff, AEF, WW I (2519)
22. Gen. Randolph M. Pate, 21st Commandant US Marine Corp. (2501)
23. Lieut. Gen. Nelson A. Miles, famous Indian fighter (1873)
24. Maj. Walter Reed, Army doctor; discovered cause yellow fever (1864)
25. Mary Roberts Rinehart, world famous authoress (4269)
26. Maj. Gen. William Starke Rosecrans, Civil War leader (1862)
27. 1st Lieut. Thomas Selfridge, USA; first military plane death (2158)
28. Maj. Gen. Daniel E. Sickles, Civil War leader (1906)
29. Kate Williams Upshur, cousin of Mrs. Robert E. Lee (1883)
30. Col. Charles Young, second Negro graduate West Point (1730)

### Section 4

31. Col. Wm. Jennings Bryan, US Vols; Presidential nominee (3121)
32. Rear Adm. Harry Hamlet, USCG; noted Coast Guard leader (2613-B)
33. Com. Zachary Landsdowne; killed in "Shenandoah" crash (3123)
34. Gen. Ben Lear, USA; commanded 2nd Army WW II (2690)
35. Ensign Frank J. Sprague, invented electric street car (2959)

### Section 8

36. Lieut. Com. John McCloy, USN; won two Medals of Honor (5246)
37. Adm. Russell A. Waesche, USCG; WW II leader (5190)

### Section 11

38. Maj. Thomas B. McGuire, USAAF; WW II ace (426)

### Section 18

39. Sgt. Edward Younger, chose WW I Unknown Soldier (1918)

### Section 34

40. Gen. H. H. Arnold, USAAF; Chief, Army Air Forces, WW II (44-A)
41. Gen. J. Lawton Collins, USA; WW II leader (121-A)
42. Gen Muir Fairchild, USAF; noted flyer; WW II leader (48-A)
43. Cpl. Ira Hayes, USMC; Iwo Jima flag-raising, WW II (479)
44. Gen. John Reed Hodge, USA; WW II leader (157-A)
45. Maj. Gen. Melvin J. Maas, USMCR; Marine hero; Congressman (4-A)
46. Gen. John J. Pershing, General of the Armies, WW I (1)
47. Gen. Walter Harris Walker, USA; Korean War leader (185-A)
48. Lieut. Gen. Ennis C. Whitehead, USAAF; WW II leader (137-A)

## MEMORIALS

49. *Argonne Cross (Section 18)*
   Honoring the memory of the thousands of World War I American soldiers buried in Europe, this 13-foot-high marble cross was erected in 1923 by the Argonne Unit, American Women's Legion, now the American Legion Auxiliary. The Cross overlooks the graves of more than 5,000 United States soldiers who died overseas in World War I and who are buried in Sections 17, 18 and 19 at Arlington.

50. *Memorial Sections (C, D, E & F—Section 3—off Porter Drive)*
   These are individual memorials to members of the United States Armed Forces lost at sea, in plane crashes or in land actions, and their bodies were never recovered. (Memorial Sections A & B are in Section 2, just below the Mansion; Memorial Section G is in Section 13, off Wilson Drive.)

51. *Peary Memorial (Section 4—off Dewey Drive)*
Resting on a square base of granite, a stone globe of the world (with a bronze star at the North Pole) commemorates the discoverer of the North Pole—Rear Admiral Robert Edwin Peary, USN. The great explorer, civil engineer and scientist and his wife rest beneath this memorial which was erected in 1922 by the National Geographic Society and dedicated by President Harding.

52. *Polar Bear Regt. (339th Inf.) Dead-Siberia: 1918–19 (Section 18)*
The Allied Expeditionary Force to Siberia in 1918–19 attempted, among other objectives, to stop the Bolsheviks there. Seven of the 230 Americans who died in Siberia are buried at Arlington. They and their comrades were thus the first Americans to lose their lives opposing Communism. All members of the 339th Infantry Regiment, nicknamed the Polar Bear Regiment, they came from in and around Detroit, Michigan. Six of the seven rest in individual graves in Section 18. They are Privates John P. Angove, Boleslaw Gotowski, James T. Ida, Nikodem Ladovich, Elmer E. Speicher and Louis A. Szymanski. The seventh is First Lieutenant Claude B. Hill who is buried nearby in Section 3 (4165). The Commanding General of the American Forces in Siberia, Major General William S. Graves, who died in 1940, is also buried in Section 3 (4177), a short distance from the others.

53. *United States Coast Guard Memorial (Section 4, off Dewey Drive)*
A bronze gull poised in flight at the granite base of this monument—a small pyramid of white marble—symbolizes the watchful and untiring efforts of the United States Coast Guard and its ideals of steadfastness and endurance. The Coast Guard motto "Semper Paratus" (always ready) is inscribed on the memorial with the names of 192 officers and crewmen who went down with the Coast Guard Cutters *Tampa* and *Seneca* or who gave their lives in performance of other duties in World War I. This memorial was erected by their shipmates in the Coast Guard in 1928.

54. *The USS Serpens Memorial (Section 34, MacArthur Circle)*
The United States Coast Guard suffered its largest single disaster of World War II when the USS *Serpens*, a Coast Guard ship transporting troops, was destroyed by enemy action off Lunga Beach, Guadalcanal, on January 29, 1945. Commemorating the 199 coastguardsmen, 50 soldiers and one Public Health Service officer who lost their lives in the sinking is this octagon-shaped monument of Georgia granite. The names of those who died on the *Serpens* and whose remains rest beneath the memorial are listed on its sides.

*Special Note 1*
Section 11 includes the site of Fort McPherson, one of the chain of forts built for the defense of Washington in the Civil War. It was named in honor of Brigadier General James Birdseye McPherson of Ohio, who was killed in action near Atlanta, Georgia, on July 22, 1864. The fort was never under hostile fire during the Civil War, and it was leveled in 1946 for additional gravesites.

*Special Note 2*
A Contraband Camp for freed Negroes was established by the Army in 1863 on the site of the present Memorial Amphitheater through Pershing Hill (Section 34) and to the south end of the present Arlington National Cemetery (Sections 8 and 18). Thousands of newly-freed Negroes from Virginia, North Carolina, South Carolina and other southern states were cared for here from 1863 to 1865 when it was renamed Freedmen's Village. Many of them remained here for long periods of time, helping to support themselves by farming small plots on the Arlington Estate. Their number had dwindled to about 800 in 1890 when the United States Government helped them move to other locations around Washington to permit the expansion of the cemetery.

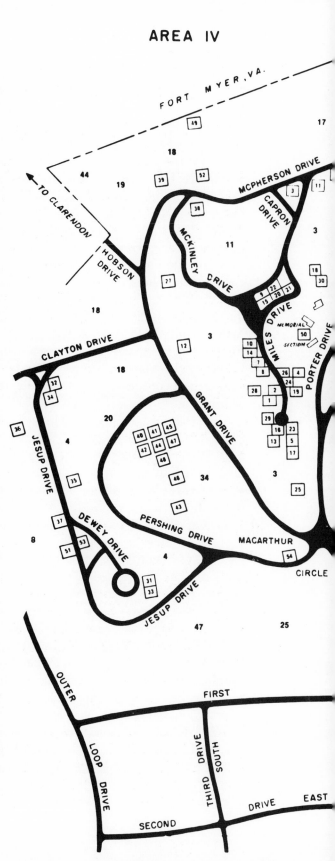

AREA IV

Directly fronting the mansion are the final resting places of Pierre L'Enfant, who planned the City of Washington; Horatio Wright, whose VI Corps saved it from capture by the Confederate Jubal Early in July, 1864; the dashing Phil Sheridan; and David Dixon Porter, naval hero of the War Between the States.

Near the gravelled walk to the south lie many other illustrious Americans: Walter O. Gresham, Brigadier General of Volunteers, Postmaster General, Secretary of the Treasury and Secretary of State; Army Surgeon General George Miller Sternberg, noted bacteriologist; John Lincoln Clem, "the drummer boy of Chickamauga"; Julius Stahel, the Hungarian patriot who became a Union General and won the Medal of Honor; John Gibbon of the Iron Brigade and Indian Wars; the remarkable Ords—headed by Edward Otho Cresap Ord, famous in the War Between the States—a family that has furnished outstanding officers for all of our wars since 1812; George Crook, the doughty Indian fighter; Arthur MacArthur—father of Douglas MacArthur, and a brilliant soldier-statesman in his own right; Chennault of the Flying Tigers; Army Generals Schofield, Corbin, Nicholson and Lawton; Elliott of the Marines; Admirals Leahy, Wilkes, Caperton, Kalfbus, Wiley; and a host of other great soldiers, sailors, airmen, marines and coast guardsmen.

To the west along Meigs Drive out towards the Fort Myer Gate, with its exquisite Colonial-style chapel, are other graves that spell out American history. Walking among the graves in Section 1, on the right, the visitor will read the names of many brave men who died fighting for their country in the War of 1812; the Seminole Wars of the 1820s; the Mexican War; the War Between the States; the Indian Wars; the Spanish-American War; the Boxer Rebellion; the Philippine Insurrection; both World Wars; and in Korea and Viet Nam. Revolutionary War veterans are also buried there. No other place in our country has this proud but sad distinction! Off to the left in Section 13 is the fenced-in Custis Family burial lot. Shaded by tall trees, are the graves of George Washington Parke Custis, builder of Arlington and adopted son of George Washington, and his wife, Mary Fitzhugh Custis.

Then, from the Fort Myer Gate there is a road that touches well-remembered episodes of American history. On the west side of McPherson Drive, in Section 17 at Jackson Circle, Moses Ezekiel's Confederate Memorial guards the graves of 391 gallant Southerners. Ezekiel himself rests at its base. Further along on the right, in front of the Argonne Cross, are buried several thousand Americans who fought and died in Europe in World War I.

Across the road from the Confederates is the Rough Riders Monument —a memorial to sixty-five members of the 1st U. S. Volunteer Cavalry who gave their lives in Cuba in 1898. Many of the men whose names are inscribed here rest in Arlington. Looking towards the east, a few score yards away, the visitor sees the mast of the ill-fated battleship USS *Maine*. In front of it are buried more than two hundred *Maine* crewmen. The mausoleum at the base of the mast contains, temporarily, the body of the great Polish patriot and musician, Ignace Jan Paderewski. It will remain there until *Polandia Restituta*—"Poland is free!"

Hundreds of Army, Navy and Air Force nurses who served so selflessly are buried in the Nurses Section—Section 21—just off to the left. A heroic-size marble statue of a nurse broods over their graves. Nearby, at the top of a small rise, are the graves of John Foster Dulles, Leonard Wood and the Spanish-American War naval commander, William T. Sampson.

A short turnoff at Capron Drive— named after the military dynasty that started with Army Captain Erastus A. Capron, killed in action at Cherubusco, Mexico, in 1847—ends at the mausoleum of Nelson A. Miles. In Section 3, as his comrades in death, are scores of others who earned their places in our history. Among them—to mention only a few—are Walter Reed, James Harbord, the Chaffees, the Davenports and the Grahams, Floyd Bennett, William Starke Rosecrans, William Shepherd Benson, George O. Squier, Hugh A. Drum, Frank R. Andrews, Jonathan Letterman and John H. Upshur. The latter's first wife, Kate Williams, and their son, Custis Parke Upshur, are buried in the same lot with him. Kate Williams Upshur was a cousin of Mary Custis Lee—Mrs. Robert E. Lee.

Back to McPherson Drive, and then along Grant Drive where, on the right off in the distance at the crest of a small hill in Section 34, is the grave of John J. Pershing. As he wished, there is only a plain GI headstone. When he was buried in 1948 the hilltop was isolated. Now the Generals and the Admirals who knew him in life have come to join him in death. Henry H. (Hap) Arnold is one of them. And up the same hillside are slowly creeping the graves of the enlisted men, who were so near to Pershing's heart. In this same area, clustering mostly around the USS *Serpens* Memorial at MacArthur Circle, are the mass graves of many air crews who died together and who, fittingly, are buried together. Flat stones bearing their names, ranks and date of death mark each grave.

Proceeding up Porter Drive to Roosevelt Drive, the visitor notes on the left the Memorial Sections to servicemen of all ranks whose bodies were never recovered. George Catlett Marshall, Walter Bedell Smith and other well-known military and naval leaders are buried just a few steps off of Roosevelt Drive in Section 7; and other leaders, among them John A. Lejeune, are buried in Section 6. Looking uphill, there are the imposing Tomb of the Unknown Soldier and the Arlington Ampitheater.

The heart of Arlington, of course, is the Tomb of the Unknown Soldier. Millions of Americans find inspiration and dedication here. The Changing of the Guard, every hour on the hour, is a simple but impressive ceremony. It is conducted by the Honor Guard—picked men of the elite 3rd U. S. Infantry (Old Guard), at Fort Myer. Organized in 1784, the 3rd has fought with distinction in thirty-nine battles in six wars and is the oldest infantry unit in active service. As the sentinel at the Tomb is relieved by another 3rd Infantryman, visitors stand in respectful silence, broken only by the commands of the Sergeant of the Guard.

Fortunate are the visitors who are present at the Tomb of the Unknown Soldier when the carillon at the Amphitheater rings out hymns dear to all faiths. It is played for 15 minutes at noon and at 4:05 P.M. every Monday through Friday, and on Saturdays and Sundays at five minutes past the hour from 9 A.M. to 5 P.M.

Down the hill from the Tomb of the Unknown Soldier, on a wooded slope in Section 2, is the simple Chaplain's Memorial—dedicated to the men who went unarmed into battle to bring the consolations of their own faiths to the fighting men. The Army's first Chief of Chaplains—Chaplain (Colonel) John T. Axton—was buried there in 1934, and its Chief of Chaplains in World War II—Chaplain (Major General) William R. Arnold—in 1965. Chaplain Arnold, first Army chaplain to attain General's rank, served later as a Catholic Auxiliary Bishop of New York. Scores of other chaplains— among them many who also became prominent in their own denominations and others who gave their lives in wartime—rest in this section and also in other parts of Arlington. Chaplain (Captain) John B. Frazier, the Navy's first Chief of Chaplains, is buried in Section 7.

Some visitors to Arlington National Cemetery leave their automobiles in parking areas near the Sheridan Gate, first on the right from the Main Gates, and walk to the Kennedy grave and Custis-Lee Mansion. The path leads along Custis Walk and through eras of American history written by men whose names are on the nearby tombstones. To cite only a few: William Howard Taft, twenty-seventh President of the United States; James V. Forrestal, Robert P. Patterson and such distinguished soldiers as Tasker H. Bliss, Peyton C. March, Charles P. Summerall, Richard K. Sutherland, Floyd L. Parks and Raymond A. Wheeler; noted naval officers, including Forrest P. Sherman, John H. Towers, Jonas H. Ingram, Richard S. Edwards and Joseph Taussig; and the Air Force's Hoyt Vandenberg, all of whose graves are in Section 30. Lawrence A. Steinhardt—the one-time Army Sergeant who rose to become a United States Ambassador to six nations—and Presidential physician, Cary T. Grayson, are among other well-known persons who rest there. Closer to the Kennedy grave among the famous who rest in Section 5, on the left of Custis Walk, are George Barnett, the Marine commandant, and Oliver Wendell Holmes, the jurist.

Others visiting Arlington prefer to enter by the Pedestrian Gate—immediately to the left of the Main Gates. They can walk past the final resting places, in Sections 2 and 2A on their left, of a galaxy of Generals and Admirals who helped bring victory in World War II. Robert L. Eichelberger heads the list for Army, while the Navy has William (Bull) Halsey, John E. Gingrich, Marc Mitscher, Luke McNamee, George D. Murray, William H. Blanding, John Dale Price, David Foote Sellers, Tom Burbridge Hill, Edward C. Ewen and Edward O. McDonnell. The Marines have Roy S. Geiger and Merritt Edson. Among other noteworthy Americans buried there are Richard E. Byrd, Frank Knox, William Gibbs McAdoo, Dwight Davis, Paul V. McNutt and Donald Quarles.

On the right, when approaching the Kennedy grave, the visitor notes a striking statue in bronze of a mounted officer. This marks the grave of Field Marshal Sir John Dill, Chief of the British Military Mission to the United States in World War II. He died on duty in Washington in 1944 and is one of several score British, French, Canadian, Dutch, Latin American, Italian and other foreign military and naval men buried at Arlington by special permission of Congress because they were wartime allies.

Now follow us through Arlington from the Memorial Bridge to the Amphitheater and see in pictures this great shrine to our service dead as it is today.

Slightly apart from the other graves is that of Pierre L'Enfant, which seems ever to be looking toward the city of Washington—the city of his dreams, laid out for the fifty states he envisioned as the goal of the new nation.

**Abbie Rowe, National Park Service**

Graves of George Washington Parke Custis and Mary, his wife.

**Patrick Hughes**

An Army funeral is an impressive sight. Here one starts out from the Chapel at Fort Myer, built in 1934 by Major General Kenyon Joyce, whose funeral from this same chapel was held on January 18, 1960.

The stately memorial to William Howard Taft, President of the United States and Commander-in-Chief of the Armed Forces, is set apart in a little oasis of green.

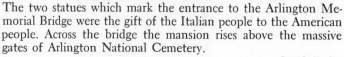

The two statues which mark the entrance to the Arlington Memorial Bridge were the gift of the Italian people to the American people. Across the bridge the mansion rises above the massive gates of Arlington National Cemetery.

Arlington's Ord-Weitzel Gate, the last gate to the north (or right) of the Main Gates, is now one of the principal entrances to the cemetery. Graves of the first soldiers buried at Arlington—in May 1864—are located in the first several rows on the left just inside the gate. On the right for a quarter of a mile from the top of the hill are the graves of 3,800 contrabands or former slaves who died in or near Washington or in a Freedmen's Camp on the Arlington Estate in 1864, 1865 and 1866.

Patrick Hughes

A little girl walks among some of the graves of the 3,800 Negroes, former slaves, buried in 1864, 1865 and 1866 in the oldest part of Arlington National Cemetery near the Ord-Weitzel Gate. Theirs, like the graves of servicemen, have been decorated with flags for Memorial Day.

Washington Post Photo

Private William Christman, 67th Pa. Inf., was the first Union soldier to be buried in Arlington National Cemetery —on May 13, 1864. Behind his grave are those of four unknown Union soldiers—the first unknowns buried in Arlington.

Abbie Rowe, National Park Service

The interior of the Custis-Lee Mansion is one of the best examples of life as it was lived in the days before the War Between the States.

Many were the concerts and family "sings" held in this drawing room.

Abbie Rowe, National Park Service

In the Lee bedroom an old-fashioned high four-poster bed required a tall step-ladder. It was in this room that Robert E. Lee prayed for Divine guidance the night he resigned his commission.

Abbie Rowe, National Park Service

The primitive kitchen contrasts sharply with the other rooms in the mansion.

Abbie Rowe, National Park Service

The headstone on the right marks the grave of the first officer buried at Arlington. He was Captain Albert H. Packard of the 4th Maine Infantry. His grave is the fourth on the gravelled path leading south from the Custis-Lee Mansion. It is in an L-shaped row of graves ordered dug in the Rose Garden by Quartermaster General Montgomery Meigs to assure that the Lees would never return to live in their former home. In the background is the Temple of Fame—a strange memorial to George Washington and eleven Union Generals, ordered built by Meigs in 1866. It was torn down in 1966 when the National Park Service restored the Rose Garden.

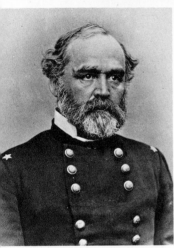

Quartermaster General
Montgomery Meigs.

This memorial to the unknown dead of the War Between the States is very close to the Custis-Lee Mansion itself. Montgomery Meigs wanted to be sure that the house was made uninhabitable, so he had the bones of 2,111 Union soldiers gathered from the fields of Bull Run and the route to the Rappahannock, and buried beside the house.

Abbie Rowe, National Park Service

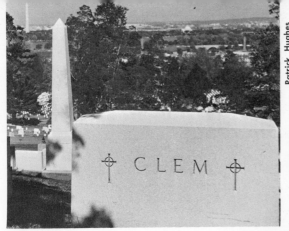

Patrick Hughes

Almost modern in its composition is this view which shows the Washington Monument, matched by a similar obelisk just below the grave of Johnny Clem, the "Drummer Boy of Chickamauga," who enlisted at the age of eleven, and grew up to be a Major General.

It is a source of great pleasure to both young and old when their visit to Arlington coincides with a review of the crack 3rd Infantry (Old Guard) at historic Fort Myer. The fort is really an integral part of Arlington, for it was created from a part of the original Arlington Estate. Reveille and Retreat and the sunset gun from Fort Myer are heard throughout the cemetery.

**U.S. Army Photograph**

Patrick Hughes

The mainmast of the USS *Maine* is the Memorial to those who went down with their ship. It is interesting that the base, being large, has held for a time the bodies of famous foreigners. President Manuel Quezon of the Phillippines rested there until the Japanese were driven out and he could return to his homeland. Ignace Jan Paderewski still waits until Poland will be free.

The magnificent Amphitheater is used for very important funerals and for special services, such as that of Memorial Day, but it is best known for its magnificent approach to the Tomb of the Unknown Soldier.

"Twin Gates of Sleep"

Seldom a weekday goes by that the visitor does not see a military funeral. In this picture the Navy is burying one of its officers.

# THE UNKNOWN SOLDIER

"HERE RESTS IN HONORED GLORY AN AMERICAN SOLDIER KNOWN BUT TO GOD."

This moving inscription has become familiar to millions of Americans who have read it on the Tomb of the Unknown Soldier at the Memorial Amphitheater at Arlington National Cemetery or in the many stories written about the most hallowed place in these United States.

The inscription is simple, the marble tomb plain. The soldier from World War I who lies here is in himself no great and dashing hero famed in song or story. Nor are his two companions from World War II and Korea, who rest with him in separate marble tombs commanding an unforgetable view across the Potomac of much of the Capital City of the nation they died to defend.

The three are more than that for they represent all American soldiers, sailors, airmen, marines and coastguardsmen, who answered their country's call and went to fight—and made the supreme sacrifice so that the principles in which all true Americans believe might not perish from the Earth.

It is more than sentiment that makes the Tomb of the Unknown Soldier the greatest of American Shrines. It is the embodiment of idealism—of the American ideal of the dignity of the individual man. For no one knows who the Unknowns are—from what background they came; where they lived; to what creed they owed allegiance; who there were to wait in vain for word, and to mourn their passing.

To these tombs have come the great of the earth to do homage. Those who fought by our side during two World Wars and in Korea have honored them. Those who fought against us have saluted them. And by the millions their fellow countrymen have come to the Tomb, marked only with the years of their sacrifice: 1917-1918 for the World War I Unknown; 1941-1945 for the World War II Unknown, and 1950-1953 for the Korean War Unknown.

144

Even before the great tomb was built for the Unknown Soldier of World War I, the Honor Guard from Fort Myer watched over him. The uniform was different but the spirit remained the same.

Kings and potentates have placed wreaths at the foot of the Tomb. So have the humblest citizens. The young Queen of Great Britain, among whose titles is "Defender of the Faith," has more than once come to this hallowed place with flowers. The stately guardian of the shrine of Mohammed at Mecca, Ibn Saud, has bowed his head before these honored dead. The aged leader of ten million Buddhists, Archibishop Rosen Takashima, brought a wreath to show his respect for the Unknowns and prayed at their Tomb.

Archbishop Rosen Takashima, seventy-eight-year-old leader of ten million Buddhists as head of the Japanese Zensoto Buddhist Section, paid his respects after laying a wreath on the Tomb of the Unknown Soldier August 4, 1963.

There have been those who stayed awhile to dream that the Unknown might be their boy, so long missing. There are those who come to muse upon a known grave too far away for them to visit. And there are those, perhaps sadder still, who mourn all warrior dead, having no son to give to their country.

There are among these visitors the old, who remember the high hopes of peace and goodwill among men and nations. There are the young who see visions of what they will do to make the world right again.

And there are the children—always the children—who, their parents hope, will carry away with them inspiration for the future, while they watch with fascination the fine-looking young men of the Honor Guard slowly pacing back and forth, back and forth.

Statistics of the millions who visit the Tomb are unimportant. What is important is that only those who care, go there. Only those who care, cross the river. There is no morbidity involved—because these warriors are unknown. Not the sculptured conquerors of old for whom great cathedrals were built, not the embalmed figure in the Red Square in Moscow, not the draped catafalques upon which our own lamented great have lain, means as much as the plain marble Tomb. "Known but to God"—but, *known to God.*

It was on Memorial Day in 1921 when, according to a Resolution of Congress, the bodies of four soldiers, one from each of the four American

President Kennedy visits the Tomb of the Unknown Soldier on Veteran's Day, November 11, 1961.

Abbie Rowe, National Park Service

National Cemeteries in France, were honored in special ceremonies at Chalons-sur-Marne—the town that lies almost halfway between Chateau Thierry and St. Mihiel. Americans had fought and died—and won—at both places. They had added new battle flags and honors to the Army's imperishable records. It was but natural that the Marne Valley which had seen their struggles should see their glory.

No one knew, no one had any way of knowing, who these soldier-dead were. They had been so arranged and rearranged that it was impossible even to tell from which cemetery the caskets had come.

Then, at last, the solemn moment came. Sergeant Edward F. Younger, who had been wounded in combat and decorated for valor, was selected from a group just brought in from Germany, to make the final choice. Slowly he approached the four caskets. Then—almost prayerfully—he laid a spray of white roses on one of the caskets.

So was the Unknown Soldier of the First World War selected. His casket, bedecked with flowers by French children, was brought to the port and placed on the cruiser *Olympia*, which had been the flagship of Admiral Dewey at Manila Bay.

In greatest honor the Unknown Soldier came home. The *Olympia* docked at the Washington Navy Yard in a soft rain in the late afternoon of November 9, 1921 to the sound of a twenty-one-gun salute and solemn dirges by service bands.

For two days while tens of thousands filed by to pay their respects, the Unknown rested in state at the Capitol on the catafalque which had borne the bodies of three martyred Presidents—Lincoln, Garfield and McKinley— and which has since borne a fourth—John Fitzgerald Kennedy.

On November 11, the Unknown Soldier was placed in the Tomb at Arlington, attended by President Warren G. Harding and hundreds of dignitaries representing all of the Allied nations as well as our own. Acting for the American people, the President conferred the nation's highest decoration—the Medal of Honor—on the Unknown warrior at the ceremonies.

The accompanying citation read, in part, that the Medal of Honor, "emblem of highest ideals and virtues," was bestowed by Congress on the Unknown Soldier "typifying the gallantry and intrepidity, at the risk of life and above and beyond the call of duty, of our beloved heroes who made the supreme sacrifice in the World War."

"They died in order that others might live," the citation concluded— a fitting epitaph to all war dead at Arlington.

For thirty-five years he rested there alone through nearly twenty years of uneasy peace, then through five years of war; through a few years of increasing turmoil and then more years of war. Was the peace for which he fought and died never to arrive?

But there was a very significant development. Arlington had become a cemetery, orginally, in order to house the Union dead of the War Between the States. Later it encompassed the Confederate dead. In the Spanish-American War, many of those who had worn the Blue fought side by side with many of those who had worn the Grey—and both fought for their country and many came home to Arlington to rest together.

In World War I the Rainbow Division, made up of American boys from North and South and East and West, fighting in a single unit against a common enemy, proved conclusively that the United States was a unified nation.

In World War II, the mixing of men from all states further proved to the World that the United States are truly *united* states.

The Korean War proved that the men of the United States were capable of world unity—without which there can be no peace—by bearing the brunt of a mission assigned by the United Nations to halt aggression by a powerful totalitarian Communist dictatorship against a weak but valiant free state.

The bill to name Unknowns from both World War II and the Korean War was signed by President Eisenhower on August 3, 1956. The selection of these Unknowns was as carefully and reverently handled as that of the first Unknown Soldier. For World War II, two caskets, equally carefully chosen, from the European and Pacific Theaters, were brought to the USS *Canberra*, a guided missle cruiser. There, off the Virginia capes in late May,

The Honor Guard changes before the Tomb of the Unknown Soldier.

Abbie Rowe, National Park Service

"Known but to God"

the choice was made by Hospitalman First Class William R. Charette, the Navy's only enlisted holder of the Medal of Honor still on active duty. On the after-missile deck of the *Canberra*, he stood for a moment before the two caskets and then placed his wreath on the one who was to be the Unknown of World War II.

For the Korean War, the selection was made in the National Cemetery of the Pacific, at Honolulu, by much decorated Master Sergeant Ned Lyle, U. S. Army, who, after standing silent before four identical flag-draped caskets, solemnly placed a wreath of carnations on the one to be known as the Korean Unknown.

As it had at the burial of the Unknown Soldier in 1921, the nation again paid its highest honors to the Unknowns of World War II and Korea. After lying in state at the United States Capitol, where multitudes of Americans paid their last respects, the Unknowns were brought to Arlington on Memorial Day, 1958 for religious and state funeral rites participated in by President Dwight D. Eisenhower and a host of other ranking United States Government officials, representatives of foreign governments, and citizens.

As their twin flag-draped caskets rested on the podium of the Arlington Amphitheater, President Eisenhower bestowed the Medal of Honor on each unknown warrior. Two brief citations were read, expressing the nation's feelings about their sacrifice.

The Unknown of World War II was honored, the first said, for "exemplifying the selflessness of all our fallen heroes of the Second World War, who, in courageous defense of the ideals of democracy against aggression, gave their lives to preserve our noble heritage."

The other citation read that the Unknown of the Korean War was honored as "symbolic of the gallantry and intrepidity above and beyond the call of duty of all members of the Armed Forces of the United States who gave their lives in the Korean conflict while defending the ideals of freedom and democracy."

At the burial of these two Unknowns, among the several thousand guests of honor, there was one group that was particularly distinguished.

The Unknown Solider of the Korean Conflict is awarded the Medal of Honor by President Eisenhower.

Abbie Rowe, National Park Service

U. S. Army Photograph

This group consisted of 212 of the 320 living holders of the Medal of Honor. Appropriately, they were given the places of honor on the steps of the Amphitheater entrance leading from the Tomb and immediately behind the President and Vice-President for the interment ceremonies.

On this occasion the great funeral procession, the gathering of dignitaries from the nations of the world led by the President of the United States and the Vice-President, the artillery's booming salute, the marching of the West Point Cadets, the Annapolis Middies, and those from the Air Force and Coast Guard Academies, as well as the regular Armed forces, and finally the volley and the bugler's rendition of the inspiring "Taps," was seen and heard not only by the thousands who thronged the hillside at Arlington, but by millions throughout the world who watched and heard it on television.

To all the world, as well as to all Americans, it proclaimed: "The people of America, conceived in the concept that all men are free, and born to defend that concept, pledge allegiance to the free people of the world and their right to remain free."

There at Arlington, in honored glory, rest the Unknowns from three wars. Like all the dead at Arlington, each of them can say, as another soldier, Saint Paul, wrote in his Second Epistle to Timothy, Chapter IV, Verse VII: "I have fought a good fight, I have finished my course, I have kept the faith."

All that these dead ask of us—the living American—is that their sacrifice shall not have been in vain and that freedom shall not perish from the Earth.

SP/5 Ambrose C. Jackson, a member of the United States Army Band (Washington, D.C.) plays "Taps" during a funeral ceremony at Arlington National Cemetery, Arlington, Virginia.

**U.S. Army Photograph**

# EPILOGUE

### THE VIETNAM WAR

The war in Vietnam has given us many new heroes. It has proven once again that men under stress do not think first or only of self.

Symbolic of the men who have died attempting to rescue others is Marine Captain Joseph L. Powell, Jr., of Arlington, Va. He was a helicopter pilot who had already earned 28 Air Medals, among other decorations, when he was killed at the age of 25.

The captain had already completed more than 300 missions when he set out on October 17, 1968. The weather was bad and there were reports of sniper fire. But he knew that there were seriously wounded men who needed help—so he took off. When he was bringing his helicopter down for a landing, it was struck by enemy fire and crashed into a hillside.

"Home they brought her warrior, dead." Karen Powell, with a Marine escort, walks behind her husband's casket to the grave.

His funeral was held at St. George's Episcopal Church, close to Arlington Cemetery. He had been married in this church and his son was baptized there. From its doors he was borne to his grave in Arlington, his wife, with a Marine escort, walked behind the caisson.

By one of those coincidences which almost seemed planned, Captain Powell was laid to rest a few yards from another hero, who was also a friend. Second-Lieutenant William A. Wilks of Silver Spring, Maryland, had been at Notre Dame with Powell and had followed him into the Marine Corps.

Captain Joseph L. Powell, U.S.M.C.          Lieutenant William A. Wilks, U.S.M.C.

Lieutenant Wilks was killed in action in July 1967. He was an artillery officer, acting as forward observer for a Marine unit that was greatly outnumbered and in danger of being overrun by the enemy. Calmly he called for fire from Marine artillery on his own position to smash the Communist advance. His cool heroic act was a deliberate sacrifice of himself to save others.

Major General Keith L. Ware, Commander of the Army's First Infantry Division, was killed in a helicopter crash in Vietnam in September 1968. His aircraft was shot down by enemy fire near the Cambodian border, while he was on a routine flight over the front lines, observing the progress of his troops.

A Fighting General at the front—Major General Keith Ware, U.S.A.

Army News Features

General Ware, a native of Denver, Colorado, was known as a "soldier's soldier." He understood the men he commanded—and they would have followed him anywhere. He entered World War II as a draftee and was the first graduate of an Officers Candidate School to become a general officer.

By his actions at Sigolsheim, France, in December 1944, he earned the Medal of Honor. Though a battalion commander, he had picked up an automatic rifle and boldly led an assault that penetrated, and eventually destroyed, a strongly fortified position.

In the years after the war he went on in his chosen profession; doing well in every assignment given him, including a turn at teaching at West Point, and duty as Chief of Information, Department of the Army, at the Pentagon just before he left for Vietnam.

The last tour of duty of Army Sergeant William R. Spates, Jr., of Washington, D. C., before he left for Vietnam was as relief commander of the Honor Guard that is in constant attendance at the Tomb of the Unknown Soldier.

Serving with the Honor Guard is considered a privilege, not a duty, for the Guard is composed of men especially chosen from the crack 3rd Infantry—the Old Guard—which garrisons Fort Myer.

Just before leaving for Vietnam, he spoke to his comrades of the Honor Guard, telling them how much that duty had meant to him and expressing the wish that, if he died in Vietnam, he could be buried as near to the tomb of the Unknown Soldier as was possible.

Sergeant Spates went to Vietnam in June of 1965 and was killed in action in November of the same year, when the Vietcong attacked a Vietnamese Ranger Battalion for which he was advisor.

When his body was brought back to Arlington, the men who knew how much it had meant to him, formed a guard of honor worthy of a general, and he was laid to rest, as he had hoped, within a few yards of the Tomb of the Unknown Soldier.

The Honor Guard buries one of its own, Staff Sergeant William F. Spates, Jr.

Private First Class Jack Kuri, a naturalized American born in Esthonia— a country which resisted Soviet Communists until completely overrun—was killed in action by Vietnamese Communists on April 29, 1967. He was a psychology major at George Washington University when he entered the Army eight months before his death.

Private Kuri was on a "search and destroy" mission in Huang Nhgia Province, Vietnam, acting as "point man" for his platoon—a unit of Company B, 2nd Battalion, 27th Infantry Regiment, 25th Division, when he spotted a Vietcong ambush. He fell mortally wounded in the first burst of fire and was posthumously awarded the Bronze Star for Valor for "his personal bravery and devotion to duty."

Many of the men who rest at Arlington were descended from families with a proud tradition of military service. Such a man was Army Lieutenant Colonel William E. Berzinec. For generations his forebears had been either soldiers or priests of the Byzantine rite, affiliated with the Roman Catholic Church, in Austria and Czechoslovakia.

Colonel Berzinec, an Army Ranger, was an honor graduate of Kent State University where he was both President of the Senior Council and Colonel of the R.O.T.C.

While commanding the 4th Battalion, 39th Infantry, 9th Division, he was fatally wounded by fragments from an enemy booby trap, while on combat patrol. Just twenty-nine days into his second tour of duty in Vietnam, he was killed on July 30, 1968. He had volunteered to return because, he said, he preferred to fight the enemy in Vietnam, rather than on American soil.

The sad duty of celebrating a Mass of Requiem for the colonel fell on his father, the Rev. George Berzinec, retired pastor of St. Nicholas Byzantine Catholic Church, Roebling, New Jersey. Father Berzinec himself had served in the Office of Strategic Services and, later, as a chaplain in World War II.

A Requiem Mass was celebrated according to the Byzantine rite for Lieutenant Colonel William E. Berzinec by his father who had been both chaplain and soldier in World War II.

Washington Post Photo

He felt that his son who had earned two Silver Stars, a Bronze Star and other decorations for bravery—all posthumously—was simply carrying on the family tradition of service to God and country.

Another soldier who, having had experience with the Communists in the Korean War, volunteered to go to Vietnam, was Staff Sergeant Arthur N. McMellon of Hamlin, West Virginia.

Sergeant McMellon was the youngest of five brothers to participate in the Korean War—and their mother was a widow. When the Red Chinese swarmed across the Yalu, the sergeant was captured, after being gravely wounded. But he managed to escape and return to duty. His wounds, however, precluded any more combat and he became a mess sergeant.

Out of the Army for a brief period, Sergeant McMellon reenlisted and became "the best mess sergeant in the whole Army," his men claimed.

Finally he went to Vietnam. His unit of the Big Red One (First Division) was stationed in an area where there had not been much pro-American feeling, thanks to the Vietcong. But when Sergeant McMellon arrived, he won over the people of Ben Cat, 35 miles from Saigon—especially the children for whom he gave a more-than-successful Thanksgiving party. In fact his success was disturbing the Vietcong. He was getting the people to rally against terrorists and guerillas. He was giving them courage to fight.

In December of 1965 when he was enroute to the village to help arrange a Christmas party, his jeep ran over a Vietcong-planted mine. He died instantly, and Ben Cat went into mourning.

Sergeant McMellon's body now rests at Arlington—but at Ben Cat there is another memorial raised by his comrades who knew what he had done. It is an orphanage for 200 children and the sign reads: "The Arthur N. McMellon Orphanage."

Sergeant Keith A. Campbell was 20 years old and had been in the Army for nearly three years, part of that time as a member of the Green Berets. Before Vietnam he had earned the Bronze Star for bravery in the Dominican Republic. He also had twelve other awards and decorations. Including the Distinguished Service Cross and another Bronze Star for Valor, he was awarded five decorations in the nineteen days he lived in Vietnam.

His death was typical of the man. He was a medic with the 503rd Parachute Regiment, 173rd Airborne Brigade, and he saw a wounded soldier lying in an exposed position without any protection. Disregarding the hail of bullets Sergeant Campbell ran to the soldier and dragged him back to the shelter of a tree where he administered first aid. The tree protected his patient, but it was too small to shield Campbell as well and he fell fatally wounded. "Greater love hath no man than this. . . ."

Today Sergeant Campbell rests in Arlington, not far from where he lived and went to school. Each Christmas his young sister, Judy, places a small fir tree on his grave. It is decorated with a very special chain which Judy and her brother had started to make before he left for Vietnam and which she has kept up ever since.

The manner of Sergeant Campbell's dying and the way in which he lived has caused the George Washington Chapter, Association of the United States

Sergeant Keith Campbell, aged 20.

Judy Campbell of Arlington, Virginia, places a decorated Christmas tree on her brother's grave.

Army, to name a memorial plaque in his honor. It is presented annually to the outstanding Green Beret enlisted reservist in the Washington area. The George Washington Chapter, to which Sergeant Campbell belonged, is composed of more than 4,000 members, including many of the Army's highest ranking generals.

An inheritance of valor is that of West Point Cadet Joseph E. Muir II, for, besides his father's name, he inherited a tradition of great courage, command performance and of faith in his country.

Marine Lieutenant Colonel Joseph E. Muir, a native of Oak Hill, Virginia, and a graduate of the University of Maryland, enlisted as a private in 1945. Twenty years later on September 11, 1965, he was killed by a land mine near Danang, Vietnam, while commanding the 3rd Battalion of the 3rd Marines.

The Medals he earned in Vietnam—the Navy Cross for "fearlessly exposing himself to intense enemy fire while leading his battalion against insurgent forces and repeatedly positioning himself in the midst of the violent action," the Legion of Merit and two Bronze Stars, each with "V" for Valor— were presented personally to the then 18-year-old Cadet Muir by General Leonard F. Chapman, Commandant of the Marine Corps, on October 5, 1966.

To the young West Point Cadet, and to his mother and four brothers and sisters as well, the loss was still greater than the tradition.

In the last two decades the helicopter has become indispensible. It is used to transport troops, equipment and supplies, for medical evacuation and rescue work. A helicopter also enables a commanding officer to be right on top of his troops and to anticipate their needs in battle.

Cadet Muir with his mother and General Chalsman, Commandant of the Marine Corps.

All three uses were being made of helicopters on Easter Sunday in 1967 in the Mekong Delta. Troops were about to be landed; a medical evac plane was in position, should anything go wrong, and at the controls of a third chopper was Colonel Jack Dempsey, commander of the unit.

Then the Vietcong opened fire from ambush. The transport helicopter was shot down. The medical evac chopper that instantly went to give aid was shot down. Colonel Dempsey located the Communists, strongly entrenched behind a bunker. He called for air coverage and said he was going in.

Ordered to wait until the air coverage arrived, he obeyed—but the air cover could not stop the fire and calling for more coverage he radioed to the other ships: "I'm going down there after my men." But five feet above the ground a bullet found its mark and he was killed.

Colonel Dempsey, originally from Fort Smith, Oklahoma, had been listed for promotion to brigadier-general. He held the Distinguished Flying Cross, the Silver Star, 31 Air Medals and other awards. Now he was awarded—posthumously—the Distinguished Service Cross.

The citation read in part: "His unimpeachable valor and profound concern for the welfare of others will serve as a constant source of inspiration to all those who knew him . . . and is in the highest traditions of the military service."

On the 23rd of July, 1968, Air Force Major General Robert F. Worley set out in an unarmed two-seater reconnaissance plane for a routine flight over the demilitarized zone, to be sure there were no signs of Vietcong activity.

One characteristic of General Worley that stood out in all his service as an officer was that he always insisted on seeing for himself what was going on.

Major General Robert F. Worley, U.S.A.F.

**U.S. Air Force Photograph**

Captain James A. Graham, U.S.M.C., who was awarded the Medal of Honor for bravery above and beyond the call of duty.

**U.S. Marine Corps Photograph**

He found the Vietcong—literally speaking, Vietnamese Communists—or rather they found him. A burst of gunfire from the ground brought down his plane killing both the general and his pilot.

In his forty-nine years the General, who was born in Riverside, California, had had an eventful life. He graduated from pilot training in May, 1941, and flew in World War II, participating in the North African, Italian and Asiatic-Pacific campaigns with 120 serial missions. Just prior to his going to Vietnam he served as Deputy Chief of Staff for Operations, Headquarters, Tactical Air Command.

At the time of his death General Worley was serving as Vice Commander of the Seventh Air Force. It was for the way he carried out this task and for the marked ability he showed that he was awarded, posthumously, the Distinguished Service Medal.

The first Medal of Honor recipient from Vietnam to be buried in Arlington was a Marine, Captain James A. Graham, of Forrestville, Maryland. He was the seventeenth Marine to receive the nation's highest honor, and it was awarded to him posthumously.

Captain Graham was killed in action on June 2, 1967, while commanding Company F, 2nd Battalion, 5th Marine Regiment, 1st Marine Division, during Operation Union 11 near Quang Tin, Vietnam. His unit was leading a battalion assault across a paddy area when it came under heavy machine gun, mortar and rifle fire. The second platoon, hit hardest, was pinned down in the open by fire from two machine guns.

Captain Graham formed an assault unit from his small company headquarters, and, according to the citation, "boldly led a fierce assault . . . forcing the enemy to abandon the first machine gun position, thereby relieving the pressure on the second platoon and enabling evacuation of the wounded to a more secure area."

Although the second machine gun continued its devastating fire, the small group held its position, Captain Graham suffering two wounds.

The citation continues: ". . . with their supply of ammunition exhausted, Captain Graham ordered those remaining in the small force to withdraw to friendly lines; and although knowing that he had no chance of survival, he chose to remain with one man who could not be moved due to the seriousness of his wounds."

The last radio transmission received from Captain Graham reported that he was being attacked by a force of about twenty-five enemy. His actions were surely "above and beyond the call of duty"—but in keeping with the traditions of the Marine Corps.

One of the youngest men to receive the nation's highest award for valor, 18-year-old Marine Corporal Larry E. Smedley of Berryville, Va., was the second Marine posthumous recipient of the Medal of Honor to be buried at Arlington.

Joining the Marines when he was 17, the young corporal was a squad leader with the 7th Marines, First Marine Division, near Da Nang on the evening of December 20, 1967. While leading a six man patrol he spotted a large enemy force with 122mm rocket launchers and mortars. He immediately recognized this hostile force as a prelude to an attack on Da Nang.

Radioing for reinforcements, Smedley immediately led his small patrol in an attack on the enemy unit nearly 20 times its size. The suddeness and fury of the attack threw the enemy off balance, but a grenade seriously wounded Smedley. Undaunted, he led another charge on the Communist position, when he was again wounded.

Although weak from loss of blood, Smedley then launched a one-man assault on an enemy machine gun position. He silenced the gun—and died at the age of 18. His heroic actions gained time for a Marine reaction force to arrive and end the enemy threat to Da Nang.

Lieutenant Colonel Levi P. Howard, Jr., one of the Army's finest Infantry leaders, rests today in Arlington close to his father who was an Infantry corporal in World War I.

The colonel was killed in action on August 19, 1969, near Da Nang when his command helicopter was shot down. At the time he was directing units of his command, the 3rd Battalion, 21st Infantry Regiment, 196th Light Infantry Brigade, which had come under intense enemy fire.

Part of the citation for the Distinguished Flying Cross conferred on him posthumously read: "Colonel Howard, at the cost of his own life, pinpointed the well camouflaged and reinforced North Vietnam force so that air strikes might effectively destroy the enemy position."

During his two tours of duty in Vietnam Colonel Howard also earned three Bronze Stars for valor, three Air Medals and other decorations. For outstanding staff work at the Pentagon before going to Vietnam he was awarded the Legion of Merit.

Colonel Howard was born in Chicago and was a star athlete at Morgan State College and a graduate of its R.O.T.C. His funeral Mass at Fort Myer Chapel was attended by hundreds of military friends, from generals to privates, and many civilians. They came to honor a gallant soldier who had left to them and to his widow and five children an imperishable tradition of service to country.

Corporal Larry E. Smedley, U.S.M.C.

Lieutenant Colonel Levi P. Howard, U.S.A.

## FIRE AT SEA

In the days of the wooden sailing ships, fire at sea was the greatest dread of all seamen. Today, despite our modern fire fighting equipment, it continues to be a tremendous hazard because of the amount of gasoline, oil and explosives carried aboard.

Such a tragedy befell the giant 76,000 ton aircraft carrier, the USS *Forrestal*, off the coast of Vietnam on July 29, 1967. The exhaust from a jet accidently touched off a missile on another plane; the missile exploded into a tank of high-test gasoline and within seconds the flight deck of one of the mightiest ships in the world was a raging holocaust.

Despite incredible heroism on the part of the crew—heroism in keeping with the traditions of the U. S. Navy—134 men died. The fire was sudden and the shock great. No one knows how many men who died on the *Forrestal* gave their lives for others.

About two score of the *Forrestal's* dead now rest in Arlington—eighteen of these under a memorial stone in front of the Amphitheater.

The same type of valor in which a man thinks first of others was evidenced in another fire at sea—also during Vietnam operations—which cost the lives of 44 officers and crewmen on another carrier, the *Oriskany*, on October 25, 1965. Some of these also are buried at Arlington.

Naval experts agree that the loss of life in both disasters would have been very much higher had it not been for the gallant courage and self-sacrifice of those who thought of self last.

## THE ASTRONAUTS

Those who cross the frontiers of oceans, mountains, land and air take their lives in their hands. It is not so much the thought of reward that drives them on as it is the insatiable desire of bold men to find out what lies beyond.

Such a breed of men, too, are the Astronauts. The nation mourned when, on January 27, 1967, Lieutenant Colonel Virgil I. Grissom, U. S. Air Force, Lieutenant Commander Roger B. Chaffee, U. S. Navy, and Lieutenant Colonel Edward H. White, 2nd, U. S. Air Force, (the man who walked in space) were killed.

White was buried above the Hudson at West Point. Grissom and Chaffee joined four other Astronauts at Arlington—equally brave and dedicated men, who had died in plane crashes not connected with their space duties.

Commander Elliot M. See, U. S. Naval Reserve, and Major Charles A. Bassett, U. S. Air Force, were killed instantly when their plane crashed at Lambert Airport, Saint Louis, Missouri, on February 28, 1966. Captain

Theodore C. Freeman, U. S. Air Force, died at Elmsdorf Air Force Base, Alaska, on October 31, 1964, when his jet crashed. Major Clifton C. Williams, U. S. Marine Corps, was lost in a plane crash near Tallahassee, Florida, on October 5, 1967.

These men did not die in war. But they died as surely for their country as they had lived for it.

President Johnson is presenting the flag to Mrs. Grissom. The President also attended the Chaffee funeral and performed the same rite.

UPI

## CHAPLAINS

Those who carry the Christian Cross or the Star of David as their insignia are weaponless. Yet they do not stay behind the lines when there is a battle. Their task is to sustain the living, comfort the wounded, anoint the dead. Their field of action is where the fighting is fiercest—and enemy bullets do not respect the insignias that set them apart. Of the 10 chaplains killed in action in Vietnam three have come home to rest in Arlington.

Chaplain (Major) Ambrosio Salazar Grandea was born in Corregidor, the Philippines, in 1912. He came to the United States with his parents and upon graduating from the Boston University School of Theology, he was ordained a Methodist minister in 1959, two years after becoming a United States citizen. He entered the Army chaplaincy as a lieutenant in 1960—and was a major at his death.

He was conducting services in a field at Chu Lai, Vietnam, on June 4, 1967, when he was critically wounded by Communist mortar fire, and died

Field service conducted by Chaplain Grandea. Born in Corregidor, educated in the United States, killed in Vietnam.

Chaplain (Major) Charles J. Watters, U.S.A.

a few days later. At the time of his death he was serving with the 3rd Brigade, 25th Infantry Division.

Chaplain Grandea was awarded a Silver Star posthumously for an action which occurred several weeks before his death. According to the citation, he left a relatively safe position during a battle, crawled to several wounded soldiers to administer first aid, shouted words of encouragement to other Americans repelling the enemy attack, and "inspired the men to fight with renewed vigor and determination." His "courageous actions were in large part responsible for the defeat of the enemy," the citation adds. But, then, the chaplain was only doing his duty.

Half a world away from the Philippines, Chaplain (Captain) William Newcomb Feaster was born in Portland, Maine. He graduated from Harvard and its Divinity School, and then was ordained a minister of the United Church of Christ in 1963. Two years later he joined the Army Chaplains Corps and was assigned to the 196th Light Infantry Brigade in Vietnam. He sustained wounds which eventually proved fatal on October 26, 1966.

Chaplain Feaster's wife also serves her country. She was an Army nurse in Korea when she was informed her husband had been critically wounded. Flown to Saigon to be with the chaplain she nursed him until he died. After his death she volunteered for duty in Vietnam and carried on their joint tradition of service.

Chaplain (Major) Charles Joseph Watters came from Jersey City, New Jersey, attended Seton Hall University and studied for the Catholic priesthood at Immaculate Conception Seminary, Darlington, New Jersey. Ordained in 1953, he did parish work in Northern New Jersey before being appointed an Army chaplain in 1965.

After a year's tour of duty in Vietnam, Chaplain Watters volunteered for an extension. He was reassigned to the 503rd Parachute Regiment, 173rd

Airborne Brigade. When his regiment assaulted Hill 875, a heavily fortified Communist position near Dak To, in one of the fiercest battles of the war in November 1967, the chaplain insisted on going with the advance units. Fearlessly and repeatedly, he risked his life to assist the wounded and dying, carrying many of them to less exposed positions. Like Chaplain Grandea, his inspiring example helped encourage his comrades to take the hill against heavy odds.

Chaplain Watters was killed by a bomb explosion on November 19, 1967. His heroism was so extraordinary throughout the four-day battle that he has been awarded the Medal of Honor.

### ROBERT F. KENNEDY

The first chapter of this book dealt with the death of a President of the United States by an assassin's bullet. John F. Kennedy had earned his resting place at Arlington not just in public office as Commander in Chief of the United States Armed Forces, but as an officer in the United States Navy on combat duty in World War II.

And now the book ends with the story of the President's brother, who also met his death by an assassin's bullet.

Robert F. Kennedy, United States Senator, presidential aspirant, and former cabinet member, was also a Navy veteran; he had served as a seaman in the United States Navy from 1945 to 1948 while still in his teens.

In adjoining gravesites the Kennedy brothers are at rest in Arlington.

Robert Kennedy's grave adjoins the burial site of his brother, the late President. The hedge in the background separates the two plots.

**U.S. Army Photograph**

Robert F. Kennedy was the first to be buried there at night. No special privilege had been asked. The burial was to take place in the late afternoon, but circumstances beyond anyone's control changed the whole schedule.

As he represented the State of New York it was only proper and right that his funeral should be held in that state—at Saint Patrick's Cathedral. The stately cathedral and the surrounding streets were jammed with mourners. Transferring the thousand friends who were to go to Washington with the casket to the railroad station took more time than expected. The funeral train was late in starting—very late, and all schedules had to be changed.

Along the tracks for the 220 miles between New York and Washington, people stood. There were throngs at every station. Each delay meant that other trains had to go forward first.

Gradually the shadows deepened. There seemed no lessening of the crowds in Washington who wanted to attend the burial.

Arlington Cemetery is not equipped for a night funeral but its staff responded nobly. And by flickering lights the burial took place. The people were massed on the gently sloping hills surrounding the grave site. Many of them joined in the hymns played by a military band. They had waited patiently, for hours.

The widow and her children, who had spent the long journey down to Washington trying to thank the friends who accompanied them, held up magnificently. It was a farewell to the father of a family and a beloved husband; no one who witnessed it will forget.

President John F. Kennedy had belonged to the Nation. In those last hours, Robert Kennedy belonged to his wife and children.

Ethel Kennedy, with her brother-in-law, Senator Edward Kennedy, and eight of her children clustered around her, stands bravely during the funeral of her husband in Arlington—the only night funeral ever held there.

**Washington Post Photo**

Arlington . . . monument to heroes. The Confederate Memorial at sunset.

Patrick Hughes

"Unknown—except to God."
The Tomb of the Unknown Soldier.

Patrick Hughes

"Home is the sailor, home from the sea."
The emblem on the Main Gate.

Patrick Hughes

"The golden evening brightens in the west;
Soon, soon to faithful warriors cometh rest."
A hillside at Arlington.

Patrick Hughes

"Angels of Mercy, Angels of Light." Detail from a tomb at Arlington.

Patrick Hughes

"I am the Resurrection and the Life . . ."
Arlington in springtime.

Patrick Hughes

". . . he who believes in Me shall never die!"
Canadian Memorial Cross.

Patrick Hughes

"Weeping may endure for a night, but joy cometh in the morning."
Detail from a tomb at Arlington.

Patrick Hughes

# APPENDIX I

# A FUNERAL AT ARLINGTON

REGARDLESS OF RANK, EVERY SERVICEMAN OR VETERAN BURIED AT Arlington is given an inspiring funeral service of great dignity. Catholic, Protestant or Jewish chaplains are available to conduct services, or a civilian clergyman may be invited to officiate. If a church service is desired by the family, arrangement can be made for the use of the Fort Myer Chapel, just outside the Fort Myer Gate. This little gem of architecture is in complete harmony with the classic lines of the nearby Custis-Lee Mansion and the architectural plan of Arlington Cemetery.

### HONORS

Honors befitting the status of the deceased are rendered by his own branch of the service. Simple honors include a burial party to carry the casket draped in the United States Flag, a firing party to fire the traditional three volley salute, and a bugler to sound "Taps."

Full honors for a commissioned officer include a military band. The casket may be mounted on a black artillery caisson drawn by seven perfectly matched black or grey horses—the last horses on active service in the United States Army.

Officers with the rank of Colonel or above, or who during their service had been mounted, are entitled to a caparisoned horse, which is led riderless behind the caisson with boots reversed in the stirrups. This is a custom dating from the days of Medieval chivalry as a symbol of the fallen warrior.

An eleven- to seventeen-cannon salute is accorded a General or flag officer or high-ranking Government official at the grave site. The rifle and cannon salutes had their origin on the battlefields of many years ago when it was the custom of opposing armies to declare a truce to bury the dead.

### "TAPS"

The hauntingly beautiful bugle call of "Taps" means a great deal to those who heard them at the end of each day in service both in this country and overseas. The notes pour out in a last farewell to the deceased after the rifles or cannon render their salutes.

It was a Union General, Daniel Butterfield, who wrote the music of

"Taps" during the Peninsular Campaign in place of the abrupt bugle call: "Extinguish lights!" But before the War Between the States was over the Confederates had adopted the call they had heard sounded over the Union lines at night.

## THE FLAG

With the sounding of "Taps," the burial party reverently folds the flag from the casket in a triangular shape, and it is handed to the Cemetery Superintendent or his representative, who presents it to the next of kin. This has been the custom in the United States Armed Forces since World War I.

## WHO CAN BE BURIED AT ARLINGTON?

Burial in Arlington National Cemetery, as in all national cemeteries, is a privilege and not a right. Until February 17, 1967, an estimated 41,000,000 Americans could be interred at Arlington.

Since then, however, because of the acute shortage of available space, burials at Arlington have been restricted to certain categories of eligibles. These comprise holders of the Medal of Honor; servicemen and women who die on active duty; members of the Armed Forces who have served long enough for full retirement, and veterans who have sat on the United States Supreme Court, in the Cabinet, in Congress or who have held other United States Government offices of great responsibility. Widows, widowers and dependent children of the above, and of those already buried there, are also eligible. The growing shortages of grave sites forced the Army in 1961 to limit each family to one grave.

From twelve to fifteen persons or more are buried at Arlington daily, Monday through Friday, except holidays. Total count as of May 1, 1969, was approximately 149,800 persons, including more than 5,000 unknowns.

The Army, in October 1966, announced a long-range master development program for Arlington National Cemetery. Under this program, which is now underway, facilities at Fort Myer, South Post—to the east toward the Potomac River—are gradually being phased out and all of the 202 acres now occupied by South Post eventually will be developed to expand the present Cemetery.

This acreage was part of the original 1,100 acres bought by John Parke Custis around 1780 on the advice of his stepfather, George Washington. When fully developed and landscaped, the new section, some parts of which are already in use as burial areas, will provide about 60,000 additional grave sites. It is estimated that by the year 1985, however, even this section will be completely filled, together with the older part of the Cemetery.

The Army's new long-range development program for Arlington seeks also to "preserve the essential qualities of the Cemetery from the impact of visiting tourists," according to its principal designer, Francis D. Lethbridge, consulting architect on the project. Well over 5,000,000 tourists now visit Arlington each year, and the number is expected to grow.

Other features of the new section include provisions for a large, two-level underground visitors' garage, 18 acres in area, and designed to accommodate 1,100 private automobiles and 80 buses; an underground visitors' center beneath the Arlington Memorial gates; a new chapel overlooking a five-acre artificial lagoon which, in turn, will adjoin a special 15-acre site to be set aside for recipients of the Medal of Honor and other distinguished members of the United States Armed Forces. The 160-foot square chapel is to be built in the new section in line with the Tomb of the Unknown Soldier and the Arlington Amphitheatre.

Tens of thousands of Arlington's honored dead rest under regulation United States Government headstones. Each headstone is of white marble and is 13 inches wide, four inches thick and 42 inches high—of which 24 inches are above ground. The name, rank, home state, unit, branch of service and decoration of the deceased serviceman or woman are carved on the stone. There are also many private markers, especially in the older sections of the Cemetery.

As at any national cemetery, there is no charge of any kind for burial at Arlington, for the officiating chaplains, for the use of Fort Myer Chapel for services, for opening the grave, or for the Government headstone.

Arlington National Cemetery is one of the eighty-five national cemeteries administered by the Office of Support Services, Department of the Army, and is under the immediate supervision of the Commanding General, Military District of Washington. It is in the charge of a resident superintendent.

The cemetery is open to visitors every day of the year during the following hours:

October 1 through March 31——8 A.M. to 5 P.M.
April 1 through September 30——8 A.M. to 7 P.M.

On gray days or sunny a funeral at Arlington is a dignified gesture of respect to the honored dead.

**U.S. Army Photograph**

# APPENDIX II

# FORT MYER–

# GUARDIAN OF ARLINGTON

FROM THE TIME ARLINGTON BECAME A CEMETERY—A CENTURY AND more ago—Fort Myer, which surrounds it on three sides, has stood guard.

Created in 1863 out of part of the original Arlington Estate, the fort is garrisoned today by the crack 1st Battalion (Reinf.), 3rd United States Infantry (Old Guard). This regiment, founded in 1784, is the oldest Infantry unit on active service. It has thirty-nine battle streamers from six wars, and its officers and enlisted men are among the best in the Army.

Originally called Fort Whipple in honor of Major General Amiel W. Whipple, who died of wounds after the Battle of Chancellorsville, Virginia, Fort Myer was established as one of the principal defenses of Washington from Confederate attack. In 1869 it became the Signal School. Its commander, until his death in 1880, was the brilliant Brigadier General Albert J. Myer, for whom the fort was named in 1881. General Myer was the Army's first Chief Signal Officer and created the Signal Corps and the United States Weather Bureau.

From 1887 until 1942 Fort Myer was, perhaps, the most famous cavalry post of that era, largely because of the thrilling riding exhibitions that brought thousands of enthusiastic spectators there. Among its commanders were the future Generals Charles P. Summerall, Jonathan M. Wainwright and George S. Patton, Jr.

Fort Myer has been the home of the Army Chief of Staff since the early years of this century. Many other top-ranking Army and Air Force Generals live on the post, which also is the headquarters for the famous United States Army Band, founded in 1922 by direct order of General Pershing, and the well-known United States Army Chorus. Composed of the finest musicians and singers, both appear at top-level military and state functions and are rated among the best in the world.

## THE OLD GUARD

Besides its primary mission of defending Washington, the 3rd Infantry, which took over that responsibility in 1948, has other unique duties. It provides the Army's official ceremonial troops to receive foreign dignitaries visiting the White House, and also participates in parades and other important events in the area. Details from the 3rd officiate at wreathe-laying ceremonies at the Tomb of the Unknown Soldier and in all military funerals at Arlington.

The singular distinction of providing the twenty-four-hour guard every day of the year at the Tomb of the Unknown Soldier falls on the Honor Guard Company—all picked men—of the 3rd Infantry. The guard is changed every hour on the hour in an inspiring ceremony that has been witnessed by millions of visitors to that hallowed place.

Visitors also are welcome at the Sunday afternoon formal reviews and other stirring military ceremonies put on by the 3rd at Fort Myer. The unit always parades with fixed bayonets, a recognition by the Army of the regiment's valor at the Battle of Chapultepec, Mexico, fought in 1847, when the 3rd led the bayonet charge that won the day.

Like Arlington National Cemetery—Fort Myer, the 3rd Infantry, and the United States Army Band and Chorus are under the immediate command of the Military District of Washington—guardian of the nation's capital.

The Fife and Drum Corps, part of the Army Ceremonial Unit, 1st Battalion, 3rd Infantry, leads the Inaugural Parade of President Richard M. Nixon on January 20, 1969. The uniforms are exact replicas of those worn by the Fife and Drum Corps that served under General George Washington in the Continental Army.

# APPENDIX III

# "ABOVE AND BEYOND

# THE CALL OF DUTY..."

THE MEDAL OF HONOR IS THE HIGHEST AWARD FOR HEROISM IN military action that this nation can bestow upon a member of its Armed Forces. There are more Medal of Honor recipients buried at Arlington (245 as of October 1, 1969) than in any other of our national cemeteries.

It was in 1862 that the Medal of Honor was first decreed by Congress. There had been a badge of Military Merit in the days of the Revolution, but with the end of that war it passed into history.

When the War Between the States got into full swing, Lincoln felt something must be done to show the nation's appreciation of exceptional bravery on the battlefield. Brevet ranks—or temporary promotions—had been tried, but they were awarded too often through political influence. Some other recognition must be devised—something above politics and really outstanding.

While the discussion continued, one General acted on his own. Major General David Birney, who had succeeded the much loved Philip Kearny whose equestrian statue rides so boldly on the greensward at Arlington, had an idea. From it, the Medal of Honor developed.

Kearny had given his men the "Kearny patch" to distinguish the Third Division. They were as proud of it as Patton's men were of another "Third" —eighty years later. But, after Kearny's death, his men wanted more—a medal to show that they had "fought with Kearny." General Birney thought it over. Kearny had demanded, expected and received the highest devotion to duty from his men. So Birney created the "Kearny Cross"—the "Cross of Valor" as it was called—to be presented to such non-commissioned officers and privates as "had distinguished themselves in battle."

The idea took hold of the public imagination and was adopted—but extended to all ranks. Why discriminate against officers?

The Navy Medal of Honor was the first enacted by Congress; then the Army's. Now the award is open to all services.

The Navy's was easily controlled, probably because deeds of heroism are more apt to be witnessed on the sea than in land fighting. By the time the dashing War Between the States Army heroes had become grizzled Indian fighters, a need was felt for more strict regulations for the award of the Medal of Honor by the Army. A Board of Review, comprised of General Alfred H. Terry, General Philip Sheridan and Colonel Samuel D. Sturgis, was appointed to set up the most rigid standards for the award of the Medal of Honor. The last two, incidentally, are buried at Arlington.

The new regulations drawn up by this Board called for a deed of extraordinary heroism to be certified by two eyewitnesses; to be clearly beyond the call of duty; to involve the risk of life; and to be the type of deed that would not bring criticism if not performed.

In short, the Medal of Honor is not given for strict performance of assigned duty—that is to be expected of any man who serves his country, no matter in what capacity. It is given for gallantry above and beyond the call of duty. In many, if not most of these cases, the deed is done to benefit others, which, after all, is the true heroism. For that reason many Medals of Honor, at least in the wars of this century, have been awarded posthumously, usually because the recipient's heroic action cost his life.

Two recipients of the nation's highest award for valor who are buried at Arlington had the unique distinction of being awarded two Medals of Honor.

One is Army Captain Frank D. Baldwin, Constantine, Michigan, who received his first Medal of Honor for heroic actions at the Battle of Peach Tree Creek, Georgia, on July 20, 1864, during the Civil War, and his second at McClellan's Creek, Texas, fighting against a greatly superior force of Indians.

The other is Chief Boatswain's Mate John McCloy, USN, Brewster, N.Y., awarded his first Medal of Honor for repeated acts of heroism with the China Relief Expedition (Boxer Rebellion) on June 13, 20, 21, and 22, 1900, and his second during the landing at Vera Cruz, Mexico, on April 22, 1914.

ARMY
1862

NAVY

The list of Medal of Honor recipients now resting at Arlington as of October 1, 1969, with their units and birthplaces, follows:

## CIVIL WAR (1861–1865)

Pvt. Robert W. Ammerman, Co. B, 148th Pa. Inf.; Center County, Pa.

Capt. Marion T. Anderson, Co. D, 51st Indiana Inf.; Decatur County, Ind.

Brig. Gen. Absalom Baird, U.S. Vols.; Washington, Pa.

Capt. Frank D. Baldwin, Co. D, 19th Mich. Inf.; Constantine, Mich. (Note: Also awarded a second Medal of Honor fighting Indians at McClellan's Creek, Texas, in 1874)

Lieut. Col. Richard N. Batchelder, Chief Quartermaster, 2nd Corps; Manchester, N.H.

Sgt. Horatio L. Birdsall, Co. B, 3rd Iowa Cav.; Butler County, Ohio

Colonel Zenas R. Bliss, 7th R.I. Inf.; R.I.

2nd Lieut. Peter M. Boehm, Co. K, 15th N.Y. Cav.; Brooklyn, N.Y.

Pvt. John G. Bourke, Co. E, 15th Pa. Cav.; Philadelphia, Pa.

Pvt. John W. Boutwell, Co. B, 18th N.H. Inf; Hanover, N.H.

Lieut. Col. Henry V. Boynton, 35th Ohio Inf.; Ohio

Pvt. James Brady, Co. F, 10th N.H. Inf.; Boston Mass.

Pvt. Felix Brannigan, Co. A, 74th N.Y. Infantry; Ireland

Cpl. Edward Brown, Jr., Co. G, 62nd N.Y. Inf.; New York, N.Y.

Capt. John H. Brown, Co. D, 12th Ky. Inf.; unknown

1st Lieut. David E. Buckingham, Co. E, 4th Del. Inf.; Del.

Maj. Charles E. Capehart, 1st W. Va. Cav.; unknown

Col. Henry Capehart, 1st W. Va. Cav.; unknown

Col. Isaac S. Catlin, 109th N.Y. Inf.; Oswego, N.Y.

1st Lieut. James I. Christiancy, Co. D, 9th Mich. Cav.; unknown

Bugler John Cook, Bat. B, 4th U.S. Art.; Hamilton County, Ohio

Lieut. Col. John Coughlin, 10th N.H. Inf.; unknown

Capt. James M. Cutts, 11th U.S. Inf.; Washington, D.C.

1st Lieut. George E. Davis, Co. D, 10th Vt. Inf.; Dunstable, Mass.

Sgt. John C. Delaney, Co. I, 107th Pa. Inf.; Honesdale, Pa.

Seaman Bartholomew Diggins, USN; Baltimore, Md.

Pvt. Michael A. Dillon, Co. G, 2nd N.H. Inf.; Chelmsford, Mass.

2nd Lieut. James R. Durham, Co. E, 12th W. Va. Inf.; Clarksburg, W. Va.

Capt. Lewellin G. Estes, U.S. Vols.; Oldtown, Maine

Cpl. Isaac Gause, Troop K, 1st U.S. Cav.; Trumbull County, Ohio

1st Lieut. Thomas P. Gere, 5th Minn. Inf.; Chemung County, N.Y.

Maj. John C. Gilmore, 16th N.Y. Inf.; New York, N.Y.

Sgt. Peter Grace, Co. G, 83rd Pa. Inf.; Berkshire, Mass.

Sgt. James H. Harris, Co. B, 38th U.S. Colored Troops; St. Mary's County, Md.

Col. Guy V. Henry, 40th Mass. Inf.; Fort Smith, Indian Territory

Capt. Charles H. Houghton, Co. L, 14th N.Y. Art.; Ogdensburg, N.Y.

Sgt. Maj. Milton M. Howard, 5th U.S. Colored Troops; Austin, Tex.

1st Lieut. Joseph E. Johnson, Co. A, 58th Pa. Inf.; Pa.
Capt. Thomas R. Kerr, Co. C, 114th Pa. Inf.; Pittsburgh, Pa.
Maj. Dennis T. Kirby, 8th Missouri Inf.; St. Louis, Mo.
1st Sgt. Gaines Lawson, Co. D, 4th East Tenn. Inf.; Hawkins County, Tenn.
Capt. Henry W. Lawton, Co. A, 30th Ind. Inf.; Ohio
Sgt. Edwin Leonard, Co. I, 37th Mass. Inf.; Agawan, Mass.
Pvt. Cyrus B. Lower, Co. K, 13th Pa. Reserves; Lawrence County, Pa.
Capt. William Ludgate, Co. G, 59th N.Y. Vet. Inf.; England
1st Lieut. Arthur MacArthur, Adjutant, 24th Wis. Inf.; Springfield, Mass.
Pvt. Patrick McGuire, Chicago Mercantile By., Ill. Light Inf.; Ireland
Capt. Martin T. McMahon, U.S. Vols.; unknown
Sgt. George Martin, Co. B, 6th U.S. Cav.; Germany
Lieut. Col. Henry C. Merriam, 73rd U.S. Colored Troops; Houlton, Maine
Col. Nelson A. Miles, 61st N.Y. Inf.; Westminister, Mass.
Pvt. Frank Miller, Co. M, 2nd N.Y. Cav.; Jamaica, N.Y.
Cpt. George W. Mindil, Co. I, 61st Pa. Inf.; Philadelphia, Pa.
1st Lieut. Alexander H. Mitchell, Co. A, 105th Pa. Inf.; Perrysville, Pa.
1st Lieut. Charles J. Murphy, Quartermaster, 38th N.Y. Inf.; New York, N.Y.
Musician Robinson B. Murphy, Co. A, 127th Ill. Inf.; Ill.
Sgt. Maj. George H. Plowman, 3rd Md. Inf.; England
2nd Lieut. James A. Purman, Co. A, 140th Pa. Inf.; unknown
Assistant Surgeon Jacob F. Raub, 210th Pa. Inf.; Weaversville, Pa.
Maj. Edmund Rice, 19th Mass. Inf.; Brighton, Mass.
Pvt. James Richmond, Co. F, 8th Ohio Inf.; Maine
Brig. Gen. Rufus Saxton, U.S. Vols.; Mass.
Maj. John M. Schofield, 1st Missouri Inf.; Mo.
Cpl. Alexander Scott, Co. D, 10th Vt. Inf.; Canada
Maj. Gen. Julius Stahel, U.S. Vols.; Hungary
Pvt. John T. Sterling, Co. D, 11th Indiana Inf.; Edgar County, Ill.
Lieut. Col. Wager Swayne, 43rd Ohio Inf.; Ohio
2nd Lieut. Walter Thorn, Co. G, 116th U.S. Colored Troops; New York, N.Y.
Pvt. Edwin M. Truell, Co. E, 12th Wisconsin Inf.; Lowell, Mass.
Pvt. M. Emmet Urell, Co. E, 82nd N.Y. Inf.; Ireland
Pvt. Wilson Vance, Co. B, 21st Ohio Inf.; Hancock County, Ohio
Col. Wheelock G. Veazey, 16th Vermont Inf.; Vt.
2nd Lieut. James D. Vernay, Co. B, 11th Illinois Inf.; Lacon, Ill.
1st Lieut. John Wainwright, Co. F, 97th Pa. Inf.; Onondaga County, N.Y.
Cpl. Francis E. Warren, Co. C, 49th Mass. Inf.; Mass.
Pvt. James Webb, Co. F, 5th N.Y. Inf.; Brooklyn, N.Y.
1st Lieut. Frank West, 6th U.S. Cav.; Mohawk, N.Y.
Maj. John F. Weston, 4th Kentucky Cav.; Ky.
Capt. Edward W. Whitaker, Co. E, 1st Conn. Cav.; Conn.
1st Lieut. H. Clay Wood, 1st U.S. Inf.; Winthrop, Maine

## INDIAN WARS (1869–1891)

1st Lieut. George E. Albee, 41st U.S. Inf.; Lisbon, N.H.

Captain Frank N. Baldwin, 5th U.S. Cav.; Constantine, Mich.

Pvt. 1st Class William C. Barnes, Signal Corps, U.S. Army; San Francisco, Cal.

1st Sgt. Sanford Bradbury, Co. L, 8th U.S. Inf.; Sussex County, N.J.

2nd Lieut. Lloyd M. Brett, 2nd U.S. Cav.; Maine

2nd Lieut. Robert G. Carter, 4th U.S. Cav.; Bridgeport, Me.

1st Lieut. William H. Carter, 6th U.S. Cav.; Nashville, Tenn.

2nd Lieut. Thomas Cruse, 6th U.S. Cav.; Owensboro, Ky.

Capt. Francis S. Dodge, Troop D, 9th U.S. Cav.; Danvers, Mass.

1st Lieut. Ernest A. Garlington, 7th U.S. Cav.; S.C.

Capt. Edward S. Godfrey, 7th U.S. Cav.; Ottawa, Ohio

2nd Lieut. Harry L. Hawthorne, 1st U.S. Art.; Minn.

2nd Lieut. Charles H. Heyl, 23rd U.S. Inf.; Philadelphia, Pa.

1st Lieut. Charles F. Humphrey, 4th U.S. Art.; New York, N.Y.

Sgt. Henry Johnson, Co. D, 9th U.S. Cav.; Boynton, Va.

Sgt. Patrick Martin, Co. G, 5th U.S. Cav.; Ireland

1st Lieut. Marion P. Maus, 1st U.S. Inf.; Burnt Mills, Md.

2nd Lieut. George H. Morgan, 3rd U.S. Cav.; Canada

Sgt. Fred Myers, Co. K, 6th U.S. Cav.; Germany

2nd Lieut. Edward J. McClernand, 2nd U.S. Cav.; Jacksonville, Ill.

1st Lieut. Henry Romeyn, 5th U.S. Inf.; Galen, N.Y.

Sgt. Thomas Shaw, Co. K, 8th U.S. Cav.; Covington, Ky.

Pvt. William H. Smith, Co. G, 1st U.S. Cav.; Lapeer County, Mich.

Surgeon Henry R. Tilton, USA; Barnegat, N.J.

Sgt. Michael Welch, Co. M, 6th U.S. Cav.; Poughkeepsie, N.Y.

Assistant Surgeon Leonard Wood, USA; Winchester, N.H.

## SPANISH AMERICAN WAR (1898)

Pvt. Dennis Bell, Troop H, 10th U.S. Cav.; Washington, D.C.

Pvt. George Berg, Co. C., 17th U.S. Inf.; unknown

Seaman Robert Blume, USN; Pittsburgh, Pa.

Blacksmith Joseph E. Carter, USN; England

Gunner's Mate George Charette, USN; unknown

Assistant Surgeon James Robb Church, 1st U.S.. Vol. Cav.; Chicago, Ill.

1st Lieut. Benjamin F. Hardaway, 17th U.S. Inf.; Benleyville, Ky.

Lieut. Richmond Pearson Hobson, USN; Greensboro, Ala.

Coopersmith Philip B. Keefer, USN; Washington, D.C.

Seaman Willard Miller, USN; Nova Scotia

2nd Lieut. Charles D. Roberts, 17th U.S. Inf.; Fort Russell, Wyo.

Pvt. George H. Wanton, Troop M, 10th U.S. Cav.; Paterson, N.J.

## CHINA RELIEF EXPEDITION (BOXER REBELLION–1900)

Capt. Andre W. Brewster, 9th U.S. Inf.; Hoboken, N.J.

Chief Boatswain's Mate Joseph Clancy, USN; unknown

Chief Carpenter's Mate William F. Hamburger, USN; Newark, N.J.

Seaman Hans A. Hansen, USN; Germany

Pvt. Clarence E. Mathias, USMC; Royalton, Pa.

Chief Boatswain's Mate John J. McCloy, USN; Brewster, N.Y. (Also won a second
    Medal of Honor at Vera Cruz, Mexico, in 1914)

Hospital Apprentice Robert Stanley, USN; unknown

Sgt. Clarence E. Sutton, USMC; Middlesex County, Va.

Gunner's Mate Third Class Martin T. Torgerson, USN; Norway

Pvt. Frank Albert Young, USMC; Milwaukee, Wis.

## PHILIPPINE INSURRECTION (1899–1909)

1st Lieut. Matthew A. Batson, 4th U.S. Cav.; Anna, Ill.

Col. J. Franklin Bell, 36th US. Vol. Inf.; Shelbyville, Ky.

Capt. William E. Berkheimer, 3rd U.S. Art.; Somerset, Ohio

Capt. Bernard A. Byrne, 6th U.S. Inf.; Newport Barracks, Va.

1st Lieut. Josephus S. Cecil, 19th U.S. Inf.; New River, Tenn.

Sgt. Clarence M. Condon, Bat. G, 3rd U.S. Art.; Brooksville, Maine

Pvt. Henry L. Hulbert, USMC; England

2nd Lieut. John T. Kennedy, 6th U.S. Cav.; Hendersonville, S.C.

1st Lieut. Charles E. Kilbourne, Signal Corps; Fort Myer, Va.

Capt. Hugh J. McGrath, 4th U.S. Cav.; Fond du Lac, Wis.

1st Lieut. Archie Miller, 6th U.S. Cav.; Fort Sheridan, Ill.

Captain David Dixon Porter, USMC; Washington, D.C.

Pvt. Peter H. Quinn, Co. L, 4th U.S. Cav.; San Francisco, Cal.

1st Lieut. George Clymer Shaw, 27th U.S. Inf.; Pontiac, Mich.

Coxswain William G. Thordsen, USN; Germany

## MEXICO (1911–1914)

Capt. Edwin A. Anderson, USN; N.C.

Ensign Oscar C. Badger, USN; Washington, D.C.

Lieut. Commander Allen Buchanan, USN; Ind.

Lieut. Guy W. S. Castle, USN; Wis.

Maj. Albertus W. Catlin, USMC; Gowanda, N.Y.

Lieut. (JG) George M. Courts, USN; Washington, D.C.

Coxswain George C. Cregan, USN; New York, N.Y.

Boatswain's Mate Percy A. Decker, USN; New York, N.Y.

Lieut. Niels Drustrup, USN; Denmark

Rear Adm. Frank Friday Fletcher, USN; Oskaloosa, La.

Capt. Julian E. Gaujot, Troop K, 1st U.S. Cav.; Keweenaw, Mich.

Lieut John Grady, USN; Canada

Boatswain's Mate, Joseph G. Harner, USN; Louisville, Ohio

Com. William Kelly Harrison, USN; Waco, Tex.

Lieut. Charles Conway Hartigan, USN; Middletown, N.Y.

Capt. Walter Newell Hill, USMC; Haverhill, Mass.

Capt. John A. Hughes, USMC; New York, N.Y.

Capt. Henry Huse, USN; West Point, N.Y.

Lieut. Jonas H. Ingram, USN; Jeffersonville, Ind.
Lieut. Commander Rufus Z. Johnston, USN; Lincolnton, N.C.
Com. Cary D. Langhorne, Medical Corps, USN; Lynchburg, Va.
Lieut. Commander James P. Lannon, USN; Alexandria, Va.
Chief Boatswain's Mate John J. McCloy, USN; Brewster, N.Y.
Ensign Edward O. McDonnell, USN; Baltimore, Md.
Lieut. Frederick V. McNair, USN; Md.
Com. William A. Moffett, USN; unknown
Lieut. Col. Wendell C. Neville, USMC; Portsmouth, Va.
Seaman Charles L. Nordsiek, USN; New York, N.Y.
Maj. George C. Reid, USMC; Lorain, Ohio
Seaman Fred J. Schnepel, USN; New York, N.Y.
Lieut. Commander Adolphus Staton, USN; N.C.
Com. Herman O. Stickney, USN; Pepperell, Mass.
Ensign Theodore S. Wilkinson Jr., USN; Annapolis, Md.

## HAITIAN CAMPAIGN (1915)

1st. Lieut. Edward A. Ostermann, USMC, 15th Co. of Marines; Columbus, O.

## WORLD WAR I (1917–1918)

1st Lieut. Deming Bronson, Co. H, 364th Inf., 91st Div.; Rhinelander, Wis.
Seaman Tedford H. Cann, USN; Bridgeport, Conn.
Sgt. Louis Cukela, USMC, 65th Co., Fifth Marines; Austria
Pvt. 1st Class George Dilboy, Co. H, 103rd Inf., 26th Div.; Greece
Lieut. Col. William J. Donovan, 165th Inf., 42nd Div.; Buffalo, N.Y.
Sgt. Michael B. Ellis, Co. C, 28th Inf., 1st Div.; St. Louis, Missouri
Lieut. Com. Alexander G. Lyle, Dental Corps, USN; Gloucester, Mass.
Cpl. John H. Pruitt, 78th Co., 6th Reg., USMC; Sadeville, Ark.
Lieut. Col. Fred E. Smith, 308th Inf., 77th Inf. Div.; Rockford, Ill.
Ensign Daniel A. J. Sullivan, USNR; Charleston, S.C.
Quartermaster Frank M. Upton, USN; Loveland, Colo.
1st Lieut. Samuel Woodfill, 60th Inf., 5th Div.; Bryansburg, Ind.

## WORLD WAR II (1941–1945)

Lieut. Richard N. Antrim, USN; Peru, Ind.
Sgt. John Basilone, 1st Bn., 7th Marines, 1st Marine Div.; Buffalo, N.Y.
Col. Merritt A. Edson, USMC; Rutland, Vt.
2nd Lieut. David R. Kingsley, 97th Bomb. Gr., 15th Air Force; Portland, Ore.
2nd Lieut. John C. Morgan, Army Air Corps; Tex.
Maj. Thomas B. McGuire Jr., 13th Air Force; Ridgewood, N.J.
Lieut. Jackson C. Pharris, USN, USS California; Columbus, Ohio
Lieut. Arthur M. Preston, USNR, Torpedo Boat Squadron 33; Washington, D.C.
Capt. Robert E. Roeder, Co. G., 350th Inf., 88th Div.; Summit Station, Pa.
Machinist's Mate 1st Class Robert R. Scott, USN, USS California; Massillon, Ohio
1st Lieut. Edward A. Silk, Co. E, 398th Inf., 100th Inf. Div.; Johnstown, Pa.

Gen. Jonathan M. Wainwright, USA; Walla Walla, Wash.

Gunnery Sgt. William G. Walsh, USMCR, Co. G, 3rd Bn., 27th Marines, 5th
  Marine Div.; Roxbury, Mass.

Lieut. Col. Keith L. Ware, USA, 1st Battalion, 15th Inf., 3rd Inf. Div.; Denver,
  Colorado

Sgt. Hulon B. Whittington, 41st Armored Inf., 2nd Armored Div.; Bogalusa. La.

2nd Lieut. Thomas W. Wigle, 135th Inf., 34th Inf. Div.; Indianapolis, Ind.

## KOREAN WAR (1950–1953)

Cpl. John W. Collier, Co. C, 27 Inf. Regt.; Worthington, Ky.

Lieut. Col. Don C. Faith, Jr., 1st Bn., 32nd Inf., 7th Inf. Div.; Washington, D.C.

Hospitalman Francis C. Hammond, USN; Alexandria, Va.

Lieut. John M. Koelsch, USN, USS *Princeton;* England

Sgt. George D. Libby, Co. C, 3rd Eng. Combat Bn.; Bridgeton, Maine

Sgt. Frederick W. Mausert, III, USMC, Co. B, 1st Bn., 7th Marines, 1st Marine
  Div.; Cambridge, N.Y.

1st Lieut. Robert M. McGovern, Co. A, 5th Cav. Regt.; Washington, D.C.

Pvt. 1st Class Walter C. Monegan, Jr., USMC, Co. F, 2nd Bn., 1st Marines, 1st
  Marine Div.; Melrose, Mass.

Lieut. Col. John U. D. Page, X Corps Art.; Luzon, Philippine Islands

Sgt. Donn F. Porter, Co. G, 14th Inf. Regt., 25th Inf. Div.; Sewickley, Pa.

2nd Lieut. Robert D. Reem, USMC, Co. H, 3rd Bn. 7th Marines, 1st Marine Div.;
  Lancaster, Pa.

2nd Lieut. Sherrod E. Skinner, Jr., USMCR, By. F, 2nd Bn., 11th Marines, 1st
  Marine Div.; Hartford, Conn.

Sgt. 1st Class Charles W. Turner, 2nd Recon. Co., 2nd Inf. Div.; Boston, Mass.

Staff Sgt. William G. Windrich, Co. I, 3rd Bn., 5th Marines, 1st Marine Div.;
  Chicago, Ill.

## VIETNAM

Captain James A. Graham, USMC, Co. F, 2nd Bn., 5th Marines, 1st Marine Div.;
  Wilkinsburg, Pa.

Cpl. Larry E. Smedley, USMC, D. Co., 1st Bn., 7th Marines, 1st Marine Div.;
  Berryville, Va.

Chaplain (Major) Charles Joseph Watters, 503rd Para. Reg., 173rd Air. Brig.;
  Jersey City, N.J.

## IN PEACE

Seaman George Breeman, USN; Passaic, N.J.

Commander Richard E. Byrd, Jr., USN; Winchester, Va.

Seaman Thomas Cahey, USN; Ireland

Lieut. Commander Robert W. Cary, USN, USS *Santiago;* Kansas City, Mo.

Chief Gunner's Mate Frank W. Crilley, USN; Trenton, N.J.

Ensign Henry C. Drexler, USN; Braddock, Pa.
Maj. General Adolphus W. Greely, USA; Newburyport, Mass.
Fireman 1st Class David Harrington, USN; Washington, D.C.
Fireman 1st Class Alexander Jardine, USN; Scotland
Seaman Johan J. Johansson, USN; Norway
Commander Claude Ashton Jones, USN; Fire Creek, W. Va.
Chief Watertender Harry Lipscomb, USN; Washington, D.C.
Chief Boatswain Isidor Nordstrom, USN; Sweden
Boatswain's Mate 1st Class Alexander Peters, USN; Russia
Hospital Steward William S. Shacklette, USN; Delaplane, Va.
Chief Boatswain's Mate Patrick Shanahan, USN; Ireland
Chief Elecrician William E. Snyder, USN; South Bethlehem, Pa.
Chief Master-at-Arms John Stokes, USN; New York, N.Y.
Boatswain's Mate James F. Sullivan, USN; Mass.
Chief Machinist's Mate Karl Westa, USN; Norway

## SOME OF THE OTHER NOTEWORTHY PERSONS BURIED AT ARLINGTON ARE:

Maj. Gen. Fred C. Ainsworth, noted Army Adjutant-General
Maj. Samuel T. Armstrong, Army surg.; Supt. Bellevue Hosp. N.Y.C.
Maj. Lillian Aubert, Army nurse; trained thousands nurses WW I
Maj. Gen. Christopher Columbus Auger, USA; Civil War leader
Col. Robert Low Bacon, USAR; Congressman, banker, financier
Fay Bainter, actress (wife of Lt. Com. Reginald S. Venable)
Maj. Nancy M. Baker, Army nurse; escaped Corregidor by sub
Com. Beatrice V. Ball, USCGR; senior officer SPARS, WW II
Rear Adm. Alan B. Banister, much-decorated WW II sub commander
1st Lieut. Eugene H. Barksdale, USAAF; pioneer Army flyer; AFB named for him
Maj. Andrew A. Barna, USAAF; first WW II burial at Arlington
Maj. Gen. George Barnett, USMC; Marine Commandant WW I
Vice Adm. Patrick N. L. Bellinger; early naval flyer; WW II leader
Constance Bennett, actress (wife of Brig. Gen. J. T. Coulter, USAF)
First Lieut. Ollie J. B. Bennett, USA; pioneer woman Army Dr. WW I
Commodore E. P. Bertholf, Commandant, USCG (1911–19)
Maj. Gen. W. P. Biddle, Commandant, USMC (1911–14)
Rear Adm. F. C. Billard, Commandant, USCG (1924–32)
Col. J. S. Billings, founded world famous US Army Medical Library
Lieut. Col. Hiram Bingham, USAR; US Senator and Governor of Conn.
Col. Arthur C. Blakeney, USA; noted psychological warfare expert
Col. Edward Bomar, USAR; well-known Associated Press writer
Lieut. Gen Albert J. Bowley, USA; WW I leader
Brig. Gen. D. L. Brainard, survivor Greely Arctic Exped. 1880s
Col. Alva Jennings Brasted; Chief, Army Chaplains (1933–37)

Lt. Gen. Lewis H. Brereton, USAAF; comm. Allied Airborne Army Europe WW I
Brig. Gen. Serano E. Brett, USA; much decorated WW I Commander
Capt. Wendell H. Brockley, USAAF; noted test pilot
Lieut. Col. Kilburn Roby Brown, USAR; advertising executive
Maj. Ralph D. Brown, USAAF; hero chaplain, died WW II prison camp
Lt. Gen. Andrew D. Bruce, USA; WW I armored leader; former pres. U. of Houston
Lieut. Wilbur M. Brucker, USA, WW I; Sec. of Army; Gov. of Michigan
Maj. Gen. Omar Bundy, USA; World War I leader
Col. Wm. W. Burrows; 1st Command. USMC (1798–1804)
Brig. Gen. Reynolds Burt, USA; officer 41 yrs; wrote West Point-Army songs
Lieut. Holt Fairfield Butt, III, USNR; Chaplain, West Point (1937–41)
Captain George F. Cahill, USAR; noted urologist
First Lieut. Loren H. Call, USAAF; pioneer Army flyer
Lieut. Gen. Ralph J. Canine, USA; first director, Natl. Sec. Agency
Gen. John K. Cannon, USAF; comm. Allied Tac. AF, Europe, WW II
Dr. James Carroll, assisted in yellow fever experiments
Brig. Gen. Paul T. Carroll, Military Aide to Pres. Eisenhower
Lieut. Thomas H. Carroll, USNR; president, George Wash. University
Brig. Gen. John J. Carty, USAR; noted inventor and engineer
Maj. Gen. James E. Chaney, USAAF; World War II leader
Lieut. Selden Chapin, USNR; Ambass.
Master Sgt. Alexander T. K. Choa, USA; oriental expert and author
Col. Bennett Champ Clark, USAR; US Senator, Missouri (1933–45)
Lieut. Col. Nellie V. Close, USAF; organized AF Nurses Corps
Vice Adm. Calvin H. Cobb, USN; World War II leader
Lieut. Gen. Henry C. Corbin, USA; noted Indian fighter
Maj. Gen. Enoch Crowder, USA; World War I Leader, Ambassador
Maj. Gen. William Crozier, USA; WW I Chief of Ordnance
Col. William S. Culberton, USAR; ambassador
First Lieut. Cushman Kellogg Davis, US Vols.; US Sen. & Gov. Minn.
Lieut. Col. Dwight F. Davis, USAR; financier, donor Davis Cup
Adm. Louis de Steigneur, WWI leader; anti-submarine expert
Gen. John L. Dewitt, USA; World War II leader
Capt. Ed. P. Doherty, 16th N.Y. Cav.; captured John Wilkes Booth
Rear Adm. Robert Donohoe, USCG; directed air-sea rescues WW II
Maj. Gen. Richard C. Drum, Indian fighter; Army Adj. Gen. (1880–89)
Capt. Simon A. Drum, USA; first of distinguished Army family
Jules Dubois, noted Chicago *Tribune* Latin-American writer
Capt. Franklin Dunham, USA WW I; noted educator; NBC exec.; church official
Col. E. P. Easterbrook, Chief, Army Chaplains (1928–29)
Brig. Gen. John Eaton, US Vols: US Comm. Education 16 years
Adm. Richard S. Edwards; World War II leader

Lieut. Col. Frederick Eglin, USAAF; test pilot; AFB named for him
Maj. Gen. George F. Elliott, Command. USMC (1908–10)
Capt. Hugh Elmendorf, USAAF; Army test pilot; AFB named for him
Maj. Gen. Hanson E. Ely, USA; World War I leader
Rear Adm. Mordecai T. Endicott, USN; noted civil engineer
Lieut. Col. John B. England, USAAF; World War II ace
Col. Luther W. Evans, well-known Army Chaplain
Rear Adm. Robley Dunglison Evans, commanded "Great White Fleet"
Vice Adm. Edward C. Ewen, USN; World War II—Korean War leader
Vice Adm. A. P. Fairfield, USN; World War II leader
Maj. Gen. Thomas F. Farrell, USA; helped develop A-Bomb
Pvt. Robert Fechner, USA, WW I; Dir., Civ. Conservation Corps.
Maj. Gen. Herman Feldman, USA; Army Quartermaster Gen. (1949–51)
Col. Francis V. Fitzgerald, pioneer Army Information officer
Col. Edward A. Fitzpatrick, USAR; noted educator and college pres.
Maj. Gen. Philip Fleming, USA; Adminis., Fed. Works Agency
Pvt. Henry P. Fletcher, US Vols. Ambass.; Undersec. State
Brig. Gen. Nathan Bedford Forrest, USAAF; noted WW II pilot
Lt. Gen. Amos Fries, USA; organized Chem. Warfare Service, US Army
Col. David D. Gaillard, USA; designed Panama Canal locks
First Lieut. Ruth M. Gardiner, first Army nurse killed WW II
Brig. Gen. Harold H. George, USAF; WW I ace; noted pilot
Gen. Thomas P. Gerrity, USAF; WW II leader; Dep. Chief of Staff, USAF
Vice Adm. Robert L. Ghormley, USN; World War II leader
Capt. F. M. Gibson, 7th Cav. relief party, Custer Massacre
Brig. Gen. R. A. Ginsburg, USAF; Asst. ed., *US News & World Report*
Capt. George Graham, USA; Sec. of War for Presidents Madison and Munroe
Brig. Gen. Edward Gruber, USA; wrote official Army song
Col. Robert Guggenheim, USAR; Ambass.
Maj. Gen. William G. Haan, USA; WW II leader
Anna Hanbury, Span. Amer. War Nurse; led nurses' training, Mexico
Vice Adm. Osborne Hardy, USN; WW II leader
Col. John Harriss, Commandant, USMC (1859–1864)
Maj. Gen. Stuart Heintzelman, USA; WW I leader
Maj. Gen. Guy V. Henry, 51 years Army service; noted equestrian
Maj. Gen. Charles Heywood, Commandant USMC (1891–1903)
Lieut. Col. Horace Hickam, USAAF; Army pilot; AFB named for him
Marguerite Higgins, Pulitzer Prize-winning war correspondent
Vice Adm. Tom Burbridge Hill, USN; WW II leader
Brig. Gen. Frank T. Hines, USA; early director, Veteran's Bureau
Maj. Donald Holleder, West Point All-American football end
Col. George V. Holloman, USAF; guided missile pioneer
Sgt. Caradine Hooten, USA WW I; ex-Gen. Sec. Methodist Bd. Social Concerns

Maj. Gen. Edgar E. Hume, USA; Pres. Soc. of Cincinnati
First Lieut. Frederic Humphreys, USAAF; one of first two Army pilots
Col. Kent Hunter, USAR; noted intelligence officer and newsman
Rear. Adm. Edward Hutchinson, USN; noted sub commander WW II
Pvt. John B. Hutson, USA WW I; Undersec. Agri.; Asst Gen. Sec. United Nations
Maj. Gen. Rufus Ingalls, USA; Civil War leader
Maj. Ralph E. Johnson, USA; well-known Negro chaplain, WW I; educator
Edward Jones, Treasury official under Pres. George Washington
Vice Adm. Edward D. Jones, USCG; WW I leader
Sgt. Louis Vaughn Jones, USA WW I; concert violinist; Howard U. professor
Adm. Edward C. Kalfbus, commanded Battle Force, US Fleet
Col. Wm. Pitt Kellogg, US Vols; US Senator; Governor
Sgt. Lawrence B. Kelly; first American killed, liberation Paris
Vice Adm. Henry S. Kendall, USN; WW II leader
Cpl. Omar B. Ketchum, USA; VFW official and legislative expert
Judge Paul J. Kilday, US Military Court of Appeals
Col. Harley M. Kilgore, USAR; US Senator (W. Va.)
Pvt. Ivory Kimball, US Vols; suggested Memorial Amphitheatre
Brig. Gen. Dan C. Kingman, USA; noted engineer
Adm. Alan G. Kirk; led US Naval Forces, Normandy Landing, 1944
Maj. Gen. Myron C. Kramer, USA; WW II Army JAG; member, Int. War Crimes
     Tribunal
Brig. Gen. Frank Lackland, pilot; AFB named for him
Lieut. Col. Rae D. Landy, Army Nurse; founded Palestine health centers
Lieut. Gen. Thomas B. Larkin, USA; WW II leader
Lt. Gen. Henry L. Larsen, USMC; World War II leader
Maj. Gen. Henry J. Lawton, USA; killed, Philippine Insurrection
Gen. Ben Lear, USA; World War II leader
Lieut. Gen. John C. H. Lee, USA; WW II leader
Capt. Wm. E. Lee, USAR; Chairman, Interstate Commerce Comm.
Col. L. R. Legendre, USAR; Director, Natl. Hq., American Legion
Lieut. Col. Anthony Leviero, USAR; Pulitzer Prize-winning newsman
Lieut. Paul W. Linebarger, Sr., US Vols; China expert; US Judge
Col. Paul W. Linebarger, Jr., USAR; Asia expert, educator, writer
Sgt. Herve J. L'Heureux, USA; WW I; State Dept. official; diplomat
Col. James McCubbin Lingan, Revolutionary War officer
Col. E. H. Liscum, USA; killed leading attack Tientsin, China, 1900
Vice Adm. Leland P. Lovette, USN; destroyer expert; author
Rear Adm. Jos. B. Lynch, USNR; led naval pilot training programs
Col. Leslie MacDill, USAAF; fighter pilot; AFB named for him
Maj. Gen. Wm. F. Marquat, USA; much-decorated WW II leader
Lieut. Gen. Horace McBride, USA; commanded XX Corps, WW II
Rear Adm. E. R. McCarthy, USCGS; directed important map work WW II

Maj. Hezekiah McClellan, USAAF; test pilot; AFB named for him
Maj. Gen. Frank R. McCoy, USA; WW I leader
Col. Michael McCoy, USAAF; B-47 commander; AFB named for him
Field Clerk Michael McDermott, USA; WW I, State Dept. Off.; Ambass.
1st Lieut. James P. McGranery, USA; WW I; US Attorney-General; Congressman
Rear Adm. Ross T. McIntyre; personal physician Pres. F. D. Roosevelt
Vice Adm. Charles H. McMorris, commanded Cruiser Task Force, WW II
Adm. Luke McNamee, USN; WW I leader
Col. Paul V. McNutt, USAR; Governor; Ambass; Natl. Com. Amer. Leg.
Col. E. A. Malmstrom, USAAF; pilot; AFB named for him
Vice Adm. B. E. Manseau, USN; naval engineer and salvage expert
Lieut. Peyton C. March, Jr., USAAF; early pilot; AFB named for him
Col. Robert A. Martino, USA; honored by Vatican for relief work
Lieut. Carl S. Mather, USAAF; fighter pilot; AFB named for him
Capt. Charles E. Merriam, USA; noted political scientist, U. of Chicago
Maj. Anne R. Metcalf, Army Nurse; Pershing Exped. Mexico; wounded, WW I
Lieut. Dennis Michie; athlete; Michie Stad., West Point, named for him
1st Lieut. George Fort Milton, USA; WW I; newspaper editor, author, historian
Mrs. Virginia Lee Montgomery (Mrs. John C.), grandniece Robt. E. Lee
Brig. Gen. James M. Moore, USA; as Eng. Captain, planned Arlington
Lieut. Commander Wayne Morris, USNR, motion picture actor
Col. James A. Moss, USA; founded U.S. flag assn.
Maj Gen. James I. Muir, USA; commanded 44th Div., WW II
Brig. Gen. A. B. Nettleton, US Vols; newsman; financier; Sec. of Treasury
Simon Newcomb, famous astronomer; professor US Naval Academy
Brig. Gen. Wm. J. Nicholson, USA; awarded DSC for valor WW I age 62
Mrs. Julia Dent Sharp Nolan; niece Pres. Grant; baptized at White House
Vice Adm. Ralph A. Oftsie, USN; noted WW II and Korean War leader
Capt. John O'Donnell, USAR; syndicated columnist N.Y. *Daily News*
Brig. Gen. William O'Dwyer, USAR; Mayor of New York City
Col. John Callan O'Laughlin, USAR; publisher and editor
Capt. Wm. O'Neill, US Vols; Rough Rider, killed San Juan Hill, Cuba
Maj. Gen. John F. O'Ryan, USA; WW I leader
Capt. Winfred Overholser, USAR; leading psychiatrist and hospital super.
Lieut. Gen. Floyd L. Parks, USA; noted combat leader WW II
Col. Rich. C. Patterson, USAR; bus. exec.; city official; Ambass.
Col. Leo Francis Paul, USAF; flew 209 combat missions WW II and Korea
Lieut. Col. Lemuel Penn, USAR; prominent Negro educator
Lieut. Col. Elmer D. Perrin, USAAF; B-26 test pilot; AFB named for him
Cpl. W. A. Pixton, Rough Riders—first Span. Amer. War dead buried Arlington
Anna Platt, first of many Civil War nurses buried at Arlington
Lieut. Col. Charles A. Powers, USAR; famous plastic surgeon
Brig. Gen. Richard H. Pratt, USA; founded Carlisle Indian School

Cadet John E. Puerifoy, US Mil. Acad.; State Dept. off.; Ambas.

Lieut. David L. Quinn, USN; heroic chaplain died Jap. prison camp WW II

Vice Adm. Van Herbert Ragsdale, USN; noted carrier Com. WW II

Rear Adm. Albert C. Read, USN; commanded first plane to cross ocean

Vinnie Ream (Mrs. Edwin Hoxie), sculptress

Maj. David J. Reilly, USMC; much-decorated Vietnam War pilot

Brig. Gen. Henry J. Reilly, USAR; first pres., Reserve Officers Assn.

Brig. Gen. Samuel Rickenbaugh, USA; Chief of Tank Corps, AEF, WW I

Adm. Claude V. Ricketts, USN; former Vice-Chief Naval Operations

Maj. Gen. James B. Ricketts, USA; Civil War leader

William R. Rivkin, State Dept. official; Ambassador

Brig. Gen. Henry M. Robert, USA; author "Robert's Rules of Order"

Brig. Gen. A. E. Robins, USAAF; air logistician; AFB named for him

Col. Henry Latrobe Roosevelt, USMCR; Asst. Secretary of Navy

Lieut. Col. Andrew Rowan, USA; carried famous "message to Garcia," 1898

Brig. Gen. Daniel Rucker, USA; Civil War leader

Maj. Gen. Benjamin Runkle, US Vols; founder Sigma Chi Fraternity

Capt. Louis Ruppel, USMCR; newspaper and magazine editor

Maj. Gen. John H. Russell, Comm. USM Corps; Commis. To Haiti

Brig. Gen. William Russell, Revolutionary War Officer from Virginia

Rear Adm. Benj. F. Sands, USN; made US Naval Observatory world-famous

Col. Ralph I. Sasse, USA; West Point football coach 1930s

George B. Schadmann, educator; trained hundreds for service academies

Col. David G. Schilling, USAF; WW II Ace; AFB named for him

Maj. Gen. Jack W. Schwartz, USA; noted urologist; a hero of Bataan death march

Capt. Evan W. Scott, USN; Chief of Naval Chaplains (1921–26)

Adm. David Foote Sellers, USN; Commanded US Fleet, battleship expert

Brig. Gen. Harry H. Semmes, USA; won 3 Distinguished Service Crosses WW I–
    WW II

Capt. C. F. Shoemaker, Com. Revenue Cutter Service (1895–1905)

Lieut. Gen. Walter C. Short, USA; Pearl Harbor commander

Pvt. Fred. W. Smith, Canadian Army, WW I; long-time Methodist minister

Maj. Gen. George W. Smythe, USA; Korean War leader; noted athlete

Brig. Gen. Oscar Solbert, USA; Chief Psycholog. Warfare, WW II

Hosp. Corpsman C. G. Sonntag, USA; volunteer, yellow fever experiment

Maj. Gen. R. H. Soule, USA; much-decorated WW II combat leader

Ens. Frank J. Sprague, USN; invented electric street car

Maj. Gen. Owen Squier, USA; noted Army Chief Signal Officer

Adm. Wm. H. Standley, USN; US Ambassador Soviet Union WW II

Col. John H. Stotensburg, US Vols; Philippine Insur. leader

Adm. Joseph Strauss, USN; WW I leader; ordnance expert

Brig. Gen. Samuel D. Sturgis, USA; Civil War leader

Maj. Gen. Alexander D. Surles, USA; armored expert
Gen. Walter C. Sweeney, USAF; noted fighter pilot; World War II leader
Rear Adm. George Synon, USCG; World War II leader
Corp. James A. Tanner, commander in chief, Grand Army of Republic
Col. Dora E. Thompson, USA; Superin., Army Nurse Corps, WW I
Vice Adm. John H. Towers, USN; early Navy pilot; WW II leader
Brig. Gen. Robt. F. Travis, USAF: WW II Ace; AFB named for him
Sergeant E. K. Turner, first Army casualty WW II buried at Arlington
1st Lieut. Sullins P. Turner, USAAF; early pilot; AFB named for him
1st Lieut. Frank B. Tyndall, USAAF; WW I pilot; AFB named for him
Com. George Tully Vaughn, USNR; famous surgeon
Maj. Gen. Edward M. Watson, USA; Military Aide Pres. F. D. Roosevelt
Maj. Emily Weder, Army Nurse Corps; widely-known in nursing
Lieut. John W. Weeks, USN; Secretary of War (1923–25)
Hosp. Corpsman C. L. West, USA; volunteer, yellow fever experiment
Gen. Thomas D. White, USAF; former Air Force Chief of Staff
Col. John H. Wigmore, USAR; Dean, Northwestern University Law School
Adm. Henry A. Wiley, USN; commander in chief, US Fleet (1927–29)
Lieut. Frank W. Wilson, USN; Chap. WW I & II; noted Episcopal Priest
Brig. Gen. T. J. Wint, USA; 46 years' military service; five wars
Capt. H. P. Williams, USA; Chaplain, Span. Amer. War; YMCA Sec. WW I
Maj. Gen. Ord Wingate, British Army; famous commando leader WW II
Lt. Col. Hubert Wood, USAR; Post.-General (1922–23) Sec. Inter. (1923–28)
Lt. Com. Hugh Wood, Jr., USN; much-decorated WW II Ace
Col. Arthur Woods, USAAF; Police Commissioner N.Y. City (1914–1918)
Lt. Gen. William Mason Wright, USA; commanded 1st Corps, WW II
Col. Jacob Wuest, USA; noted intelligence officer and Far East expert
Maj. Gen. Paul B. Wurtsmith, USAF; noted pilot; AFB named for him
Surgeon H. C. Yarrow, USA; well-known zoologist
Rear Adm. Wm. Brent Young, USN; WW II leader; famous military family
Rear Adm. Ellis Zacharias, USN; intelligence expert and author